NAME	DESCRIPTION
.override	States that the method overrides
.pack	States the field boundary size
.param	Defines default values for option
.permission	Defines security access information about one resource
.permissionset	Defines security access information about zero or more resources
.property	Defines a property in the class
.publickey	Defines the public key used to sign the assembly
.publickeytoken	Contains 8 bytes of a referenced assembly's public key
.removeon	Allows clients to unregister event notifications
.set	Defines the modification method for a property
.size	UDefines a block of memory in a class
.subsystem	States the user interaction preference
.try	Defines a try block
.ver	Either states the current version of the assembly or the desired version of a referenced assembly
.vtentry	States which slot the method should be in the v-table
.vtfixup	Defines a v-table for exported methods

CIL Programming:
Under the Hood™ of .NET

JASON BOCK

CIL Programming: Under the Hood™ of .NET

Copyright © 2002 by Jason Bock

ISBN: 1-59059-041-4

Printed and bound in the United States of America 12345678910

Technical Reviewer: Dan Fergus

Editorial Directors: Dan Appleman, Peter Blackburn, Gary Cornell, Jason Gilmore, Karen Watterson, John Zukowski

Managing Editor: Grace Wong

Copy Editor: Ami Knox

Compositor: Diana Van Winkle, Van Winkle Design

Indexer: Carol Burbo

Artist and Cover Designer: Kurt Krames

Manufacturing Manager: Tom Debolski

Marketing Manager: Stephanie Rodriguez

Distributed to the book trade in the United States by Springer-Verlag New York, Inc., 175 Fifth Avenue, New York, NY, 10010
and outside the United States by Springer-Verlag GmbH & Co. KG, Tiergartenstr. 17, 69112 Heidelberg, Germany.
In the United States, phone 1-800-SPRINGER, email orders@springer-ny.com, or visit http://www.springer-ny.com.
Outside the United States, fax +49 6221 345229, email orders@springer.de, or visit http://www.springer.de.

For information on translations, please contact Apress directly at 2560 9th Street, Suite 219, Berkeley, CA 94710.
Phone: 510-549-5930, Fax: 510-549-5939, Email: info@apress.com, Web site: http://www.apress.com

The source code for this book is available to readers at http://www.apress.com in the Downloads section. You will need to answer questions pertaining to this book in order to successfully download the code.

IN MEMORANDUM

Ronald F. Bock

1939–2001

For all that you did for me,

for the encouragement you gave me,

and for being my dad.

I'll miss you on the golf course.

Brief Contents

Contents

Chapter 8 Dynamic Proxies in .NET *271*

Chapter 9 CIL Tips *317*

About the Author

Jason Bock is a senior consultant for Magenic Technologies, a Microsoft Gold Certified consulting firm. He has worked on a number of business applications using a diverse set of tools and technologies such as VB, COM, and Java. He is also the author of *Visual Basic 6 Win32 API Tutorial* and has written articles and given presentations on technical development issues regarding VB. He has a bachelor's degree and a master's degree in electrical engineering from Marquette University.

When he's not developing programs, writing books, or giving presentations, Jason enjoys spending time with his wife Liz, golfing, biking, reading, listening to and playing music, and watching *The Simpsons* whenever he can. Visit his Web site at http://www.jasonbock.net.

About the
Technical Reviewer

Dan Fergus is the president and lead developer and architect at Forest Software Group (http://www.forestsoftwaregroup.com). His most recent employment was with NuMega Technologies working on several of their debugging tools. Most recently he was the development lead for the CodeReview and FailSafe products. Dan travels the world teaching and presenting sessions on a range of topics including debugging, the .NET Framework, Web services, and Windows CE programming. Dan has had many articles and white papers published over the years and continues to write for several magazines and also for Apress.

When he is not sitting at a keyboard, Dan is busy with his four young sons on the baseball fields around Fort Worth, Texas.

Acknowledgments

While this book only has one author's name on the cover, there are a number of people who have contributed in different ways to making this book better than it ever could have been without them. First, I must thank my wife, Liz, for putting up with me being in front of the computer every night until late in the evening instead of being with her as I wrote this book. Your patience and support is forever appreciated. I love you.

To my mom, Mary, thanks for everything you have done for me. You have gone through such a difficult time in your life—I can't imagine how hard it's been. You've always encouraged me whenever I take up a project like this, and I truly appreciate the support.

The Apress staff has been great. I thank Gary Cornell for talking to me about Apress a year and a half ago (it's been that long?) and letting me write a book on CIL when everyone else was writing a book on how to create .NET assemblies with C#. The road has been difficult, but rewarding, and I'm glad you gave me the opportunity to write this book. Thanks also go to Dan Appleman, Stephanie Rodriguez, Grace Wong, Ami Knox, and anyone else at Apress who has been involved with this book—you turned my writing into a far better product than what I could've done on my own. I also thank Dan Fergus for taking the time to edit the book—your suggestions were very helpful.

The technical staff at Magenic Technologies has been awesome. I have never worked for a company where the developers are so willing to share their knowledge as well as help people out with technical issues. A number of times, I ran into some weird issues with CIL, and people would dive into the discussions to try and figure the problem out. Thanks go to Wade Baron, Jeff Ferguson, Tom Fischer, Fred Johnson, Ross Johnson, Robert Knutson, Rocky Lhotka, Steve Lundeen, and anyone else who helped but I forgot to include in this list.

I also thank John Gough for helping me out with Component Pascal syntax and Jay Freeman and Joe Hummel for helping me solve one of the first problems I had with the Emitter classes.

Finally, to the rest of my friends and family, thanks for just being there.

Introduction

"It is also tempting to compile several different languages into the same inter-mediate language and use a common back end for the different front ends, thereby obtaining several compilers for one machine. However, because of subtle differences in the viewpoints of different languages, there has been only limited success in this direction."

—Alfred V. Aho, Ravi Sethi, and Jeffrey D. Ullman, *Compilers: Principles, Techniques, and Tools* (Addison-Wesley Publishing Co., 1985)

When I first saw .NET, I was overwhelmed by the influx of new ideas and concepts. Web developers were getting a vastly improved framework with ASP.NET and Web services. Visual Basic was getting a major overhaul with VB .NET, adding inheritance and free threading into the mix along with removing some long-standing BASIC compatibility. A new language was introduced—C#—that looked a lot like Java with some subtle yet substantial differences. Security was markedly improved, allowing users to prevent code from running based on the code itself and not just on the current user's credentials.

Slowly but surely, bit by bit (and then byte by byte) I became familiar with .NET. However, there was one aspect that I became very interested in. One of the first presentations I saw on .NET demonstrated how a class in C# could be the base class in VB .NET. Debugging between the two languages was seamless. I had never seen anything like this before; using COM as the interop layer between C++ and VB just did not cut it. But how did it work? How could I create classes in one language that could be used in another? How could Microsoft claim that there were a large number of languages targeting the .NET platform?

Then I found out about ILDasm. After I loaded my first assembly and saw my first disassembled method, it was all downhill from there.

Target Audience

If you've spent some time with C# or VB .NET and you want to know what the results are when you press Ctrl-Shift-B (which compiles your code), or you want to know how code in one language can be used so seamlessly in another, then this book is for you. You may have heard about the Common Intermediate Language, or CIL, or you may have heard about the fact that in .NET you can generate code on the fly. Either way, you're not really comfortable with words like `ldfld` or `.assembly`, but you want to figure them out. I wrote this book to help you understand what these statements are doing and how you can use them in your future .NET projects.

Granted, learning CIL isn't easy. I've spent a lot of late nights trying to figure out what was going on with my CIL code. The bugs can be subtle and insidious to root out. But I think that by learning CIL, you gain tremendous insights into the inner workings of .NET. C#, Component Pascal, Mondrain . . . none of these languages truly speak the .NET truth. Only CIL can fully express what can be done in .NET.

Source Code

I have created a number of applications that demonstrate CIL in action. You can download the code from Apress's Web site at `http://www.apress.com`. I have made every attempt to ensure that the code compiles and behaves as expected, but mistakes can occur. If you find a bug in the source code, or you find an erroneous statement in the book itself, please contact me at `jason@jasonbock.net` and I'll make sure that updates are made accordingly.

Partition Documents

Throughout the book, I'll make references to a set of specification documents known as the Partition documents. These documents were sent to ECMA as part of the standardization process of .NET—they contain valuable information about how .NET is structured. When you install VS .NET, you should be able to find them in the following folder: Program Files\Microsoft Visual Studio .NET\FrameworkSDK\Tool Developers Guide\docs. You can also find them online at `http://msdn.microsoft.com/net/ecma/`.

CHAPTER 1

Language Interoperability

Java. Smalltalk. C++. Pascal. Eiffel. JavaScript. Perl. Ruby. Python. Visual Basic. Ada. Scheme . . . the list of programming languages goes on and on. I'm sure that you've used at least one language in your development career as your primary vehicle for creating programs. You may have added other languages to your programming toolbox, and not necessarily by your own choice. You've been comfortably creating your in-house applications in language X until someone gets the bright idea that all code should now be written in language Y. Time and money have been wasted over and over again in corporations because these language changes have forced developers to rewrite entire applications. The reason? The new code couldn't use the old code's logic. But that changes in .NET.

In this chapter, I'll give you an overview of .NET from the view of language interoperability. I'll cover how different languages can target .NET to create applications and also use and extend these applications produced by different compilers. I'll discuss the basics of these .NET applications and define their structures, a clear understanding of which will help you make the most of the material presented in the rest of this book.

Language Interoperability in Action

To start, I'm going to go through a hypothetical situation that can occur in .NET. Rather than define a bunch of terms about what is going on underneath the scenes, I'll show you what developers can do by using .NET from a comfortable, high-level language perspective. Then I'll start to dig beneath the code to define what's really going on.

Let's say that a .NET developer, savvy in the ways of C#, has been assigned the task to create a Person class as defined by a UML diagram shown in Figure 1-1.

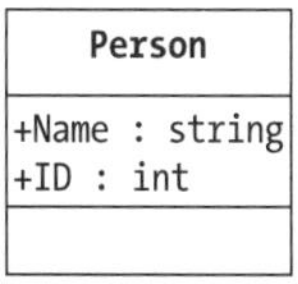

```
┌─────────────────┐
│     Person      │
├─────────────────┤
│+Name : string   │
│+ID : int        │
├─────────────────┤
│                 │
└─────────────────┘
```

Figure 1-1. Person class

She starts by writing an interface definition for the Person type:

```
using System;

namespace PersonDefinition
{
    public interface IPerson
    {
        string Name
        {
            get;
            set;
        }

        int ID
        {
            get;
            set;
        }
    }
}
```

However, being an ambitious programmer, she decides to leave the company for a potentially lucrative venture before needed additions are made. Therefore, a consultant is brought in to implement IPerson. An avid Oberon developer, he creates the following code:

```
MODULE PersonImpl;
    TYPE Person* = OBJECT IMPLEMENTS PersonDefinition.IPerson;
        VAR m_Name: System.String;
            m_ID: INTEGER;

        PROCEDURE NEW*(Name: System.String; ID: INTEGER);
        BEGIN
            m_ID := ID;
            m_Name := Name;
        END NEW;

        PROCEDURE get_ID*() : INTEGER
            IMPLEMENTS PersonDefinition.IPerson.get_ID;
        BEGIN
            RETURN m_ID;
        END get_ID;
```

```
        PROCEDURE set_ID*(newValue : INTEGER)
            IMPLEMENTS PersonDefinition.IPerson.set_ID;
        BEGIN
            m_ID := newValue;
        END set_ID;

        PROCEDURE get_Name*() : System.String
            IMPLEMENTS PersonDefinition.IPerson.get_Name;
        BEGIN
            RETURN m_Name;
        END get_Name;

        PROCEDURE set_Name*(newValue : System.String)
            IMPLEMENTS PersonDefinition.IPerson.set_Name;
        BEGIN
            m_Name := newValue;
        END set_Name;
    END Person;
END PersonImpl.
```

However, due to favorable results in the weekend lottery drawing, he suddenly leaves the project.

But the change requests don't stop. The IPerson-based type now needs to use a COM server that contains two classes, Order and OrderItem, to make purchases. The original source code has been lost; all that is left is the DLL file and a class layout, shown in Figure 1-2.

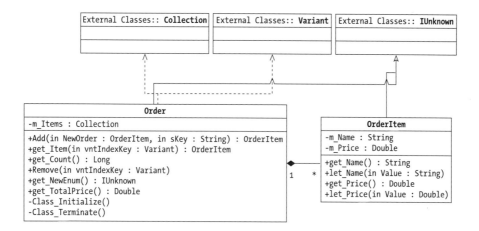

Figure 1-2. Orders UML diagram

Two contractors, one who knows C# and the other who knows VB .NET, are brought in. The first contractor decides to extend IPerson to ICustomer to have a Wallet property in C#. His new ICustomer code looks like this:

```csharp
using System;
using PersonDefinition;
using PersonImpl;

namespace CustomerDefinition
{
    public interface ICustomer : IPerson
    {
        double Wallet
        {
            get;
            set;
        }
    }
}
```

He then aggregates Person in a new Customer class that implements ICustomer:

```csharp
namespace CustomerDefinition
{
    public class Customer : ICustomer
    {
        private Person m_Person;
        private double m_Wallet;

        public Customer(string Name, int ID, double Wallet)
        {
            this.m_Person = new Person(Name, ID);
            this.m_Wallet = Wallet;
        }

        public string Name
        {
            get
            {
                return this.m_Person.get_Name();
            }
            set
            {
                this.m_Person.set_Name(value);
```

```
            }
        }

        public int ID
        {
            get
            {
                return this.m_Person.get_ID();
            }
            set
            {
                this.m_Person.set_ID(value);
            }
        }

        public double Wallet
        {
            get
            {
                return this.m_Wallet;
            }
            set
            {
                this.m_Wallet = value;
            }
        }
    }
}
```

Finally, the second contractor creates the UI application in VB .NET that ends up looking like the window in Figure 1-3.

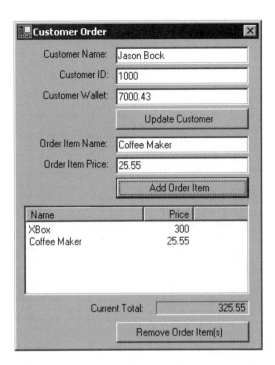

Figure 1-3. Customer order UI application

Here's how she coded the three button click events. First, when a user clicks the Update Customer button, an internal Customer object is updated:

```
Private Sub btnCustomerUpdate_Click(ByVal sender As System.Object, _
    ByVal e As System.EventArgs) Handles btnCustomerUpdate.Click
    UpdateCustomer(Me.txtCustomerNameValue.Text, _
        CInt(Me.txtCustomerIDValue.Text), _
        CDbl(Me.txtCustomerWalletValue.Text))
End Sub

Private Sub UpdateCustomer(ByVal Name As String, _
    ByVal ID As Integer, ByVal Wallet As Double)
    If Me.m_Customer Is Nothing Then
        Me.m_Customer = New Customer(Name, ID, Wallet)
    Else
        Me.m_Customer.Name = Name
        Me.m_Customer.ID = ID
        Me.m_Customer.Wallet = Wallet
    End If
End Sub
```

Once the customer is defined, order items can be purchased by clicking the Add Order Item button:

```
Private Sub btnAddOrderItem_Click(ByVal sender As System.Object, _
    ByVal e As System.EventArgs) Handles btnAddOrderItem.Click
    AddOrderItem(Me.txtOrderNameValue.Text, _
        CDbl(Me.txtOrderPriceValue.Text))
End Sub


Private Sub AddOrderItem(ByVal Name As String, _
    ByVal Price As Double)
    If Me.m_Customer Is Nothing Then
        MessageBox.Show("You have not defined the customer yet.")
    Else
        Dim bAdd As Boolean = True

        If Me.m_Order Is Nothing Then
            Me.m_Order = New Order()
        Else
            Dim possibleTotal As Double = Me.m_Order.TotalPrice() + Price
            If Me.m_Customer.Wallet < possibleTotal Then
                bAdd = False
                MessageBox.Show("The total price would be " + _
                    possibleTotal.ToString() + _
                    ", but you only have " + Me.m_Customer.Wallet.ToString())
            End If
        End If

        If True = bAdd Then
            Dim orderKey As Guid = Guid.NewGuid()
            Dim anItem As OrderItem = New OrderItem()
            anItem.Name = Name
            anItem.Price = Price
            Me.m_Order.Add(anItem, orderKey.ToString())

            Dim lvi As ListViewItem = New ListViewItem(Name)
            lvi.Tag = orderKey.ToString()
            lvi.SubItems.Add(Price.ToString())
            Me.lstOrderItems.Items.Add(lvi)
            Me.lblCurrentTotalValue.Text = Me.m_Order.TotalPrice().ToString()
        End If
    End If
End Sub
```

Finally, items can be removed by clicking Remove Order Item(s):

```
Private Sub btnRemoveOrderItems_Click(ByVal sender As System.Object, _
    ByVal e As System.EventArgs) Handles btnRemoveOrderItems.Click
    RemoveOrderItems()
End Sub


Private Sub RemoveOrderItems()
    If 0 < Me.lstOrderItems.SelectedItems.Count Then
        Dim listItem As ListViewItem
        For Each listItem In Me.lstOrderItems.SelectedItems
            Me.m_Order.Remove(listItem.Tag)
            Me.lstOrderItems.Items.Remove(listItem)
        Next
        Me.lblCurrentTotalValue.Text = Me.m_Order.TotalPrice().ToString()
    End If
End Sub
```

SOURCE CODE *All of the source code in this section can be found in the Chapter 1 directory when you download the code for this book at* http://www.apress.com. *Specific notes on how to compile the code and use the assemblies can be found in the readme.txt file.*

Language Interoperability in Theory

When you stop to think about what I was able to show you in the hypothetical example in the previous section, it's pretty amazing. I don't mean that you'd be amazed that I could design a class that modeled a person; in fact, the designs are sparse and are not stellar examples of code. But it's the interaction between all of the different pieces that result from the compilation of the code that's interesting. Figure 1-4 lays out the interactions and dependencies.

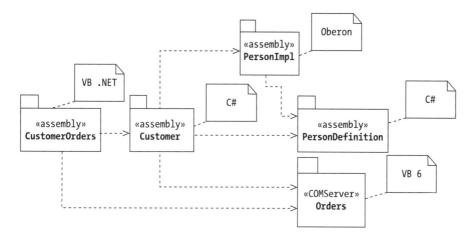

Figure 1-4. Assembly dependencies

Before .NET, if you tried to create a C++ class that you wanted to inherit in Java, you just could not do it. The reason was actually pretty simple—it's analogous to the problem that occurs when someone from America (like myself) is trying to communicate with a person from Norway. If I say to the Norwegian, "I am typing a paragraph in my book on CIL," that person will have no idea what I'm saying. Similarly, if the Norwegian asks me, "Hvordan har du det?",[1] I'll have a look of total confusion on my face. The problem is that we're both talking about the same concept (writing material for a book), but the language is getting in the way.

To overcome the increasing headaches that occur when multiple languages enter into the picture, let's say I create an intermediate human language (call it IHL) that allows a human to take his or her language and translate it to IHL. It's not necessary for me to know what IHL looks like, or how human languages are translated to and from IHL. So long as I have a tool that makes these translations for me, I can answer my Norwegian friend's question, "How is it going?"

Figure 1-5 illustrates how such a process would work with human conversations.

---

1. By the way, I don't know Norwegian; I had to have my friend Geir Olsen make the translation for me.

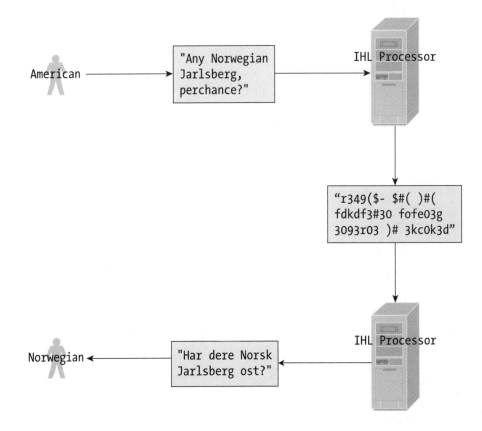

Figure 1-5. Human language IHL translations

As you can see, the IHL looks pretty much like garbage. But because of the IHL translator, my question is carried through to the Norwegian on the other side.

Now, in the real world, this procedure isn't that easy. There are subtleties with human languages that make defining such a base language that captures these tricky nuances difficult at best.[2] But with computer languages, it's not quite as complicated.[3] And that's exactly one of the more appealing aspects of .NET: it's an object-oriented substrate that multiple languages can target to produce code that can not only run within their language, but also be consumed by other code in other languages.

---

2. For an excellent read on the translation of languages, I strongly recommend *Le Ton Beau De Marot: In Praise of the Music of Language* by Douglas R. Hofstadter (Basic Books, 1997).

3. It's not a trivial problem either—Chapter 6 will talk about what happens when you compile the code examples in this chapter.

Let's back up to the example I briefly mentioned at the beginning of this section. You create a C++ class that you want to inherit in Java. Let's say your C++ class looks like this:

```
class EasyCPlusPlusClass
{
    public:
        int AMethod(void);
    private:
        int m_AMemberVariable;
};
```

Now, you want to inherit EasyCPlusPlusClass and make a new ExtendedJavaClass:

```
public class ExtendedJavaClass extends EasyCPlusPlusClass
```

You might as well stop there. There's no way Java could ever take the header file that contains ExtendedJavaClass and allow you to extend it in Java. Why? For starters, Java wouldn't understand the public: and private: access specifiers. A Java version of EasyCPlusPlusClass would look like this:

```
public class EasyJavaClass
{
    private int m_AMemberVariable;
    public int AMethod() {}
}
```

The accessibility is specified with the field or method itself in Java, so there's already a disconnect between the two languages. It's one that, as a human, you could solve, but compilers might not, as they are very picky when it comes to incorrect syntax.

Another problem is with Java methods. All methods in Java are virtual; AMethod() in EasyCPlusPlusClass is nonvirtual. Even if Java could somehow get around the public: mystery, it would interpret AMethod() as virtual because that's all it knows. If you wanted to make AMethod() virtual in C++, you'd do this:

```
int virtual AMethod(void);
```

But then Java wouldn't understand the virtual keyword!

It gets worse when the code is compiled and packaged into a file. What's Java going to do with a Windows DLL or EXE that contains EasyCPlusPlusClass? And if the situation were reversed, what would a C++ compiler do with an

EasyJavaClass.class file? Neither one of them "knows" what they contain. If you had the source code, you at least might have a chance at altering the syntax of the C++ class in a .java text file, but there are a number of concepts and keywords in both languages that would make such a translation problematic at best.

Now, it's not that C++ is better or worse than Java. Throw a bunch of other languages into the mix, and the problem continues to grow. This isn't a debate over programming languages; the issue is the absence of one ideal programming language. Because people gravitate toward certain languages for a number of reasons (first language used on the job, comfort with the syntax and available tools, and so on), we have a lot of code written in many, many languages. What would make this binary Tower of Babel start to crumble is an intermediate language that all language compilers would target so code written in one language could easily be used in another. That's one of problems .NET tries to address with its Common Intermediate Language, or CIL, which is what this book is all about.

Language Interoperability in Practice

So what does CIL look like? And how does it work? The second question is what the rest of the book will answer, but let's take some time looking at the first one in this chapter. Getting a good feel for the basics will be necessary for your understanding of the concepts I present in the rest of this book. Start by looking at the C# version of the EasyXXX classes from the previous section:

```csharp
public class EasyCSharpClass
{
    private int m_AMemberVariable;
    public void AMethod()
    {
        int x = 0;
        x++;
        x += CalledMethod();
    }
    private int CalledMethod()
    {
        return 4;
    }
}
```

I've changed AMethod() to have some implementation code—you'll see why in a moment. If you add this code to a text file and call it EasyCSharpClass.cs, you can create what's known as an assembly by running the following program at the command line:

```
csc /target:library EasyCSharpClass.cs
```

NOTE *Throughout this book, I'm going to use .NET tools from the command line. If Windows can't find a particular program when you try to execute it, run the corvars.bat file, which can be found in Program Files\Microsoft Visual Studio .NET\FrameworkSDK\Bin\.*

An *assembly* is defined in Partition I as "a configured set of loadable code modules and other resources that together implement a unit of functionality."[4] This definition becomes a bit clearer if you load the assembly into a tool that comes with the .NET Framework called ILDasm. This stands for Intermediate Language[5] Disassembler, and it's a wonderful tool for finding out just how an assembly works. Let's get the new assembly loaded into ILDasm to see what the tool looks like. Enter the following at the command line:

```
ildasm EasyCSharpClass.dll
```

NOTE *By changing the value of the /target switch, you can create EXEs as well; it was just easier to use a DLL for this example.*

You should see a window that resembles the one in Figure 1-6.

---

4.   See Section 4 of Partition I.

5.   You'll see the acronym IL used all the time in .NET circles. I will use the more complete acronym "CIL" in this book, but realize that in the context of .NET they both mean exactly the same thing.

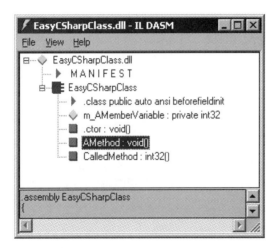

Figure 1-6. ILDasm

This looks like a simple class browsing tool of sorts. You can see your EasyCSharpClass class in the DLL along with its field and methods. You'll also notice that another method called .ctor() appears as well. You can probably guess that this is the default constructor for the class, but don't worry about that for now. Despite its appearances, however, this tool is anything but simple. Double-click the MANIFEST node and a window similar to the one in Figure 1-7 will be displayed.

```
MANIFEST                                                    _ □ ×
.assembly extern mscorlib
{
  .publickeytoken = (B7 7A 5C 56 19 34 E0 89 )
  .ver 1:0:3300:0
}
.assembly EasyCSharpClass
{
  // --- The following custom attribute is added automatica
  //   .custom instance void [mscorlib]System.Diagnostics.De
  //
  .hash algorithm 0x00008004
  .ver 0:0:0:0
}
.module EasyCSharpClass.dll
// MVID: {E09B2443-B98A-49AF-841F-536A294564FF}
.imagebase 0x00400000
.subsystem 0x00000003
.file alignment 512
.corflags 0x00000001
// Image base: 0x03510000
```

Figure 1-7. Assembly manifest

If the text doesn't make a lot of sense right now, that's perfectly fine—you've got the rest of the book to help you figure it out. For now, I want you to understand two things. First, the *manifest* (which is always part of the assembly) is used to contain information about the assembly, such as version numbers and any external assemblies that the current assembly is dependent on. You'll also note that it defines *modules* that contain the executable code. This is a little confusing at first, because it's easy to make the association that the DLL is the assembly. That's not quite true—the DLL is a module that just so happens to duplicate as the assembly file. It's possible to create an assembly file that doesn't contain a module, just a manifest. The module will be a separate file that doesn't contain any manifest information.

The second thing to note is that you'll see a bunch of words that begin with a period, like `.assembly` and `.module`. These are known as *directives*. These directives are used to set up the structure of an assembly, such as the definition of a class or one of its methods. Directives don't define executable code; they simply define information about the assembly, like the module name or a new class. Chapter 2 will cover directives in detail.

Now, double-click the AMethod node. You should see another window like the one in Figure 1-8 pop up.

```
EasyCSharpClass::AMethod : void()                              _ □ ×
.method public hidebysig instance void  AMethod() cil managed
{
  // Code size        16 (0x10)
  .maxstack  2
  .locals init (int32 V_0)
  IL_0000:  ldc.i4.0
  IL_0001:  stloc.0
  IL_0002:  ldloc.0
  IL_0003:  ldc.i4.1
  IL_0004:  add
  IL_0005:  stloc.0
  IL_0006:  ldloc.0
  IL_0007:  ldarg.0
  IL_0008:  call        instance int32 EasyCSharpClass::CalledMethod()
  IL_000d:  add
  IL_000e:  stloc.0
  IL_000f:  ret
} // end of method EasyCSharpClass::AMethod
```

Figure 1-8. CIL code

Again, you see another directive, `.method`, which is used to define a method. This time, though, what you're interested in is the following line of code:

```
IL_0000:  ldc.i4.0
```

That's CIL! The first part (IL_0000:) is known as a *code label,* and the second part is known as the *opcode.* Code labels aren't required in front of every opcode; they're usually added to define a spot you need to jump to in a method depending on certain conditions being true or false.[6] The opcodes can also vary in size, but usually they will be 1 byte in size. To see what value the opcode stands for, select View ➤ Show bytes. When this menu option is checked, you'll see a different view of a method's implementation. Figure 1-9 shows what AMethod() looks like with the bytes inline.

```
EasyCSharpClass::AMethod : void()                                    _ □ ×
.method public hidebysig instance void  AMethod() cil managed
// SIG: 20 00 01
{
  // Method begins at RVA 0x2050
  // Code size       16 (0x10)
  .maxstack  2
  .locals init (int32 V_0)
  IL_0000:  /* 16  |                       */ ldc.i4.0
  IL_0001:  /* 0A  |                       */ stloc.0
  IL_0002:  /* 06  |                       */ ldloc.0
  IL_0003:  /* 17  |                       */ ldc.i4.1
  IL_0004:  /* 58  |                       */ add
  IL_0005:  /* 0A  |                       */ stloc.0
  IL_0006:  /* 06  |                       */ ldloc.0
  IL_0007:  /* 02  |                       */ ldarg.0
  IL_0008:  /* 28  | (06)000002            */ call      instance int32 EasyCShar
  IL_000d:  /* 58  |                       */ add
  IL_000e:  /* 0A  |                       */ stloc.0
  IL_000f:  /* 2A  |                       */ ret
} // end of method EasyCSharpClass::AMethod
```

Figure 1-9. .NET methods with inline byte values

As you can see, the add opcode is 0x58 and stloc.0 is 0x0A. ILDasm will add this new information in with the comment tags so they don't interfere with the code. The .NET runtime looks at these values when the code is loaded and just-in-time activated (or JITted) to figure out what the method wants to do.

Now, there's something interesting that pops up when you show the byte values. Take a look at the line of code labeled IL_0008:. Notice that there's a value of 0x06000002 after the opcode value for call (which is 0x28). Even though I'll cover this opcode in Chapter 3, you can guess by its name that it's used to call a method. But what does that 0x06000002 stand for? It's actually a method token,

---

6.   ILDasm will always show dummy code labels for all CIL code, no matter what the code is doing.

which is used by the .NET runtime as metadata to determine information about the method. Tokens are prevalent within .NET assemblies, as they are the keys to figuring out what an assembly contains.

> **NOTE** *By the way, you may notice that the value is formatted as (06)000002 in Figure 1-9. It's the same value, but ILDasm is breaking up the token into its two main parts—the 1-byte metadata table index, and a 3-byte relative identifier (RID). 0x06 refers to the method table, and 0x000002 means that you're to call the method identified by the second method on that table. See Section 21 of Partition II for more details.*

You can see all of the tokens within the assembly by selecting View ➤ Show token values. Now, when you double-click the AMethod node, you'll see even more information (as shown in Figure 1-10).

```
EasyCSharpClass::AMethod : void()

.method /*06000001*/ public hidebysig instance void
        AMethod() cil managed
// SIG: 20 00 01
{
  // Method begins at RVA 0x2050
  // Code size       24 (0x18)
  .maxstack  2
  .locals /*11000001*/ init (int32 V_0)
  IL_0000:  /* 16  |                      */ ldc.i4.0
  IL_0001:  /* 0A  |                      */ stloc.0
  IL_0002:  /* 06  |                      */ ldloc.0
  IL_0003:  /* 17  |                      */ ldc.i4.1
  IL_0004:  /* 58  |                      */ add
  IL_0005:  /* 0A  |                      */ stloc.0
  IL_0006:  /* 06  |                      */ ldloc.0
  IL_0007:  /* 02  |                      */ ldarg.0
  IL_0008:  /* 28  |  (06)000002          */ call      instance int32 EasyCSl
```

Figure 1-10. .NET methods with token values

You can see AMethod()'s token at the top—0x06000001. It's not too hard to figure out that if you brought up CalledMethod()'s implementation in ILDasm, you'd see that its token value is 0x06000002. You can also observe that your local variable x (which is called V_0) has a metadata token as well—0x11000001. A large number of rules govern how tokens are formatted, but for our purposes here, you can assume that these tokens are correct.

Now that you know how CIL works and what tokens are, let's see how these tokens allow you to interoperate with other .NET code. To see this in action, write a piece of VB .NET code that calls AMethod():

```
Public Class VBConsumer
    Public Sub CallCSharpClass()
        Dim X As EasyCSharpClass = New EasyCSharpClass()
        X.AMethod()
    End Sub
End Class
```

To compile the VBConsumer.vb file, you need to change your command line a bit:

```
vbc /target:library /r:EasyCSharpClass.dll VBConsumer.vb
```

You're now using VB .NET's compiler, but you're also referencing the assembly that contains EasyCSharpClass via the /r switch. Now load VBConsumer.dll into ILDasm:

```
ildasm VBConsumer.dll
```

Turn on the token and byte value menu options,[7] and double-click the CallCSharpClass node. Here's what the resulting CIL looks like:

```
.method /*06000002*/ public instance void
        CallCSharpClass() cil managed
// SIG: 20 00 01
{
  // Method begins at RVA 0x2058
  // Code size       13 (0xd)
  .maxstack  1
  .locals /*11000001*/ init (class [EasyCSharpClass
    /* 23000003 */]EasyCSharpClass/* 01000002 */ V_0)
  IL_0000:  /* 73   | (0A)000002       */ newobj     instance void
    [EasyCSharpClass/* 23000003 */]EasyCSharpClass
    /* 01000002 */::.ctor() /* 0A000002 */
  IL_0005:  /* 0A   |                  */ stloc.0
  IL_0006:  /* 06   |                  */ ldloc.0
  IL_0007:  /* 6F   | (0A)000003       */ callvirt   instance void
    [EasyCSharpClass/* 23000003 */]EasyCSharpClass
    /* 01000002 */::AMethod() /* 0A000003 */
  IL_000c:  /* 2A   |                  */ ret
} // end of method VBConsumer::CallCSharpClass
```

---

7. This is one annoying thing about ILDasm—it doesn't remember your choices from a previous usage, so you have to switch them all back on.

The first thing you may note is that CallCSharpClass()'s token is the same as CalledMethod(). That's okay, because method tokens don't have to be unique across assemblies (and usually aren't). In fact, you'll notice that when you call AMethod(), you're not using the value of 0x06000001, you're using 0x0A000003! Where did that value come from?

To answer that question, you need to shut down the ILDasm instance that loaded VBConsumer.dll, and reload VBConsumer.dll using another switch:

```
ildasm /adv VBConsumer.dll
```

The undocumented /adv switch stands for "advanced options." If you look at the menu options under View, you'll now see a couple of added options. Select MetaInfo ➤ Show! (Ctrl-M), and you'll get a text dump of all the token values within the assembly. Scroll through the information—you should find a section that looks like the screen in Figure 1-11.

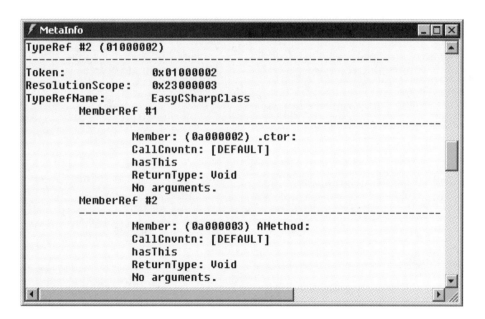

Figure 1-11. Metainfo screen

Now you can see where the 0x0A00003 token value is coming from. This is a MemberRef token;[8] it's made whenever you reference code from another assembly. This method is part of the type defined by the TypeRef token 0x01000002, which is part of the referenced assembly defined by the AssemblyRef token 0x23000003. This token is defined later on in the Metainfo dump under the Assembly section (shown in Figure 1-12).

---

8.   See Section 21.23 of Partition I for more details.

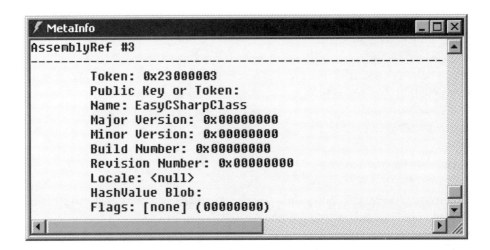

Figure 1-12. AssemblyRef values in Metainfo

Essentially, when VB .NET's compiler parses VBConsumer.vb, it finds a call to a method on an object that isn't contained in VBConsumer.vb. Therefore, it looks to see if an assembly name was given to it via the /r switch that contains a type called "EasyCSharpClass" with a method called "AMethod()" that has the correct signature. The VBConsumer class doesn't care that EasyCSharpClass was written in C#. So long as the assembly contains tokens that followed the .NET rules, it can make the method invocation.

If you get tired of drilling down through the tree view display, you can dump the contents to an .il file by selecting File ➤ Dump (Ctrl-D). The nice thing about this option is that you can take the .il file, tweak it, and recompile it using the Intermediate Language Assembler tool, or ilasm.[9] In fact, let's do this. Open VBConsumer.dll in ILDasm (without the /adv switch to keep the output small), and dump the contents to a file called VBConsumer.il. Find the line of code within CallCSharpClass() that looks like this:

```
IL_0007:  callvirt   instance void [EasyCSharpClass]EasyCSharpClass::AMethod()
```

Change it to this:

```
IL_0007:  callvirt   instance void
[EasyCSharpClass]EasyCSharpClass::CalledMethod()
```

---

9. This is why ILDasm comments out things like token values; otherwise, it would be invalid CIL code that ILasm couldn't compile.

Now try to compile the code with ilasm:

```
ilasm /dll VBConsumer.il
```

If you thought the resulting compilation would succeed and overwrite the current VBConsumer.dll file, you'd be right. ilasm is blissfully unaware that `CalledMethod()` is not visible to `VBConsumer` (because it's private). Of course, the code won't work if it's run—you'll see in Chapter 5 how you can find these errors before the code is invoked.

Remember, the whole point of this discussion is that it doesn't matter what .NET language you use. The compiler that creates the assemblies from the source files may produce inefficient code, but the fact remains that one .NET language can use types created in other languages and extend them as well. This is all due to the common language format that is CIL, and the focus of this book is to understand how CIL works.

 SOURCE CODE *The EasyCSharpClass folder contains the relevant .cs, .vb, and .il files for the code in this section.*

Conclusion

In this chapter, you saw that .NET allows a language to create and consume code written in other languages. This is accomplished by having compilers create assemblies that generate code written in an intermediate language. In the next chapter, you'll see how you can start to write assemblies in CIL by defining the directives that frame the assembly's structure.

CHAPTER 2

ilasm Directives and Attributes

In this chapter, I'll talk about the different ilasm directives and attributes that are available for the CIL developer. I'll work from the essential directives that are needed for any valid assembly to the directives that define the custom types and their associated elements (for example, methods and fields).

 NOTE *While I've included code samples in this chapter, they won't be that useful because I won't cover implementation specifics (that is, CIL opcodes) until the next chapter. However, I encourage you to compile the examples to learn how to use ilasm and to then view the results with ILDasm.*

General Assembly ilasm

When you create an assembly in CIL, the first thing you need to do is define some aspects of your assembly. Let's start the ilasm tour by defining how these directives and attributes function.

Defining the Assembly

Let's begin by looking at the `.assembly` directive. Not surprisingly, this directive is required for any assembly. Essentially, this directive defines the assembly by giving it a name:

```
.assembly BasicAssembly {}
```

While this directive seems easy enough to use, a number of subdirectives can be used with `.assembly`. I'll cover those later in this chapter.

The `.assembly` directive is also used to reference other assemblies so you can access their services. To do this, all you need to do is add the `extern` keyword:

```
.assembly extern mscorlib {}
```

In this case, I'm referencing the core library of .NET: mscorlib.dll.[1] Note that you can only have one .assembly directive in your assembly, but you can have multiple external references. You don't have to include a reference to mscorlib if you don't want to. Since this assembly contains many of the BCL types, the ilasm compiler will automatically add the reference anyway if your code doesn't.

Although naming your assembly gives you a way to identify it, that may not be sufficient. For example, if you want your assembly to live in the Global Assembly Cache (or GAC), then you need to give your assembly a strong name. To do this in ilasm requires you to add some extra directives under .assembly. Let's go over the pertinent ones[2] in detail.

Using Attributes to Store Metadata

.NET allows you to add metadata to your assembly and its contained elements via attributes. You can do this in ilasm through the .custom directive. It's a pretty simple process—just define which constructor on the attribute you wish to invoke:

```
.custom instance void
    [mscorlib]System.Reflection.AssemblyKeyFileAttribute::.ctor(string) =
    (01 00 1E 44 3A 5C 50 65 72 73 6F 6E 61 6C 5C 41
    50 72 65 73 73 5C 6B 65 79 50 61 69 72 2E 73 6E
    6B 00 00)
```

In this case, I'm giving my assembly a strong name. To do that, I use the AssemblyKeyFileAttribute attribute. I call the constructor that takes one argument, a string that defines the location of the key file, and pass in the correct informa- tion. In this case, the value is "D:\Personal\APress\keyPair.snk". Note that if I called a constructor that took no arguments, I don't have to define the array with all of the hexadecimal values. As you can see, though, the hard part here is if you have to call a constructor with arguments. How do you define that binary array correctly? Let's break down the byte array shown in the previous example and describe how it works.[3] One thing to keep in mind with this blob—it's in little- endian format. Other than the length for literal strings, the least significant bytes are first.

---

1. To understand how the runtime actually resolves which assembly to load, check out the article entitled "How the Runtime Locates Assemblies" in the SDK.

2. I won't discuss .os and .processor, as they are only used for documentation purposes in an assembly. See Section 6.2.2.3 of Partition II for more information.

3. See Sections 21.10 and 22.3 of Partition II for more detailed information on how to declare custom attributes.

First, you must begin the byte array with a prolog value of 1—that's the (01 00) value at the start (remember, it's little-endian!). You can then use named arguments and/or fixed arguments—in this example, I'm using fixed arguments, and there's only one fixed argument. Now, strings in custom byte blobs are defined using a SerString format, so you must state how long the string is. The key file location contains 30 characters, so that's the (1E) value. As this is the length of the string, it is not in little-endian format. The next 30 values are the ASCII values of the string; note that the string is *not* null terminated. Finally, the last two values, (00 00), are the number of named arguments. In this case, there are no named arguments.

> **NOTE** *If there's ever a case to be made for using a language like C# or VB .NET, this is it. I personally don't find figuring out what the value of the byte array should be for a custom attribute a pleasant experience; it's far easier to do in a higher-level language.*

Assembly Hash Algorithms

The .hash directive tells the runtime which hash algorithm was used to compute a hash value of the current assembly or a referenced file (I'll explain how to do that in the "Referencing Files and Resources" section). Technically, there are three values that could be used here,[4] but in reality only one is correct:

```
.hash algorithm 0x00008004
```

This sounds rather confusing, but essentially what the Partition docs state is that SHA1 (0x8004) is the most widely used hashing algorithm. Rather than burden any .NET implementation to support more than one hash algorithm, the spec indicates that this is the only one required and the only one that is valid.

The .hash directive can also be used to specify the hash value of a referenced assembly:

```
.assembly extern ReferencedAssembly
{
    .hash = (1F 99 2A 37 ...)
}
```

---

4.   See Section 22.1.1 of Partition II.

Referencing Files and Resources

You can add references to files and resources within a module via the `.file` and `.mresource` directives. Let's look at adding files first. It's pretty easy—you just add the filename after the directive:

```
.file nometadata BasicInfo.xml
```

Adding the `nometadata` attribute allows the file to have any format; if you don't include this attribute, the file must be a managed portable executable (PE). If you're referencing a PE file, you can also add an `.entrypoint` directive to specify that this file contains the entry point of the assembly:

```
.file entrypoint.exe .entrypoint
```

When you reference the file, you can't use drive letters and directories; you can only use the filename plus the extension. You should also add a hash value after the filename:

```
.file nometadata BasicInfo.xml .hash  = (5F 04 23 …)
```

If you declared the hash algorithm with `.hash`, then that algorithm is used to determine if the hash value for the file matches the one given here.

Adding resources is just as easy:

```
.mresource public BasicAssembly.res {}
```

You can make the resource private by using the `private` attribute in place of `public`. Public resources can be used by other assemblies; private ones are only available to the current assembly.

You refer to other resources by adding other directives. If you want to use resources in another assembly, add the `.assembly` directive:

```
.mresource public BasicAssembly.res
{
    .assembly extern ResourceSource
}
```

Or, if the resource is in a file, add a `.file` directive, except in this case, you specify a byte offset within the file where the resource is located:

```
.mresource public BasicAssembly.res
{
    .file ResourceSource.dll at 56
}
```

Defining the Culture

With .NET you can explicitly state which culture your assembly is targeted for. The `.locale` directive is used in this case. The values that you use must follow the RFC 1766 specification,[5] but you can just look up the `System.Globalization.CultureInfo` class in the SDK to get the list. The following example demonstrates an assembly targeted for the Swedish culture:

```
.locale "sv"
```

Signing Assemblies

If the `.publickey` directive is used, the value given after `.publickey` is the public key value for verifying a signature:

```
.publickey = (00 24 00 00 04 80 00 00 …)
```

The encrypted hash value is stored in the header of the assembly. (As an assembly designer, you don't have to worry about how this header information is created because ilasm.exe handles that for you.) When the assembly is loaded, the hash value of the assembly is computed, and the encrypted signature is decrypted based on `.publickey`'s value. If that result matches the value in the header, the signature verification passes. This checks that the assembly was not tampered with in any way. If someone tried to reverse-engineer the assembly and recompile it, this verification process would fail because that person wouldn't have the original private key to generate the correct signature value.

When you reference another assembly, you can use `.publickey`. However, public keys can take up a fair amount of space. If you don't want to carry around the entire public key's value, you can use the `.publickeytoken` directive to specify the last 8 bytes of the hashed public key value:

```
.publickeytoken (B7 7A 5C 56 19 34 E0 89)
```

---

5.   See http://www.freesoft.org/CIE/RFC/Orig/rfc1766.txt for more details.

Versioning

The `.ver` directive defines the current version number of the assembly. This can be up to four integers separated by colons, as the following two examples demonstrate:

```
.ver 1:2:3:4
.ver 1
```

You don't have to include all four numbers, and there are no explicit rules that you must follow on how you should version your assemblies with version numbers. The scheme that you decide on is up to you.[6]

This directive can also be used when you are referring to another assembly:

```
.assembly extern AnotherAssembly
{
    .ver 4:0:1:515
}
```

Declarative Security Information

The last bit of descriptive information you can add to your assembly is security information. Two directives enable you to describe the permissions your assembly does or does not need. They are `.permissionset` and `.permission`, but you'll only use `.permissionset`.[7] The only attribute you'll add states the security action:

```
.permissionset reqmin = (…)
```

In this case, the code is stating that the permission set defined in parentheses (which I'll describe in a moment) must be granted to the assembly for it to work—that's what `reqmin` stands for. Table 2-1 lists all of the valid security actions.

With `.permissionset`, you need to specify a byte array that describes the permission set information. The array is basically a byte representation of the result from a `ToXML()` call on the permission set in question. For example,

---

6. Section 6.2.1.4 of Partition II defines some conventions you should use, though, when employing `.ver`.

7. See Section 21.11 of Partition II to find a detailed explanation of why `.permission` isn't used to declare security metadata.

Table 2-1. Security Actions

ACTION	VALUE (HEX)	DESCRIPTION
assert	0x3	Prevents stack walks by ensuring that the code has the permission
demand	0x2	Specifies all callers must have the permission
deny	0x4	Denies the ability for any downward calls to use the permission
inheritcheck	0x7	Specifies subclasses must have the permission
linkcheck	0x6	Indicates callers must have the permission
noncasdemand	0xD	Similar to demand, but the permission must not derive from CodeAccessSecurity
noncaslinkdemand	0xE	Similar to linkcheck, but the permission must not derive from CodeAccessSecurity
permitonly	0x5	Allows the permission and no others
prejitgrant	0xB	If granted, persists at compile (JIT) time (Microsoft-specific implementation)
reqopt	0x9	Requests the permission if possible, but allows the assembly to load even if it's not granted
reqmin	0x8	Indicates the desired permission must be granted for the code to execute
reqrefuse	0xA	Does not allow the permission to be granted
request	0x1	Requests the permission if possible, but does not allow the assembly to load if it's not granted

if you were using a set that contained ReflectionPermission that needed the ability to emit code, here's how you'd get that byte array with a small piece of VB .NET code:[8]

```
Dim rpa As _
    New ReflectionPermissionAttribute( _
        SecurityAction.RequestMinimum)
rpa.Flags = ReflectionPermissionFlag.ReflectionEmit

Dim rp As IPermission = rpa.CreatePermission()

Dim ps As PermissionSet = New PermissionSet(PermissionState.Unrestricted)
ps.SetPermission(rp)
Dim psXML As SecurityElement = ps.ToXml()
Dim strXML As String = psXML.ToString()
Dim bytXML As Byte() = Encoding.Unicode.GetBytes(strXML)
```

---

8. For more information on security in .NET, I encourage you to read my book, *.NET Security* (Apress, 2002).

bytXML will now contain the information that you must insert in the
.permissionset statement. Here's what the string representation of the set looks like:

```
<PermissionSet class="System.Security.PermissionSet" version="1">
    <IPermission
        class="System.Security.Permissions.ReflectionPermission, mscorlib,
            Version=1.0.2411.0, Culture=neutral,
            PublicKeyToken=b77a5c561934e089"
        version="1"
        Flags="ReflectionEmit"/>
</PermissionSet>
```

Defining the Modules

Each assembly needs to have at least one logical name for reference purposes,
which is defined via the .module directive:

```
.module MyAssembly.dll
```

This should match the name of the file that this module resides in.[9] If you don't
declare it, ilasm will add a default value for you. You can have as many modules
within an assembly as you'd like, but these extra modules must be declared with
the extern attribute:

```
.module extern OtherAssembly.dll
```

Defining the UI

If your assembly needs to interact with the user via a graphical interface, you can
define this using the .subsystem directive. Currently, two valid values exist for
.subsystem. If you use 2, then the runtime knows that you need to run in a
standard GUI environment (like MS Word). The other value, 3, is used for
console-based programs (like cmd in Windows). For example, here's how you'd
tell the runtime that you need a console window available for your assembly:[10]

```
.subsystem 3
```

---

9. See Section 21.27 of Partition II.

10. Interestingly enough, in VS .NET, VB .NET, and C#, a Windows application emits a 2 for
    .subsystem, but a C# class library application emits a 3, whereas a VB .NET class library
    application emits a 2.

Concurrent Assembly Execution

Although .NET attempts to overcome the world of DLL Hell by allowing side-by-side installation of assemblies, there may be situations when you do not want more than one version of your assembly running at the same time.[11] Three attributes of the .assembly directive allow you to control this kind of loading behavior: noappdomain, nomachine, and noprocess. The following example demonstrates how you can have only one version of SimpleAssembly running on a machine:

```
.assembly nomachine SimpleAssembly
```

Be careful when using one of these options. You are effectively locking out other versions of your assembly from running concurrently.

Defining Data Segments

You can define data constants via the .data directive:

```
.data Miscellaneous = bytearray(54 A0 0D 20)
```

Miscellaneous is simply a 4-byte value.

Using bytearray to define the data is the most general declaration; you can also use standard value types:

```
.data Int16Data = int16(3)
```

Note that the type of the data is not preserved when you compile your code.

.data declarations can be made at the module, type, or method level. I'll show you how you can access the information in a data segment when I show you how to define fields.

SOURCE CODE *The BasicAssembly folder contains the BasicAssembly.il file, which contains examples of the directives discussed so far.*

---

11. For more information on what DLL Hell is all about, please read Steven Pratschner's article, "Simplifying Deployment and Solving DLL Hell with the .NET Framework," which can be found at http://msdn.microsoft.com/library/en-us/dndotnet/html/dplywithnet.asp?frame=true.

Type-Specific Directives

Now that I've covered the assembly-related directives, let's move on to the ones that deal with the specifics of type declaration and definition.

Defining the Type

To declare a type in your code, all you need is the `.class` directive. The type exists within a module—the simplest way to define a type is to give it a name:

```
.class SimpleType {}
```

However, there are a number of attributes that can enrich your type definition. Let's cover each of these in detail.

Type Kind

Three kinds of type can be created: value, reference, or interface. If you want your type to be an interface, add the `interface` attribute:

```
.class interface SimpleInterface {}
```

If you don't include this attribute, the type will be a reference type *unless* you explicitly extend `System.ValueType`:

```
.class SimpleStruct extends [mscorlib]System.ValueType {}
```

In this case, the type will be a value type. You can eliminate some typing through the `value` attribute, as it signifies that the type extends `System.ValueType`: [12]

```
.class public value SimpleValueType {}
```

---

12. To be valid, though, both `SimpleStruct` and `SimpleValueType` should contain at least one member, like a field, but I haven't covered type members yet.

Type Inheritance

As you may already know, .NET only supports single implementation inheritance; however, multiple interface inheritance is allowed. Figure 2-1 shows a UML diagram of a type inheritance scenario that is valid in .NET, whereas the layout in Figure 2-2 is invalid.

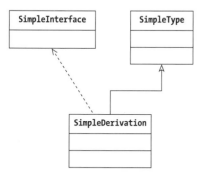

Figure 2-1. Acceptable .NET inheritance

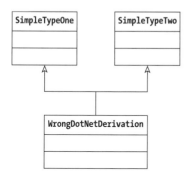

Figure 2-2. Invalid .NET inheritance

To have a type inherit the implementation of another type, use the extends keyword:

```
.class RefinedMemoryStream
    extends [mscorlib]System.IO.MemoryStream {}
```

You must fully qualify the type that you are extending by its assembly name in brackets along with its class name. If you don't include `extends` in your type definition, the compiler will automatically add an inheritance relationship to `System.Object` in `mscorlib` (as all types must directly or indirectly inherit from this base type).

If you want your class to implement one or more interfaces, use the `implements` keyword:

```
.class MyPermission implements [mscorlib]System.Security.IPermission,
    [mscorlib]System.Security.ISecurityEncodable {}
```

Of course, you're free to have both the `extends` and `implements` keywords in a `.class` declaration:

```
.class ExtendedType
    extends SimpleType
    implements SimpleInterface {}
```

Later on you'll see how to implement and/or override base methods.

Type Extensibility

Now that you know how you can use inheritance with your types, let's look at how you can control how other types can inherit from your types. Two attributes enforce special inheritance rules: `abstract` and `sealed`. Defining your type as abstract means that your type's implementation is incomplete and must either be completed by an inheriting type or deferred to another inheriting type:

```
.class abstract AbstractType {}
```

You can also create the reverse scenario—that is, a type that cannot be extended—by using the `sealed` attribute:

```
.class sealed SealedType {}
// The next line will compile,
//  but it will cause a TypeLoadException.
.class BadDesign extends SealedType {}
```

Note that value types should be declared with `sealed`—ilasm will generate a warning if you don't, as it needs to add the attribute at compile time to make the types valid.

Type Layout

Although you may have been familiar with the concept of inheritance, you may not know about the layout of the type. Essentially, these attributes define how the fields of your type are laid out in memory. There are three values you can give: auto (the default), explicit, and sequential. Here's how you define a type with the default layout:

```
.class auto SimpleAutoType {}
```

With reference types, you'll probably use auto. In this case, you're stating that you don't care how or where the fields are located in memory. However, with value types, you'll use sequential as this following example demonstrates:

```
.class public sequential
    sealed value SimpleStruct
{
    .field public float64 FieldOne
    .field public int8 FieldTwo
    .field public int32 FieldThree
}
```

What the runtime will do is lay the fields out in memory in sequential order on a 4-byte boundary, as Figure 2-3 shows.

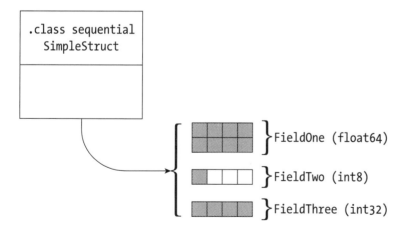

Figure 2-3. Sequential layout

However, if you use the `explicit` layout attribute, you now have the finest control over the layout as possible. For example, you can use bracketed integer values to specify the precise location of the field in memory:

```
.class public explicit
    sealed value SimpleExplicitStruct
{
    .field [0] public float64 FieldOne
    .field [12] public int8 FieldTwo
    .field [24] public int32 FieldThree
}
```

Figure 2-4 shows what this explicit layout looks like. As you can see, in this case, this explicit layout takes up more memory than the sequential example.

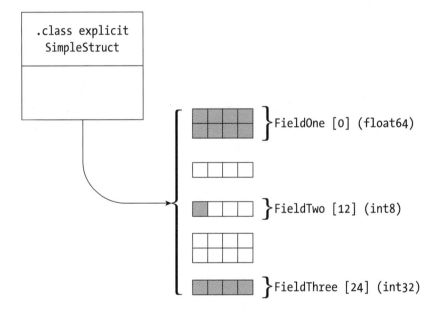

Figure 2-4. Explicit layout

You can also overlap fields and alter the natural 4-byte boundary with the `.pack` directive.[13] For example, if you add `.pack` to your SimpleStruct definition:

---

13. See Section 9.7 of Partition II for more information on layouts.

```
.class public sequential
    sealed value SimplePackedStruct
{
    .pack 1
    .field public float64 FieldOne
    .field public int8 FieldTwo
    .field public int32 FieldThree
}
```

you'll get the layout shown in Figure 2-5.

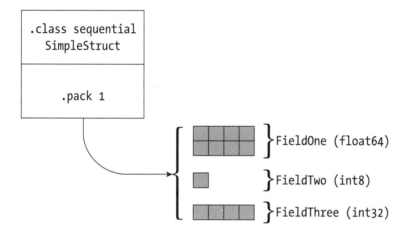

Figure 2-5. Packed layout

Now the layout is "compressed"—there are no 4-byte address alignments. Valid values for .pack are 0 to 128, so long as the value is a power of 2 (for example, 64 is valid, but 65 is not).

Furthermore, you can overlap fields by specifying the same field array slot to create a union:

```
.class public explicit
    sealed value UnionType
{
    .field [0] public int32 anInt32
    .field [0] public int32 anotherInt32
    .field [4] public string aString
}
```

Finally, you can declare a type that is nothing more but a block of memory via the `.size` directive:

```
.class public
    sealed value MemoryBlock
{
    .size 64
}
```

SOURCE CODE *The SimpleTypes folder contains the SimpleTypes.il file, which holds examples of the types shown in this section.*

Type Visibility and Accessibility

There are a number of ways that you can affect how other assemblies can use your types. Essentially, the rules are broken down via two criteria: top-level and nested types. The following code snippet shows the difference between these:

```
.class TopLevelType
{
    .class nested NestedType {}
}
```

Note the addition of the `nested` attribute for the nested type. Let's take a look at the first case (which is what I've been demonstrating so far). A top-level type controls the visibility of itself and any contained types. It can do this with two attributes: `public` and `private`. For example, take a look at the following code:

```
.assembly Visibility {}
.class public VisibleType {}
.class private InvisibleType {}
```

If another assembly uses the assembly that contains these types, it would be able to create `VisibleType`, but not `InvisibleType`:

```
.assembly extern Visibility
.assembly UseVisibility {}
.class ExtendVisibleType extends VisibleType
//  The following declaration is invalid
.class ExtendInvisibleType extends InvisibleType
```

However, note that it's legal for any code in VisibleType to create an instance of InvisibleType.[14]

Now, nested types cannot control their visibility, but they can control their accessibility. Although these two terms sound similar, they are used to define two different situations. Types control whether or not they are visible to other assemblies, and they control if their members are accessible to other assemblies. Let's alter the last code snippet to clarify this:

```
.class public VisibleType
{
    .class public nested VisibleNestedPublicType {}
    .class private nested VisibleNestedPrivateType {}
}
.class private InvisibleType
{
    .class public nested InvisibleNestedPublicType {}
    .class private nested InvisibleNestedPrivateType {}
}
```

Even though InvisibleNestedPublicType is defined as public, it won't be seen by any other assemblies because InvisibleType is private. However, VisibleType and VisibleNestedPublicType can create InvisibleNestedPublicType. Finally, InvisibleNestedPrivateType can only be created by InvisibleType and InvisibleNestedPublicType.

More accessibility attributes are available than just public and private. Table 2-2 lists all of these attributes and how they work.

Table 2-2. Accessibility Attributes

VALUE	DESCRIPTION
public	Accessible to all
private	Accessible to only the enclosing type and any other nested types
nested assembly	Accessible to all types within the assembly
nested famandassem	Accessible to types that meet the qualifications for nested assembly and nested family
nested family	Accessible to the enclosing type and any other types that inherit from the enclosing type
nested famorassem	Accessible to types that meet the qualifications for nested assembly or nested family
nested private	Accessible to only the enclosing type and any other nested types
nested public	Accessible to all

---

14. Actually, this isn't correct given the code here—you could compile it and it would work fine. Once you've read the discussion on constructors, though, come back to this example and add constructors to these types; you'll find out that ExtendInvisibleType won't work anymore. The code sample has the constructor added for these types.

SOURCE CODE *The Visibility folder contains the Visibility.il and UseVisibility.il files, which demonstrate visibility and accessibility issues.*

Type Interoperability

If you need to work with unmanaged code (for example, making a Win32 API invocation), and either one or more of the method's arguments and/or its return value is a string, then you can employ three attributes to specify what kind of marshalling should take place if a method within the class does not define it. You can use ansi (8-bit), unicode (16-bit), or autochar (which will vary depending on the underlying OS). For example, here's how you'd specify using Unicode strings for marshalling:

```
.class unicode SomeType {}
```

Type Miscellanea

You can add two special attributes to your type: beforefieldinit and serializable.[15] They result in some very interesting behaviors when you include them in your type definition. If you use serializable, you're stating to the runtime that your type's fields can be serialized into a stream:

```
.class serializable PersistableType {}
```

You'll see how object serialization works when you get to the .field directive discussion later on in the section "Adding Fields to a Type."

The beforefieldinit attribute controls when your type initializer is called, but since I haven't talked about methods and constructors yet, I'll defer discussion of this attribute until later, in the section "beforefieldinit Redux."

---

15. There are two other attributes you can use, specialname and rtspecialname, but they're ignored by the runtime. See Section 9.1.6 of Partition II.

Declaring Namespaces

Before leaving this discussion of type definitions, I'd like to cover the `.namespace` directive. You may have seen it if you've looked at your assemblies in ILDasm. For example, let's say you have the following C# class definition:

```
using System;

namespace Apress
{
    public class Book
    {
        public Book() {}
    }
}
```

If you compile this class and look at the resulting IL, you'll see something like this (I've deleted most of the results for brevity):

```
.assembly NamespaceTest
.module NamespaceTest.dll
.namespace Apress
{
    .class public auto ansi beforefieldinit Book
        extends [mscorlib]System.Object {}
}
```

A namespace is not part of any metadata; it's simply a way to logically group similar types together while allowing higher-level languages to perform less typing. For example, the `Book` type's official name is actually `Apress.Book`, but you can use `Book` within C# or VB .NET, (provided that you use type-qualification via the `using` keyword in C# or the `Imports` keyword in VB .NET). However, in CIL you'll always need to use the full type name whenever you reference a type.

Adding Fields to a Type

Types basically consist of two properties: data and behavior. In the next section, I'll cover how the behavior is defined; for now, let's look at how you can store information for your type via fields. You already saw how fields are declared when I covered type layouts, so I'll address other field declaration issues in this section.

Fields are usually scoped to the type that contains them. You define them using the .field directive. Here's one of the simplest ways you can define a field for a type:

```
.class SimpleFieldDefines
{
    .field private string m_string
    .field private static int32 m_int
}
```

The enclosing brackets are used to scope the field with the type. .NET does support the notion of a global field where the field can be accessed by any type within the module, so the following code is valid:

```
.field public string g_string
.class SimpleFieldDefines
{
    .field private string m_string
    .field private static int32 m_int
}
```

Each field must have a type name that defines what kind of field it is, such as string or int32.

As you can see in the previous code snippet, you can employ a number of attributes with a .field directive. All of the accessibility attributes (for example, private, family) were covered in the previous section. Let's take a closer look at the newer ones.

Field Scope

If a field is not global, then it is associated with a type. However, using the static attribute with a field declaration changes the accessibility of the field within the type. For example, your SimpleFieldDefines type from the previous section has two fields, m_string and m_int. m_int is a static field, so any SimpleFieldDefines instance will have access to this field, and there will be only one instance of m_int.[16] However, m_string is not static, so every SimpleFieldDefines instance gets its own m_string instance. Figure 2-6 shows this field scenario.

---

16. Although it's out of the scope of this discussion, keep in mind that there may be issues with static fields in multithreading scenarios.

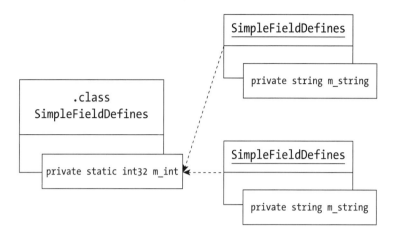

Figure 2-6. Static fields

Field Initialization

Two attributes define how fields are initialized: initonly and literal. If you use literal, you are in essence defining a constant:

```
.field private static literal int32 m_const_int = int32(44)
```

Note that m_const_int doesn't exist in memory, although it does exist as metadata. Compilers will replace the value of m_const_int in code with 44. Also, the declaration syntax to define the value of m_const_int can be done for a number of different types—the following code snippet gives an example of the field initializers in action:[17]

```
.field public static literal bool CT_BOOL = bool(true)
.field public static literal char CT_CHAR = char(0x0062)
.field public static literal float32 CT_FLOAT = float32(0x42631EB8)
.field public static literal float64 CT_DOUBLE = float64(12.34)
.field public static literal int8 CT_BYTE = int8(0x02)
.field public static literal unsigned int8 CT_UBYTE = int8(3)
.field public static literal int16 CT_SHORT = int16(0x0004)
.field public static literal unsigned int16 CT_USHORT = int16(0x0005)
.field public static literal int32 CT_INT = int32(6)
.field public static literal unsigned int32 CT_UINT = int32(0x00000007)
.field public static literal int64 CT_LONG = int64(0x8)
.field public static literal unsigned int64 CT_ULONG = int64(9)
.field public static literal string CT_STRING = "Constant string."
.field public static literal object CT_OBJECT = nullref
```

---

17.   See Section 15.2 of Partition II for the full documentation on the field initialization syntax.

initonly is similar to a constant, but it does not have to be initialized in the .field declaration. If the field is static, it must be initialized in the type initializer; otherwise, the field must be set in an instance constructor (I'll cover these methods later on in the section "Type and Instance Initializers"). Here's a sample declaration of an initonly field:

```
.field private initonly int32 m_init_once_int
```

You can also initialize a field to the value located in a data segment:

```
.data SomeData = bytearray(01 02 03 04)
.class DataInit
{
    .field static int32 UseData at SomeData
}
```

Note that only static fields can be mapped to data segments.

serializable Redux

In the section "Type Miscellanea," I mentioned that you could add the serializable attribute to a type to indicate that your instances could be serialized. However, if you want to prevent a field from being serialized, you use the notserialized attribute. Let's take a look at the following code snippet:

```
.class serializable SimpleSerialization
{
    .field private notserialized string m_string
    .field private static int32 m_int
}
```

In this case, whenever a SimpleSerialization instance is serialized, only the value of m_int will be serialized; m_string's value will be lost in the serialization process. Note that this attribute only has meaning for instance fields, as static fields are not serialized.

SOURCE CODE *The Fields folder contains the Fields.il file, which includes the types shown in this section.*

Adding Methods to Types

Having the ability to add fields to types is not enough; you'd like to be able to add behavior to your types. This is done by adding methods to a type via the .method directive. Following is a code snippet for a simple method definition:

```
.class SimpleClass
{
    .method public void SomeMethod() {}
}
```

Of course, with methods you'll usually have some kind of implementation. I'll cover how to do that with CIL in Chapter 3. As with type and field definitions, there are a number of attributes you can add to .method. Furthermore, with a method you can add other directives for the method body. Let's drill down into these aspects in detail.[18]

Type and Instance Methods

Similar to fields, methods can either belong to the type or to a specific type instance. If you use the static attribute, the method can be invoked without creating an instance of the type; otherwise, an instance must be around to invoke the method. Take a look at the following code snippet:

```
.class SimpleMethodDefines
{
    .field private string m_string
    .field private static int32 m_int
    .method public void SomeMethod() {}
    .method public static void SomeStaticMethod() {}
}
```

Calling SomeStaticMethod() does not require a SimpleMethodDefines instance, whereas SomeMethod() does.

---

18. I won't cover accessibility attributes again for methods, as I've already covered them with fields.

NOTE *Again, I'm jumping ahead of myself. If you try to compile and use* SimpleMethodDefines, *it won't work, because the methods have no implementation. In the downloadable code, I've included as little CIL as I could to get the samples to compile—that's why the code here and in the downloads will look a little different.*

Method Implementation Details

I'll deal with method implementation code in the next chapter, but for now you need to know that you have to specify a couple of attributes for the kind of implementation the method has. The first one is cil—specifying this attribute means the implementation is done completely with CIL. You can also use the runtime attribute if you're dealing with delegates—I'll talk about those near the end of this chapter in the section "Adding Events to Types."

You can also use two mutually exclusive attributes to describe the implementation. managed is used when the method is CIL-based (you'll usually use cil and managed in concert). The unmanaged attribute applies to P/Invoke calls (although it is not required). You'll see code snippets that include these implementation attributes later on in the chapter.

A number of other attributes control implementation details. For example, if you want to ensure that your method's implementation is executed by only one thread at a time, add the synchronized attribute. However, use care when including this attribute, as you can easily run into deadlocking issues.[19]

Another available attribute is noinlining. When this attribute is present, the runtime will not inline the method. *Method inlining* occurs when a compiler takes the implementation of a method and puts it directly into another method's implementation instead of making a method call. There are technical reasons why a compiler will choose to inline a method's implementation, so unless you know that your method should never be inlined for any reason, I'd suggest leaving this attribute alone.[20]

Calling Conventions

Take a look at this method:

```
.class SimpleType
{
    .method public instance void SomeMethod(int32 arg1) {}
}
```

---

19. If you want to know more about multithreading "gotchas" like deadlocking, read Chapter 2 of Allan Holub's book *Taming Java Threads* (Apress, 2000).

20. There are two other attributes, forwardref and internalcall, but they are for internal use only and you should not use them. See Section 14.4.3.3 of Partition II for further details.

Now, what do you think the type of the first argument to SomeMethod() is? Hint: it's not an int32! It's actually a reference to the current instance of SimpleType. Static methods don't receive an instance reference, but instance methods (those methods defined with the instance attribute) do.[21] Since it's pretty easy to determine what the type of the current instance is, this information isn't explicitly stated in any of the metadata.

Other attributes are available for controlling how the arguments are passed to the method. Two of them, default and vararg, are used for managed methods. Most of the methods you create will be of the default kind, but that's assumed if you don't specify anything. If you have a number of variable arguments to your method, then you must use the vararg attribute:

```
.method instance vararg int32 VariableArguments(
    int32 arg1, string arg2)
```

In this case, the caller must provide values for arg1 and arg2, but the caller can also supply a number of extra argument values.

CROSS-REFERENCE *See "Variable Argument Lists" in Chapter 3 to see how you would actually iterate through the variable arguments.*

Four other arguments are used with the unmanaged attribute and define well-known calling conventions: cdecl, stdcall, fastcall, and thiscall. You'll probably never need them, but if you must make a P/Invoke call to a CDECL-based method, you know it's possible.[22]

NOTE *If you want more information on how these calling conventions work, read the article "Calling Conventions Demystified" by Nemanja Trifunovic, at* http://www.codeproject.com/useritems/ calling_conventions_demystified.asp.

---

21. That's how C# gets its this reference and VB .NET gets its Me reference.

22. Section 14.3 of Partition II hints that there are 10 other attributes for different calling conventions, but it doesn't explicitly state what they are.

Passing Arguments

Passing arguments to a method is pretty simple—the last section showed some code snippets in which an int32 was passed into a method. Generally, you pass arguments by stating the type first, and then the name of the argument:

```
.class SimpleType
{
    .method public instance int64 SomeMethod(int32 arg1, float64 arg2,
        class [System.Windows.Forms]System.Windows.Forms.Form thisForm) {}
}
```

In this case, you have four arguments:[23] the instance pointer, an int32 named arg1, a float64 named arg2, and a Form reference named thisForm.

You can also add three attributes to the parameters that are pointer types (arguments declared with the & symbol[24]): in, out, and opt. All of these are enclosed in brackets when you use them, like this:

```
.method public instance void SomeMethod([out] int32& arg1) {}
```

in means that the caller must supply a valid pointer type before the method is called. out indicates that the method must set the argument to the correct type before the method completes; the caller does not have to supply a valid value for the argument when the method is invoked. opt means the argument is intended to be optional. However, since the runtime requires that all parameters have a value, you need to set the value to a default via the .param directive—I'll cover this later on in the section "Method Body Directives."

Unmanaged Calls

My guess is that you'll usually stay within .NET's managed space—that is, you'll stick to using the classes that are available in the .NET Framework whenever possible. However, there's too much legacy code out there that wasn't created with a .NET language. Unmanaged code can be called in .NET, but you'll need to make some additions to the method declaration. For example, let's say you wanted to call FormatMessage(), which exists in kernel32.dll. Here's what it looks like in the SDK:

---

23. I realize you just read a discussion about instance methods and the instance reference being the first argument, so in this case you have five arguments. To avoid confusion, I won't mention or include this implicit instance argument unless I have to clarify a specific issue.

24. See Section 13.4 of Partition II for more information on pointer types.

```
DWORD FormatMessage(
    DWORD dwFlags. LPCVOID lpSource,
    DWORD dwMessageId, DWORD dwLanguageId,
    LPTSTR lpBuffer, DWORD nSize,
    va_list *Arguments
);
```

Here's one way to declare this method in CIL:

```
.method private hidebysig
    static pinvokeimpl("kernel32.dll" autochar winapi)
    int32 FormatMessage(int32 Flags,
    native int& MessageSource,
    int32 MessageID, int32 LanguageID,
    native int& Buffer, int32 BufferSize,
    int32 Arguments) cil managed {}
```

You'll notice that the method is declared as `static`—only static methods can be used for P/Invokes. The method must also be declared with the `pinvokeimpl` attribute and the executable where the method exists given. `winapi` states that the runtime should use the standard calling convention of the target OS—as I mentioned before, other valid calling conventions are `cdecl`, `fastcall`, and `stdcall`. `autochar` defines how strings will be marshaled to the method—other mutually exclusive string marshalling attributes include `ansi` and `unicode`. (I'll demonstrate how this method is called in Chapter 3.)

 NOTE *There's COM interoperability to worry about as well, but this is handled at a level above ilasm and CIL, so I won't cover it here. Readers interested in learning more about .NET and COM interoperability should read Andrew Troelsen's book* **COM and .NET Interoperability**. *(Apress, 2002).*

Type and Instance Initializers

Speaking of creating instances, you can add initializers, or constructors, to your types. There are two kinds of initializers: type and instance. A *type initializer* is called before any methods are invoked or fields are accessed on a type (this can be changed a bit; I'll explain how in the next section). An *instance initializer* is called when a new instance of a type is created.

To create an initializer, you must use the rtspecialname and specialname attributes. The type initializer must be static, it can take no arguments, and it must be named .cctor. Instance initializers must have the instance attribute, and must be named .ctor. There can only be one type initializer, but you can have any number of custom constructors, so long as they all have different method signatures.

To see how these initializers are defined in a type, take a look at the following code snippet:

```
.class SimpleInitializers
{
    .method public specialname rtspecialname instance void
        .ctor() cil managed {}
    .method public specialname rtspecialname instance void
        .ctor(int32 arg1) cil managed {}
    .method private specialname rtspecialname static void
        .cctor() cil managed {}
}
```

This type has two instance initializers and one type initializer.

beforefieldinit Redux

Now that I've covered type initializers, I'd like to come back to a type attribute that I mentioned before but didn't cover in any detail: beforefieldinit. If you don't include this attribute, the runtime has to fulfill three guarantees:[25]

- A type initializer will only be run once, unless called again by user code.

- Method invocations on the type cannot be made until the type initializer is complete, unless the initializer calls the method(s).

- The type initializer will be run when either a static or an instance field is accessed, or any method on the type is called.

One problem with these rules is that it can become difficult to ensure that the type initializer runs before any methods can be run. Therefore, you can relax these guarantees by adding the beforefieldinit attribute. If you add this attribute, then it's possible that a static method will be run before the type initializer is completed.

---

25. See Section 9.5.3 of Partition II for all of the gory details on type initializers.

So when should you use this attribute? Well, if you don't have a type initializer, you should use it as there's no reason to let the runtime be more efficient with your type's usage. If you also know that a static method doesn't access static fields, then it's also safe to use this attribute. But if you must have that guarantee that the type initializer completes before anything else is done, then you shouldn't use this attribute.[26]

Exporting Methods

It is possible to create methods that can be called directly from unmanaged code. This is done with the `.vtfixup`, `.corflags`, `.vtentry`, and `.export` directives. Here's an example of how it works:

```
.corflags 0x00000002
.vtfixup [1] int32 fromunmanaged at ENTRY_1
// ...
.method public static int32 UnmanagedInt32()
{
    .vtentry 1:1
    .export [1] as UnmanagedInt32
    // ...
}
// ...
.data ENTRY_1 = int32(0)
```

The `.corflags` directive is usually set to 0x00000001. This stands for `COMIMAGE_FLAGS_ILONLY`, which indicates the file is all managed code, so you usually won't set this. Setting this directive to 0x00000002 (or `COMIMAGE_FLAGS_32BITREQUIRED`) limits the code to being loaded into 32-bit processes. However, this is required if you export a method for unmanaged access, which is the real reason it's being set.[27]

The `.vtfixup` directive states that a virtual table (or v-table) should be created at the data address specified. In this case, you only have one method to export, so you only need one v-table. If you were exporting more methods, you would change the `.data` declaration as follows:

```
.data ENTRY_1 = int32[4]
```

---

26. Although I'll cover VB .NET and C# compiler results in Chapter 6, I'd like to note here that the C# compiler will always add `beforefieldinit` if a type does not have a type initializer. If there is a type initializer, this attribute is not added.

27. See Section 24.3.3.1 of Partition II.

With this declaration, there would be four slots in the v-table. Note that you could also reverse these definitions and create four v-tables, each with one slot:

```
.vtfixup [1] int32 fromunmanaged at ENTRY_1
.vtfixup [2] int32 fromunmanaged at ENTRY_2
.vtfixup [3] int32 fromunmanaged at ENTRY_3
.vtfixup [4] int32 fromunmanaged at ENTRY_4
.data ENTRY_1 = int32(0)
.data ENTRY_2 = int32(0)
.data ENTRY_3 = int32(0)
.data ENTRY_4 = int32(0)
```

If you need to export more than one method, the choice between the two is up to you. There's really no difference between them—they'll work the same in the end. Personally, I'd choose creating one v-table with the necessary number of slots—it's less typing.

The `int32` attribute specifies the size of the slot entry—`int64` is also valid, but the two attributes cannot be used together (note that `int32` is the default if you don't specify either one). The `fromunmanaged` attribute states that the target method of this slot should be called from unmanaged code, which is what you want to do. Finally, the reference to `ENTRY_1` defines the v-table entry location in memory.

Now, in the method, you use the `.vtentry` directive. The first number specifies which v-table the method will be located in. Since you only have one v-table, you use 1. The second number specifies which slot the method will be located in the v-table—again, you only have one slot, so you use 1. The `.export` directive specifies an ordinal number along with the name that an unmanaged program (like VB 6) can use to call the method. In both directives, the values are 1-based.

So what does all of this v-table mess mean? It comes down to this: the compiler will create the necessary information in the resulting module such that an unmanaged client can call the managed method. The v-tables and v-table slots are there primarily as a mechanism for the .NET runtime to find the managed method and create a thunk (or a marshalling layer) to allow the unmanaged method to call the managed method. Therefore, a VB 6 client can now call the module that contains `UnmanagedInt32()` like this:

```
Private Declare Function UnmanagedInt32 Lib "Methods.dll" () As Integer

Private Sub cmdInvoke_Click()
MsgBox "UnmanagedInt32 = " & CStr(UnmanagedInt32())
End Sub
```

SOURCE CODE *The Methods folder contains the Methods.il file, which holds method declaration samples. The VBTest subfolder contains a VB 6 application that calls the* UnmanagedInt32() *method.*

Method Body Directives

Now that you know how to declare methods, let's move on to the method body directives. These directives are not CIL instructions, but they get you closer to the method's implementation, as some of them allow you to declare variables and state the stack size.

Declaring an Entry Point

You may have written a VB application with a Main() method in a code module or a Java application with a static main() method. In both cases, these are well-known entry points that represent the starting points of the application. By convention, the entry point method is given a conventional name ("main"), and the compiler makes the necessary adjustments in the executable such that this method is the one that is called when the application starts. However, in ilasm you're not confined to one specific name for your entry point. Simply add the .entrypoint directive to the method body to define that method as the entry point:

```
.class public SimpleEntryPoint
{
    .method public static void AnEntryPointMethod()
        cil managed
    {
        .entrypoint
    }
}
```

There are a couple of restrictions for an entry point method. It must be static, and it can only return an int32 or an unsigned int32 (or void if nothing will be returned). As AnEntryPointMethod() shows, the entry point doesn't have to take any arguments, but if it does, it must take only one argument, an array of System.String values. Also, you can have only one entry point method per assembly. The method's accessibility doesn't matter, as the runtime will call it no matter what it is.

Adding Custom Attributes

As you've seen before with types, you can add metadata to your method via attributes. You use the .custom directive to specify which attribute you'd like to use to decorate your method:

```
.method public instance int32
    ObsoleteMethod() cil managed
{
    .custom instance void
        [mscorlib]System.ObsoleteAttribute::.ctor(string,bool) =
        ( 01 00 0F 44 6F 6E 27 74 20 75 73 65 20 74 68 69
        73 21 01 00 00 )
}
```

In the previous code snippet, I'm using the ObsoleteAttribute attribute to mark ObsoleteMethod as obsolete. I'm also passing two values to its constructor; it's easier to see what's going on by viewing its C# counterpart:

```
[Obsolete("Don't use this!", true)]
public int ObsoleteMethod() {}
```

Declaring Local Variables

More often than not, you'll need to use local variables within your methods. Declaring them is pretty easy—just use the .locals directive:

```
.method public instance int32 AMethod() cil managed
{
    .locals ([0] class [mscorlib]System.Type someType,
        [1] class [System.Windows.Forms]System.Windows.Forms.Form formRef,
        [2] int32 i)
}
```

In this example, I'm giving the index of the locals explicitly via the bracketed numbers, but you don't have to do this (it helps, though, as a mnemonic for some of CIL codes you'll see in the next chapter). You can declare a number of local variables so long as you enclose them via parentheses. Technically, the variable names (for example, someType, i) aren't required, but I'd suggest declaring local variables with names for clarity's sake.

You don't have to declare all of your variables at the top of the method body. It is possible to declare local variables within CIL code. To do this, enclose them within braces:

```
.method public instance int32 AMethod() cil managed
{
    .locals ([0] int32 i, [1] int32 j)
    //  CIL code goes here.
    {
        .locals([2] int32 k)
        //  More CIL goes here.
    }
}
```

In fact, if two variables are of the same type, you can reuse variable array slots:

```
.method public instance int32 AMethod() cil managed
{
    .locals ([0] int32 i, [1] int32 j)
    //  CIL code goes here.
    {
        .locals([2] int32 k)
        //  More CIL goes here.
    }
    {
        .locals([2] int32 l)
        //  More CIL goes here.
    }
}
```

This allows you to perform some optimizations by reusing previous variable declarations.

You can also add the init attribute when you declare local variables:

```
.method public instance int32 AMethod() cil managed
{
    .locals init ([0] int32 i, [1] int32 j)
}
```

When you use this attribute, the variable will be automatically initialized to its default value. I'd suggest adding init whenever you declare a variable as it'll keep things consistent in terms of knowing what state your variables will be in when you use them the first time.[28]

Finally, you can add the pinned attribute to local variable declarations:

```
.method public instance int32 PinnedVariables() cil managed
{
    .locals init ([0] int32 floating,
        [1] int32 pinned fixedInPlace)
}
```

This tells the runtime that it should not move the variable in memory. Therefore, as PinnedVariables() executes, the location of floating may change, but fixedInPlace will always exist at the exact same place in memory.

Optional Arguments

It is possible to define a method with optional arguments. Take a look at the following example:

```
.class public OptionalArgs
{
    .method public
        instance void OnlyOneIsNeeded(int32 X,
        [opt] string Name) cil managed
    {
        .param [2] = "Jason"
    }
}
```

Technically, every argument in a .NET method is required to be given a value by the caller. However, some languages (like VB .NET) have optional arguments. This syntax supports the concept. By declaring the argument Name as being optional via the [opt] keyword and supplying a default value for Name via the .param directive, VB .NET developers can call this method as follows:

```
Dim oa As OptionalArgs = New OptionalArgs()
oa.OnlyOneIsNeeded(3)
```

---

28. It'll also keeps your methods verifiable—see Section 14.4.1.3 of Partition II for details.

In this case, the VB .NET compiler will look at the default value for Name and automatically add it to the assembly's generated code. The index value after .param specifies which argument is mapped to the value. Note that 0 specifies the return value, 1 specifies the first argument value, and so on (the instance reference cannot be set as an optional argument). It is not up to the runtime to set the value of Name if it is not given to OnlyOneIsNeeded(); if you design a language that supports optional arguments, you need to pass in the default value if the coder doesn't include it in a method call.

Specifying the Maximum Stack Size

As your method executes and the CIL opcodes run, you'll inevitably put values onto the stack. To tell the runtime the maximum number of variables that will be on the stack during method execution, use the .maxstack directive:

```
.method public instance int32 AMethod() cil managed
{
    .maxstack 10
}
```

Note that this only specifies the maximal number of values that you think will be on the stack at one time; it doesn't relate in any way to the memory size of these values.

This directive is optional; if you don't include it, ilasm will automatically include this directive in your method body and set the size to 8. This doesn't mean that you're limited to only eight values on the stack at a time. In fact, if you know that the maximal stack size will be bigger than this default value, you should use .maxstack to set this size. If you don't and the method in question is executed, the runtime will throw a VerificationException exception.

CROSS-REFERENCE *See ".maxstack Calculations" in Chapter 3 to see why calculating this maximum value isn't as easy as it looks.*

SOURCE CODE *The MethodBody folder contains the MethodBody.il file—it demonstrates the method body declarations I just covered.*

Overriding Methods

The last method body directive to discuss is .override. I'm also going to backtrack a bit and talk about a few of method attributes I didn't mention before: abstract, virtual, hidebysig, and newslot. As you'll use these in concert, I thought it would make sense to define them in the same section. However, before you look at actual code, you need to make sure you know what a method signature is prior to overriding methods.

A method signature is comprised of a number of parts:

- The calling convention

- The argument types (if any exist)

- The return type

Let's take a look at a couple of methods:

```
.method public int32 Method1(float64 arg1) cil managed
.method private void Method2(float64 arg2) runtime managed
.method family int32 Method3(byte arg3)
.method famorassem int32 Method4(float64 arg4)
.method private vararg int32 Method5(float64 arg5)
.method int32 Method6(char arg6a, int32 arg6b)
.method int32 Method7(int32 arg7a, char arg7b)
```

Out of these five methods, only Method1() and Method4() have the same method signatures. Their calling conventions are the same (it's not explicitly declared in either method, so it's the default convention), their return types match (int32), and they have the same number of arguments with the same types (one float64).

CROSS-REFERENCE *See "Overloading Methods in CIL" in Chapter 6 to see how this can lead to an interesting situation with what can be done in ilasm and CIL, but not in VB .NET or C#.*

Now that you have the definition of a method signature, let's start the method overriding discussion by looking at the `virtual` attribute:

```
.class public BaseClass
{
    .method public virtual instance void BaseMethod()
        cil managed {}
    .method public instance void NoOverrideBaseMethod()
        cil managed {}
}
```

When you use this attribute, types that extend `BaseClass` can override the implementation of the method in question. In this case, `BaseMethod()` can be overridden, but `NoOverrideBaseMethod()` can't. Note that you can only override instance methods; static methods cannot be overridden.

To override the virtual method's implementation, you can declare a method that matches the virtual method's name:

```
.class public SubClass extends BaseClass
{
    .method public virtual instance void BaseMethod()
        cil managed {}
}
```

That's all you need to do to override a method.

However, you can have more control over the overriding process if you want it. So far, I've shown you how to override methods based on name only. If you add the `hidebysig` attribute, then you'll only override a base method if the derived method matches the base's signature and the name:

```
.class public BaseClassHiding
{
    .method public virtual instance void BaseMethodBySignature(int32 arg1)
        cil managed {}
    .method public virtual instance void BaseMethodByName(float64 arg1)
        cil managed {}
}
.class public DerivedClassHiding extends BaseClassHiding
{
    .method public hidebysig virtual instance
        void BaseMethodBySignature(int32 arg1)
```

```
        cil managed {}
    .method public virtual instance
        void BaseMethodByName()
        cil managed {}
}
```

In this case, both base methods are overridden by DerivedClassHiding's methods. However, BaseMethodByName() overrides BaseClassHiding.BaseMethodByName(), even though it doesn't take a float64 argument.

If you use the abstract attribute with a virtual method, you force the user to provide an implementation in a subclass (or continue to defer the implementation):

```
.class abstract public AbstractClass
{
    .method public abstract virtual
        hidebysig instance void AbstractMethod()
        cil managed {}
}
.class abstract public MiddleClass extends AbstractClass {}
.class abstract public ImplementationClass extends MiddleClass
{
    .method public virtual hidebysig
        instance void AbstractMethod()
        cil managed {}
}
```

In this case, AbstractClass defines an abstract method, AbstractMethod(). MiddleClass defers the implementation of this method by not overriding it. ImplementationClass decides to implement this method by providing a virtual method with the correct signature.

The other attribute, newslot, affects when a virtual method is really defined:

```
.class public BaseClassNewSlot
{
    .method public virtual instance void BaseMethod()
        cil managed {}
}
.class public SubClassNewSlot
    extends BaseClassSlot
{
    .method public hidebysig virtual newslot instance
        void BaseMethod()
        cil managed {}
}
```

Even though you have a method that should override
`BaseClassNewSlot.BaseMethod()`, `SubClassNewSlot.BaseMethod()` won't. By adding
`newslot`, the runtime will create a new virtual method that will not override
`BaseClassSlot.BaseMethod()`. Therefore, the correct place to add this attribute
is in the base class and not the extending class:

```
.class public BaseClassNewSlot
{
    .method public hidebysig virtual newslot instance
        void BaseMethod()
        cil managed {}
}
.class public SubClassNewSlot
    extends BaseClassNewSlot
{
    .method public hidebysig virtual instance
        void BaseMethod()
        cil managed {}
}
```

This expresses the intent of your design. You want `BaseMethod()` in
`BaseClassNewSlot` to be a new virtual method, and adding `newslot` guarantees this.

Finally, you can use the `.override` directive in the method body to control
which method you are overriding. This is useful if you want to use one method to
implement a number of virtual methods, since you won't be able to match all of
the abstract method names. Let's take a look at an example of how this works:

```
.class interface public InterfaceOne
{
    .method public virtual
        hidebysig instance void MethodOne()
        cil managed {}
}
.class interface public InterfaceTwo
{
    .method public virtual
        hidebysig instance void MethodTwo()
        cil managed {}
}
.class public OverrideClass implements InterfaceOne, InterfaceTwo
{
    .method public virtual
        hidebysig instance void MethodOneAndTwo()
        cil managed
    {
        .override InterfaceOne::MethodOne
        .override InterfaceTwo::MethodTwo
    }
}
```

61

OverrideClass provides an implementation for both MethodOne() and MethodTwo() via MethodOneAndTwo(). Therefore, if someone ran the following VB .NET code:

```
Dim oOverride As OverrideClass = New OverrideClass()
Dim oIOne As InterfaceOne = oOverride
oIOne.MethodOne()
Dim oITwo As InterfaceTwo = oOverride
oITwo.MethodTwo()
```

the same method would be called twice.

SOURCE CODE *The Overrides folder contains the Overrides.il file, which has all of the overriding cases just demonstrated.*

Defining Properties in Types

Properties are essentially thin method wrappers around fields. They're useful in providing a way to encapsulate access to and/or modification of your type's data such that the client doesn't have to know the underlying implementation details. However, to a client, it appears as though it's accessing a field even though it's really calling a method.

To define a property for a type, you use the .property directive. Here's a simple example of having a read-only property:

```
.class public AgeStorage
{
    .field private int32 m_Age
    .property instance int32 Age()
    {
        .get instance int32 get_Age()
    }
    .method public specialname instance int32 get_Age() cil managed
    {
        //  CIL code to return m_Age goes here.
    }
}
```

A VB .NET developer would get the value of the age like this:

```
Dim oAge As New AgeStorage
Dim iAge As Integer = oAge.Age
```

To the developer, it looks like he or she is accessing a field called Age, but the developer is really calling get_Age(). To allow a user to set the age, you use the .set directive:

```
.class public AgeStorage
{
    //  Assume the "get" code still exists…
    .property instance int32 Age()
    {
        .set instance int32 set_Age()
    }
    .method public specialname instance void set_Age(
        int32 value) cil managed
    {
        //  CIL code to return m_Age goes here.
    }
}
```

When you declare a property, the type name that precedes the property name must match the type that's returned by the getter and accepted by the setter (denoted via the .get and .set directives). You don't need to specify both a getter and a setter, but you must have at least one. The getter and setter methods must be marked with the specialname attribute, and they must be instance methods.

Now, if you've done .NET programming with a higher-level language, creating properties may not be that big of a deal for you. But did you know that properties are not limited to just getters and setters? In ilasm, you can use the .other directive to specify extended property behavior. Let's modify AgeStorage to create an initialization property (I'll show how C# and VB .NET handles extended property methods in Chapter 6):

```
.class public AgeStorage
{
    .field private int32 m_Age;
    //  Assume the get/set methods still exist…
    .method public specialname instance void init_Age() cil managed
    {
        //  CIL code to initialize m_Age goes here.
    }
    .property instance int32 Age()
    {
        .other instance void init_Age()
    }
}
```

SOURCE CODE *The Properties folder contains the Properties.il file, which demonstrates how to create a property.*

Adding Events to Types

The last set of directives and attributes that I'll cover are related to events. However, as events are based on delegates, I'll start the discussion there.

Delegates are nothing more than specialized reference types that derive from System.MulticastDelegate.[29] Delegates are a way to provide a type-safe function pointer to .NET developers. Let's take a look at how you would declare a delegate for the following method:

```
.method void OnRandomNotify(int32 NewRandomValue)
```

Here's how it would look:

```
.class sealed public RandomDelegate
    extends [mscorlib]System.MulticastDelegate {}
```

The .class declaration is simple—you just need to ensure that the delegate type is sealed. However, when it comes to method declarations, there are some special rules you must follow. First, let's take a look at the constructor:

```
.method public specialname rtspecialname
    instance void .ctor(object Instance,
        native int Method) runtime managed {}
```

With any method declared in a delegate, you must use the runtime attribute. This means that the runtime will provide an implementation for the method when it executes. You cannot provide any method implementation details for delegates.

Now, when it comes to the delegate's constructor (which you must define), you have to declare two arguments. The first one specifies if the target method is an instance or a static method. If it's an instance method, you pass in the associated instance to Instance; otherwise, you pass in null. The second argument is used to pass in the method pointer.

---

29. Read Section 13.6 of Partition II for an interesting note on why you can't derive from System.Delegate directly.

The second method you are required to declare is `Invoke()`:

```
.method public virtual instance void
    Invoke(int32 NewRandomValue) runtime managed {}
```

This method must have the same method signature as the target method. In this case, you need to pass in an `int32`, and you need to have a return type of `void`.

CROSS-REFERENCE *See "Method Pointers" in Chapter 3 where I show you the implementation details to handle delegates, like passing a method pointer.*

By declaring these methods, you have the ability to invoke methods in a synchronous fashion. However, you can declare two more methods in the delegate if you want to have asynchronous invocations. The first one is `BeginInvoke()`:

```
.method public virtual
    instance class [mscorlib]System.IAsyncResult BeginInvoke(
    int32 NewRandomValue,
    class [mscorlib]System.AsyncCallback callback,
    object Instance) runtime managed {}
```

With this method, you need to have the same arguments as the target method. After they're declared, you must have `AsyncCallback` and `object` arguments. Also, the return type must be an `IAsyncResult` type.

If you declare `BeginInvoke()`, then you must declare `EndInvoke()`:

```
.method public virtual instance
    void EndInvoke(
    class [mscorlib]System.IAsyncResult result)
    runtime managed {}
```

`EndInvoke()` should have the same return type as the target method. It should also list as arguments any managed pointer types. In this case, there are none. After those arguments, an `IAsyncResult` type should be given.

These are the essentials of creating a delegate. For the sake of completeness, I'd like to cover the `.event` directive, as .NET's event architecture relies upon delegates.

An event for a type is defined using a delegate:

```
.class public RandomEvent
{
    .event RandomDelegate NewRandom {}
}
```

This tells clients of the class that they can hook up to your event. But how do they hook up to the event? That's where the .addon and .removeon directives come into play:

```
.event RandomDelegate NewRandom
{
    .addon instance void addNewRandom(class RandomDelegate Handler)
    .removeon instance void removeNewRandom(class RandomDelegate Handler)
}
.method public specialname
    void addNewRandom(class RandomDelegate value)
    cil managed synchronized {}
.method public specialname
    void removeNewRandom(class RandomDelegate value)
    cil managed synchronized {}
```

The two directives define which methods clients can call to hook into the event. Of course, it is your responsibility to have a field that the addXXX() and removeXXX() methods can access to store the client's wishes. In this case, you should have a private RandomDelegate field such that you can add and remove delegate invocations:

```
.field private instance RandomDelegate m_randomDelegate
```

The reason you make it private is to prevent clients from circumventing the event architecture by directly using m_randomDelegate.

You can also use the .fire directive to declare which method is used to fire the event:

```
.event RandomDelegate NewRandom
{
    .fire instance void fireNewRandom(int32 NewRandomValue)
}
.method private specialname void
    fireNewRandom(int32 NewRandomValue)
    cil managed {}
```

As with the field you use to store event notification requests, you need to declare the firing event with the proper accessibility to prevent the client from accidentally calling the method.

Conclusion

In this chapter, I went through a number of ilasm directives and attributes. The directives allowed you to define assemblies, modules, types, fields, and methods. You also saw how the attributes permitted you to adjust the behavior of specific .NET elements. In the next chapter, you'll look at the CIL opcodes that are used to implement method definitions.

CHAPTER 3

CIL Opcodes

IN THIS CHAPTER, I'll talk about the different opcodes that are available for the CIL developer. I'll start by showing you how the virtual execution stack works in .NET and how the opcodes are structured. Next, I'll move on to some basic opcodes that allow you to load and store information into variables. Then you'll see how to perform operations on these variables via CIL. Finally, I'll wrap up by demonstrating how to create objects and call virtual and nonvirtual methods on objects.

Basic Stack Information

Let's start by looking at how the virtual execution stack is designed. It's pretty simple in that you push information onto the stack for performing a number of tasks: finding values in arrays, calling methods on objects, and so on. The main point to keep in mind with the stack is the number of types that it can contain—it's different from the number of types that are defined in .NET. In fact, there are only seven:

- Four numeric types: `int32`, `int64`, `native int`, and `F`

- One object reference type: `O`

- Two pointer types: `native int` and `&`

Let's go over these in more detail. You're probably familiar with the first two numeric types, but the last two may be new to you. The `native int` type is different depending on what the underlying processor is. For example, on a Pentium III, a `native int` is 4 bytes in size, but on an IA-64 it's 8 bytes.[1] The `F` type is just an internal type that the runtime uses to store floating-point values. Although standards for dealing with floating-point values[2] are available, various systems may handle the implementations of this standard differently. Therefore, the `F` type abstracts this detail away, and makes implicit conversions between the `float32` and `float64` data types when they're manipulated on the stack. Since there

---

1. `Native ints` are usually used for calling methods via a method pointer; I'll show you how to do this later on in the section "Method Pointers."

2. .NET uses the IEC 60559:1989 standard to handle floating-point operations and encodings.

are only four value types that can be stored on the stack, implicit conversion will take place if you store a 1-byte value on the stack (it'll expand into a 4-byte value). You'll see later on how you can manage these conversions when you need to pull values off of the stack.

The object reference type, 0, is an opaque object reference. As the description states, it stores references to objects so you can call methods on them and compare them to other 0 values to see if they are the same type. The & type, a managed pointer, is used to actually point to a value—this is needed when you want to pass information to a method by reference. The big difference between this pointer type and an unmanaged pointer (native int) is verifiable code. By using unmanaged pointers, you've basically made your code unverifiable, since the runtime cannot determine in most cases what the unmanaged pointer is pointing to and what the results of certain operations are. In contrast, managed pointers are reported to the garbage collector and hence can be verified.[3]

Opcode Essentials

Before taking a look at the opcodes, I'd like to spend a brief amount of time talking about their structure and stack behavior. First, let's look at their structure. An opcode is actually nothing more than a sequence of bytes that the runtime can interpret to generate native code. The size of the opcode can be one or more bytes in length.[4] For example, the add opcode is equal to 0x58, and arglist is equal to 0xFE00. The functionality of the opcode can also affect code size. For example, pop only takes up 1 byte of space, 0x26. However, newobj takes up 5 bytes, 0x73 and 4 bytes that represent the instance's constructor method as a token (for example, 0x0A000002). Furthermore, some opcodes have alternate representations to express the same thing, but each one is different in code size. For example, ldc.i4.0 only takes up 1 byte, 0x16. There's also a short form of this opcode, ldc.i4.s 0. This takes up 2 bytes (0x1F00). Finally, the general form of this opcode, ldc.i4 0, takes up 5 bytes (0x2000000000). They all do the same thing (push 0 onto the stack), yet their code sizes vary considerably.

Another aspect of the opcode you need to know about is its stack behavior. Some opcodes push a value onto the stack, such as ldc.i4. Others, such as ceg, take one or more values off of the stack, evaluate them in some way, and push a new value onto the stack. Some, such as jmp, don't do anything to the stack. And some opcodes' stack alteration behavior varies, such as call. Knowing what is on

---

3.   See Section 1.1.4 of Partition III for more details on pointers.

4.   See Section 1.2.1 of Partition III for information on reserved and experimental byte values.

the stack is essential in some cases—you'll see in the section "Handling Exceptions" why this is so. Furthermore, figuring out what is on the stack is crucial to calculating the maximum stack size, an issue I'll briefly cover in the section ".maxstack Calculations."

Basic Opcodes

Now that you know what constitutes an opcode, let's see how you can use it to load values from variables of different locations onto the stack. These opcodes are fairly simplistic, and they'll illustrate the fundamentals of how the opcodes work with the stack.

Using Local Variables

Let's say you have the following method:

```
.method public hidebysig instance void
    BasicMethod()
    cil managed
{
    .maxstack  1
    .locals init ([0] int32 var1,
        [1] int32 var2)
    ldloc 0
code_label: stloc 1
    ret
}
```

Although this CIL is pretty easy, I'll cover it in detail so you know exactly what is going on. The `ldloc` instruction pushes the contents of a local variable onto the virtual stack, and `stloc` pops the current value on the stack and stores it in a local variable. `ret` is used to leave a method—you should always have at least one `ret` statement in a method. If the method needs to return a value, that value must be at the top of the stack.

You can also use variable names in place of the index values:

```
.method public hidebysig instance void
    BasicMethod()
    cil managed
{
```

```
.maxstack  1
.locals init ([0] int32 var1,
    [1] int32 var2)
ldloc var1
code_label: stloc var2
ret
}
```

Figure 3-1 shows what is going on with the stack in this code snippet.

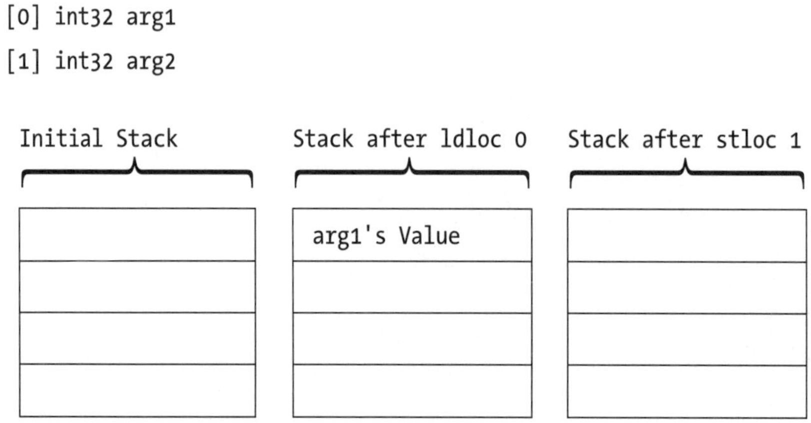

```
[0] int32 arg1
[1] int32 arg2
```

Figure 3-1. ldloc *and* stloc *behavior*

Since var1 and var2 are initialized to 0, this code doesn't do much other than waste processing cycles (you'll see in a moment how you can change the variables). As this code snippet demonstrates, you can add a code label in front of any opcode. This isn't required, but you'll see later on when I discuss branch instructions that this is a necessity.

Now, there are a couple of variants of ldloc and stloc. So far, in the examples you've been referencing which local variable you want to use by stating its index. However, if you're using a local variable with an index position between 0 and 3 inclusive, you can use ldloc.x and stloc.x, where x can be 0, 1, 2, or 3. Therefore, you can change the previous snippet as follows:

```
.maxstack  1
.locals init ([0] int32 var1,
    [1] int32 var2)
ldloc.0
stloc.1
```

Similarly, if your index value is between 4 and 255 inclusive, you can use the "short" form of ldloc to load the variable's contents, ldloc.s:

```
ldloc.s 5
```

As I mentioned before, the code snippet isn't doing much because var1 and var2 are equal to 0. To change the value of a variable, you can use the ldc opcode in concert with stloc:

```
.method public hidebysig instance void
    BasicMethod()
    cil managed
{
    .maxstack  1
    .locals init ([0] int32 var1,
        [1] int32 var2)
    //  Set var1 = 2.
    ldc.i4 2
    stloc.0
    //  Set var2 = 5.
    ldc.i4 5
    stloc.1
    ret
}
```

To use ldc (which is short for "load constant"), you need to do two things. First, you specify the type of the value that you want to push onto the stack; valid values are i4, i8, r4, and r8. Next, you specify the value that you want to push. As you saw with ldloc, there are efficient ldc variants for values between –1 and 8, and there are short form variants for values between –128 and 127. Here are some examples of these encodings:

```
ldc.i4.2
ldc.i4.m1
ldc.i4.s -100
```

Now, while ldloc is pushing the value of the variable onto the stack, you can use ldloca to push the variable's address onto the stack:

```
ldloca var1
```

To "dereference" the pointer, you use ldind, giving it the valid type that you want to push onto the stack (similar to what you saw with ldc):

```
ldloca var1
ldind.i4
```

ldind takes the previous stack value, which should be a pointer type, and loads the value located at that address.

There's also a stind opcode that allows you to store a value at a given address. The pointer is loaded first, and then the desired value is pushed onto the stack:

```
ldloca var1
ldc.i4 7890
stind
```

In this case, var1 would be equal to 7890.

Conversions

Now, you may have noticed that I've only been using 32-bit integers to load and store information. Of course, there are other kinds of value types, like Booleans and doubles. What happens when these types are used? The answer is based on the primitive types that the stack can store—therefore, implicit widening and narrowing conversions will take place when other types are loaded. For example, take a look at the following code snippet:

```
.method public hidebysig instance void
    BasicMethod() cil managed
{
    .maxstack  1
    .locals init ([0] bool b1
        [1] int64 l1, [2] float64 d1,
        [3] int32 i1)
    // b1 = true;
    ldc.i4.1
    stloc.0
    // d1 = 123.4;
    ldc.r8 123.4
    stloc.s d1
    // l1 = 789789789890;
    ldc.i8 789789789890
    stloc.1
```

```
//  l1 = 2222222;
ldc.i4 2222222
conv.i8
stloc.1
//  i1 = (int)l1;
ldloc.1
conv.i4
stloc.3
ret
}
```

Let's look at each conversion issue in detail.[5] First, you have the case where you're setting a Boolean to true. This is pretty easy—you put 1 on the stack as an int32 via ldc.i4.1. No implicit conversion takes place, as this is a type that the stack supports. However, when you call stloc.1, you narrow the value from 4 bytes to 1 to accommodate the size of a Boolean.[6]

The next four opcodes don't do very much, other than showing how you change the value of floating-point and 8-byte integer variables. ldc.r8 puts 123.4 on the stack as the F type, and stloc.s takes that value and puts it into d1. Similarly, ldc.i8 puts 789789789890 onto the stack as a 64-bit integer value, which is put into l1 via stloc.2.

The next three opcodes are where things get interesting. Note that I'm having you set l1 to 2222222. However, you don't include ldc.i8 (although that would be perfectly valid). Rather, you use ldc.i4, and then you use a new opcode, conv.i8. You can probably guess what conv does—it's a conversion instruction. It takes the current value on the stack, converts it to the type given (in this case, an int64), and then leaves the new value on the stack. In this example, you take that converted value and store it in l1 via stloc.1.

Usually, you'll see conv when you need to explicitly narrow the value currently on the stack. For example, the last set of opcodes are taking the value of l1 and putting it into i1. To do this, you need to use conv.i4, as the type that's on the stack after ldloc.1 does not match the target type denoted by stloc.3.[7] But what happens if the target can't handle the current value on the stack? Let's say that you have the following code:

---

5.   I've inserted the C# code to help illustrate what the CIL code is doing.

6.   A Boolean takes up 1 byte—see Section 1.1.2 in Partition III. Actually, you could set a Boolean to any nonzero value to make it true, so ldc.i4.7 would work just as well.

7.   See Section 3.63 of Partition III.

```
//   l1 = 789789789890;
ldc.i8 789789789890
stloc.1
//   i1 = (int)l1;
ldloc.1
conv.i4
stloc.3
```

In this case, i1 will be equal to 1138630338 because l1's value is too big to store in an int32. No exception is thrown if you employ conv; however, you can use conv.ovf to create an exception if any data would be lost on the conversion:

```
 //   l1 = 789789789890;
ldc.i8 789789789890
stloc.1
//   i1 = (int)l1;
ldloc.1
conv.ovf.i4
stloc.3
```

In this case, you'd get an OverflowException at the conv.ovf.i4 opcode.

With conv, you can convert to most of the data types you're familiar with, rather than the primitive stack types. For example, conv.i1 takes the current value on the stack and coverts it to a 1-byte value. However, the size of the value on the stack is still 4 bytes.

Finally, to complete this discussion of the basic stack operations, I'll demonstrate a couple of opcodes that manipulate the stack. If you want to get rid of the topmost value on the stack, use pop:

```
.method public hidebysig instance void
    PopTheStack() cil managed
{
    .maxstack 2
    .locals init ([0] int32 result)
    ldc.i4.32
    ldc.i4.42
    ldc.i4.52
    pop
    stloc result
    ret
}
```

When this code is run, result will be equal to 42.

You can also take the current value on the stack and duplicate it by using dup:

```
.method public hidebysig instance void
    DuplicateTheStack() cil managed
{
    .maxstack 3
    ldc.i4.32
    dup
    dup
    ret
}
```

Running DuplicateTheStack() will put three 32 values onto the stack.

Finally, if you want to add an opcode that won't do anything, you can use nop:

```
.method public hidebysig instance void
    UselessMethod() cil managed
{
    .maxstack 0
    nop
    ret
}
```

Using Method Arguments

Now that you know some of the basic CIL opcodes, let's see how you can use method arguments. The opcodes are similar to the ones in the last section. For example, to load an argument's value onto the stack, you use ldarg. As with ldloc, ldarg has four optimized encodings: ldarg.x, where x is between 0 and 3 inclusive. It also has a short form, ldarg.s, to reference arguments 4 through 255. However, remember that the static and instance method attributes affect the index value. Take a look at the following two methods:

```
.method public hidebysig instance void
    StoreAValue(int32 ValueToStore) cil managed
{
    .maxstack 1
    .locals init (int32 aLocalInt)
    ldarg.1
    stloc.0
}
```

```
.method public hidebysig static void
    StaticStoreAValue(int32 ValueToStore) cil managed
{
    .maxstack 1
    .locals init (int32 aLocalInt)
    ldarg.0
    stloc.0
}
```

As you can see in StoreAValue(), the index value is 1 because the current instance reference is always passed as the first argument value. In StaticStoreAValue(), the index value is 0.

Of course, you can generalize the issue by using the name of the argument if you'd like:

```
ldarg ValueToStore
```

With method arguments, you will only store a value when the argument is a pointer to a type. In that case, you use stind to put a value into a by-reference argument. The following code snippet demonstrates how stind works:

```
.method public hidebysig instance void
    UseArgument(int32& ValueToUse) cil managed
{
    .maxstack 2
    //  Set ValueToUse = 22
    ldarg.1
    ldc.i4.s 22
    stind.i4
    ret
}
```

What UseArgument() does is take an int32 by reference and puts 22 into ValueToUse. To do this with stind requires you to perform two tasks. First, you need to load the argument's pointer value onto the stack—that's what ldarg.1 is doing. Next, you push the value that you want to store into the argument. Finally, you call stind, specifying the type of the argument. stind works just like ldind, except that this time, you're storing the value (22) into the value type (ValueToUse).

Using Type Fields

Type fields are manipulated similarly to method arguments. Again, you need to know if the field is an instance or a static field to know which opcode to use. Let's look at the following code snippet to see how you can work with fields:

```
.class public beforefieldinit FieldTest
    extends [mscorlib]System.Object
{
    .field private int32 m_IntField
    .field private static int32 m_StaticIntField
    .method public hidebysig instance
        void UseFields() cil managed
    {
        .maxstack  2
        // Set m_StaticIntField = m_IntField
        ldarg.0
        ldfld int32 CILTest.CT::m_IntField
        stsfld int32 CILTest.CT::m_StaticIntField

        ldarg.0
        // Set m_IntField = m_StaticIntField
        ldsfld int32 CILTest.CT::m_StaticIntField
        stfld int32 CILTest.CT::m_IntField
        ret
    }
}
```

The first new opcode, ldfld, will take the value of the designated field—m_IntField in this case—and push it onto the stack. However, before ldfld is called, the correct object reference must be pushed onto the stack—that's why ldarg.0 was included in the code snippet. To store that value into the static field m_StaticIntField, you use stsfld, specifying which field should get the value on the stack.

The other opcodes do the reverse of what you just saw. ldsfld takes a value out of a static field and puts it onto the stack. stfld requires you to push the target object reference onto the stack first, and then the value that will be stored into the target field—that's why the ldarg.0 precedes ldsfld.[8] Remember to push the instance value onto the stack before you use instance fields; your assembly won't be verifiable if you don't and you'll end up throwing an exception.

---

8. Note that you can use ldfld and stfld to load and store static fields. However, you cannot use ldsfld and stsfld for instance fields.

Basic Operations

Now that you know how to use the stack to push and pop values from different
locations, let's investigate how you can perform operations on these stack values.

Arithmetic Operations

Let's start by looking at operations that perform familiar arithmetic functions. As
you may expect, there are opcodes that allow you to add, subtract, multiply, and
divide—add, sub, mul, and div, respectively. Here's a code snippet showing all four
in action:

```
.class public beforefieldinit BasicMath
    extends [mscorlib]System.Object
{
    .method public hidebysig instance int32
        Add(int32 X, int32 Y) cil managed
    {
        .maxstack 2
        ldarg.1
        ldarg.2
        add
        ret
    }
    .method public hidebysig instance int32
        Subtract(int32 X, int32 Y) cil managed
    {
        .maxstack 2
        ldarg.1
        ldarg.2
        sub
        ret
    }
    .method public hidebysig instance int32
        Multiply(int32 X, int32 Y) cil managed
    {
        .maxstack 2
        ldarg.1
        ldarg.2
        mul
        ret
    }
```

```
.method public hidebysig instance int32
    Divide(int32 X, int32 Y) cil managed
{
    .maxstack 2
    ldarg.1
    ldarg.2
    div
    ret
}
}
```

Each of the four opcodes requires you to push the two values that you want to use before you perform the mathematical function.[9] For add and mul, it really doesn't matter which order you push the values onto the stack, but it does for sub and div. In all four cases, the second value pushed is either added to, subtracted from, multiplied to, or divided into the first value. Therefore, if you altered Subtract() to this:

```
ldarg.2
ldarg.1
sub
ret
```

Calling Subtract(4, 3) would return –1 instead of the expected 1.

As you saw with conv, you can add .ovf to all of these opcodes (except div) to generate an OverflowException if the result can't be properly represented. div will throw DivideByZeroException if the second value is equal to 0.[10]

If you want to get the negation of a value, use neg:

```
.method public hidebysig instance int32
    Negate(int32 X) cil managed
{
    .maxstack 1
    ldarg.1
    neg
    ret
}
```

neg works for both integral and floating-point values.

---

9. Those who remember Reverse-Polish Notation calculators will have no problems writing CIL-based mathematical code.

10. This only happens for integral types; it doesn't happen with F types. See 3.31 of Partition III for more details.

Finally, there's rem. This opcode works like div, except that it pushes the remainder onto the stack:

```
.method public hidebysig instance int32
    Mod(int32 X, int32 Y) cil managed
{
    .maxstack 2
    ldarg.1
    ldarg.2
    rem
    ret
}
```

When Mod(15, 4) is called, 3 is returned (15/4 = 3 with remainder 3).

Now, with floating-point numbers, you won't get an exception if you divide by 0. The resulting value will be "not a number," or NaN. However, the ckfinite opcode will determine if either a NaN or a positive or negative infinity value is on the stack:

```
.method public hidebysig instance float64
    DivideWithCheck(float64 X, float64 Y) cil managed
{
    .maxstack 2
    ldarg.1
    ldarg.2
    div
    ckfinite
    ret
}
```

If the current stack value is one of these weird values, an ArithmeticException is thrown. Otherwise, the stack value is left on the stack. DivideWithCheck(4.5, 1.2) would therefore return 3.75, but DivideWithCheck(4.5, 0.0) would not.

SOURCE CODE *The BasicMathTest.il file contains the* BasicMath *type that shows you how each of the mathematical operations work. The BasicMathTestClient project is a C# console application that uses the BasicMathTest assembly.*

Binary Operations

Some opcodes allow you to perform binary functions on values. They are and, or, not, and xor. Here's a code snippet demonstrating them in action:

```
.method public hidebysig instance void
    BasicBinaryOps() cil managed
{
    .maxstack  2
    .locals init ([0] int32 someValue,
        [1] int32 anotherValue, [2] int32 andValue,
        [3] int32 orValue, [4] int32 xorValue,
        [5] int32 complementValue, [6] int32 shiftRightValue,
        [7] int32 shiftLeftValue)
    //  Set someValue to 12 and anotherValue to 7.
    ldc.i4.s 12
    stloc.0
    ldc.i4.7
    stloc.1
    //  andValue will equal the and of someValue and anotherValue.
    ldloc.0
    ldloc.1
    and
    stloc.2
    //  orValue will equal the or of someValue and anotherValue.
    ldloc.0
    ldloc.1
    or
    stloc.3
    //  xorValue will equal the xor of someValue and anotherValue.
    ldloc.0
    ldloc.1
    xor
    stloc.s xorValue
    //  complementValue will equal the not of someValue.
    ldloc.0
    not
    stloc.s complementValue
    ret
}
```

The first three opcodes—and, or, and xor—are straightforward to use. You push the two values you want to use onto the stack, and then you use the appropriate opcode. The resulting value is pushed onto the stack, so that's why the stloc opcodes are needed to store the results. not is a bit different in that you only need to put one value onto the stack. With this code snippet, andValue will be 4, orValue will be 15, xorValue will be 11, and complementValue will be –13.

Two other operators, shl and shr, shift the binary values left and right, respectively:

```
.method public hidebysig instance void
    BasicShiftOps() cil managed
{
    .maxstack  2
    .locals init ([0] int32 someValue,
        [1] int32 shiftRightValue, [2] int32 shiftLeftValue)
    // Set someValue to 12.
    ldc.i4.s 12
    stloc.0
    // Shift-right someValue 2 bits and store in shiftRightValue.
    ldloc.0
    ldc.i4.2
    shr
    stloc.1
    // Shift-left someValue 2 bits and store in shiftLeftValue.
    ldloc.0
    ldc.i4.2
    shl
    stloc.2
    ret
}
```

Both shl and shr require you to push two values onto the stack. The first value is the value that you want to shift, and the second value is how many bits you want to shift over. shl shifts the bits to the left, filling in 0-bit values, whereas shr shifts the bits to the right, and it fills the empty bits with the value of the highest bit. It also preserves the sign of the value. Therefore, in this code snippet, shiftRightValue will be 3 and shiftLeftValue will be 48.

You can also use shr.un, which acts a bit differently from shr. It shifts bits to the right, but it acts like shl in that it fills the empty slots with 0-bit values, and it does not preserve the sign. Here's a code snippet demonstrating the difference between shr and shr.un:

```
.method public hidebysig instance void
    ShiftRightDifferences() cil managed
{
    .maxstack  2
    .locals init ([0] int32 someValue,
        [1] int32 shrValue,  [2] int32 shrunValue)
    //  Set someValue to -14.
    ldc.i4.s -14
    stloc.0
    //  Shift-right someValue 2 bits and store in shrValue.
    ldloc.0
    ldc.i4.2
    shr
    stloc.1
    //  Shift-right someValue 2 bits with shr.un and store in shrunValue.
    ldloc.0
    ldc.i4.2
    shr.un
    stloc.2
    ret
}
```

shrValue will be –4, but shrunValue will be 1073741820.

SOURCE CODE *The BinaryOpsTest.il file contains the* BinaryOps *type that shows you how each of the binary operations work. The BinaryOpsTestClient project is a C# console application that uses the BinaryOpsTest assembly.*

Comparison Operations

CIL also gives you the ability to compare two values to see how they are different. ceq tells you if two values are equal:

```
.maxstack  2
.locals init ([0] int32 valOne,
    [1] int32 valTwo, [2] bool ceqRes,
    [3] bool cgtRes, [4] bool cltRes)
ldc.i4.s 12
ldc.i4.s 21
ceq
stloc.2
```

You push the two values in question onto the stack—ceq will push 1 onto the stack if they are equal and 0 if they're different. In this case, ceqRes will be false.

cgt and clt work like ceq in that they compare the two topmost stack values. cgt pushes 1 onto the stack if the deeper stack value is greater than the top stack value, otherwise it pushes 0; clt is the exact opposite of cgt (assume that this code snippet is an extension of the previous one):

```
ldc.i4.s 12
ldc.i4.s 21
cgt
stloc.3
ldc.i4.s 12
ldc.i4.s 21
clt
stloc.s cltRes
```

When this code is run, cgtRes will be false, but cltRes will be true.

Note that cgt and clt also have .un variations. These operators (cgt.un and clt.un) work just like their cousins, except they consider the two stack values to be unsigned if they're integer values. If they're F types, the operators work as expected unless the first pushed value is unordered, or a not-a-number symbol (NaNS). If the first value is NaNS and the second value is ordered, both cgt.un and clt.un return 1.

SOURCE CODE *The CompareTest.il file contains the* Compare *type that shows you how each of the compare operations work. The CompareTestClient project is a C# console application that uses the CompareTest assembly.*

Object Instructions

So far, you've only seen value types. You haven't really looked at how you can handle reference types and call methods on them. In the following sections, I'll show you the CIL opcodes that you can use to manipulate reference types.

Creating Type Instances

The first thing you need to do is create an instance of the type—that's what newobj is for. Listing 3-1 shows a simple object creation case.

Listing 3-1. Creating Objects

```
.class public beforefieldinit SimpleType
    extends [mscorlib]System.Object
{
    .field private int32 m_FieldOne
    .field private int32 m_FieldTwo

    .method public hidebysig
        specialname rtspecialname
        instance void .ctor() cil managed
    {
        //  TODO:  Implementation code goes here.
    }

    .method public hidebysig
        specialname rtspecialname
        instance void .ctor(int32 FieldOne, int32 FieldTwo)
        cil managed
    {
        //  TODO:  Implementation code goes here.
    }

    .method public hidebysig static class SimpleType
        CreateThyself() cil managed
    {
        .maxstack 1
        newobj instance void SimpleType::.ctor()
        ret
    }

    .method public hidebysig
        static class SimpleType
        CreateThyself(int32 FieldOne,
        int32 FieldTwo) cil managed
    {
        .maxstack 2
        ldarg.0
        ldarg.1
        newobj instance void SimpleType::.ctor(int32,
            int32)
        ret
    }
}
```

Since I haven't officially covered how to call methods yet, I can't show you the constructor's implementation code; I'll get back to that in the next section.

When you call `newobj`, you need to specify the type that you want to create along with the constructor that you want to call. In the first `CreateThyself()` call that takes no arguments, you use the default constructor, but the other `CreateThyself()` uses the constructor that takes two `int32`s. When you call constructors that take arguments, you need to push the arguments onto the stack in order from left to right. Therefore, in the code snippet, the first argument will be equal to `FieldOne`, and the second one will be equal to `FieldTwo`. Make sure you have the constructor method signature correct; otherwise you'll get a `MissingMethodException`.

You can also set an instance to null by loading a null reference onto the stack via `ldnull`. This allows the runtime to collect the object's memory at the next garbage collection cycle:

```
.locals init ([0] class
    SimpleType newBT)
//  Set newBT = new SimpleType instance
newobj instance void
    SimpleType::.ctor()
stloc.1
//  Set newBT = null
ldnull
stloc.1
```

Calling Methods

Now that you know how you can create objects, let's see how you can call their methods.

Virtual Methods

Let's say you added the following method to `SimpleType`:

```
.method public hidebysig newslot virtual
    instance void VirtualMethod(int32 FieldTwo) cil managed
{
    .maxstack 2
    //  Set m_FieldTwo = FieldTwo
    ldarg.0
    ldarg.1
```

```
    stfld int32 SimpleType::m_FieldTwo
    ret
}
```

To call this method, you use `callvirt`:

```
newobj instance void SimpleType::.ctor()
ldc.i4.6
callvirt instance void SimpleType::VirtualMethod(int32)
```

To call a virtual method, you need to first push the object instance onto the stack (in this case, `newobj` takes care of this for you). Next, any arguments that the method takes need to be pushed onto the stack. Finally, when `callvirt` is used, the method signature in the method token that follows must match a method on the type whose instance was initially pushed onto the stack.

In this case, you have a virtual method on `SimpleType` called `VirtualMethod()` that takes an `int32` as its only argument, so the call will succeed. If the runtime cannot find the method on the target type, it will look at the type's superclasses to see if a match can be found. Therefore, if you had the following inheritance structure:

```
.class public beforefieldinit DerivedType
    extends SimpleType
{
    //  Implementation code goes here…
}
```

this CIL would work:

```
newobj instance void DerivedType::.ctor()
ldc.i4.6
callvirt instance void DerivedType::VirtualMethod(int32)
```

Since `DerivedType` doesn't override `VirtualMethod()`, the runtime will call `SimpleType::VirtualMethod`.

Note that if the method returns a value, it will be pushed onto the stack.

Nonvirtual and Static Methods

To call a nonvirtual or static method, you use `call`. For example, let's say you added the following method to `SimpleType`:

```
.method public hidebysig instance void
    NonVirtualMethod(int32 FieldOne) cil managed
{
    .maxstack 2
    // Set m_FieldOne = FieldOne
    ldarg.0
    ldarg.1
    stfld int32 SimpleType::m_FieldOne
    ret
}
```

Now, to create a SimpleType instance with CreateThyself() and then call NonVirtualMethod() on the new instance, you would code it like this:

```
ldc.i4.1
ldc.i4.2
call class SimpleType
    SimpleType::CreateThyself(int32,
    int32)
ldc.i4.5
call instance void
    SimpleType::NonVirtualMethod(int32)
```

This works just like callvirt—you push the arguments in the correct order (including the type instance if the method is an instance method), and then you make the invocation. As you see, with CreateThyself() no type instance is pushed onto the stack, but with NonVirtualMethod() you need one (it's the return value from CreateThyself()).

In fact, you can use call to invoke virtual methods:[11]

```
ldc.i4.1
ldc.i4.2
call class SimpleType
    SimpleType::CreateThyself(int32,
    int32)
ldc.i4.5
call instance void
    SimpleType::VirtualMethod(int32)
```

---

11. With callvirt and call being so close in behavior, you may wonder why there are two different opcodes. I'll cover that discussion in Chapter 6.

Constructors

Now that you know the basics of method invocation, let's go back and finish off SimpleType's constructors:

```
.method public hidebysig
    specialname rtspecialname
    instance void .ctor(int32 FieldOne, int32 FieldTwo)
    cil managed
{
  .maxstack 2
  ldarg.0
  call instance void [mscorlib]System.Object::.ctor()

  // Set m_FieldOne = FieldOne
  ldarg.0
  ldarg.1
  stfld int32 SimpleType::m_FieldOne

  // Set m_FieldTwo = FieldTwo
  ldarg.0
  ldarg.2
  stfld int32 SimpleType::m_FieldTwo

  ret
}
```

In the default constructor, a base class's constructor needs to be called as well. After that is done, any instance fields should be initialized. If you have a type initializer, static fields would be initialized in that constructor. With this custom constructor, you set m_FieldOne and m_FieldTwo to the related argument value; in the no-argument constructor, these field values are set to 0.

Unmanaged Method Calls

Recall in Chapter 2 that I said I'd show you how to call an unmanaged method—specifically, FormatMessage(). The reality is that once the method has been declared, it's not too hard to call the unmanaged method. But when you call an unmanaged method, the chances are that you may need to use some .NET Framework classes to help you out. Let's see what the CIL looks like:

```
.locals init(/* SimpleType's Main locals
    go here… */
    [3] native int bufferPtr,
    [4] native int messageSource,
    [5] int32 retVal,
    [6] string strRetVal)
// …
// Load the values to call FormatMessage()
ldc.i4 0x1100  // FORMAT_MESSAGE_FROM_SYSTEM |
    // FORMAT_MESSAGE_ALLOCATE_BUFFER
ldloca messageSource
ldc.i4 0x24  // ERROR_SHARING_BUFFER_EXCEEDED
ldc.i4.0
ldloca bufferPtr
ldc.i4.1
ldc.i4.0
call int32 SimpleType::FormatMessage(int32, native int&,
    int32, int32, native int&, int32, int32)

// Now convert the buffer to a string.
stloc retVal
ldloc bufferPtr
ldloc retVal
call string
    [mscorlib]System.Runtime.InteropServices.Marshal
    ::PtrToStringAuto(native int, int32)
stloc strRetVal
```

The first value, 0x1100, is a combination of two Win32 constants, FORMAT_MESSAGE_FROM_SYSTEM and FORMAT_MESSAGE_ALLOCATE_BUFFER. The first constant specifies FormatMessage() should look for a message resource from the operating system, and the second constant states that the Buffer argument should point to this message when the function is finished. The second value will be ignored since the first value doesn't contain FORMAT_MESSAGE_FROM_HMODULE or FORMAT_MESSAGE_FROM_STRING. The third value is the error code you're looking for—in this case, it's ERROR_SHARING_BUFFER_EXCEEDED. The next parameter instructs FormatMessage() to find the message in a language based on a set of preexisting rules—using 0 basically picks the default language of the system. Buffer will contain the pointer to the string value when the method completes. Because you only want one string, you set BufferSize to 1. Finally, you're not dealing with formatted messages, so you can set Arguments to 0.

To invoke FormatMessage(), you use call. Once the method completes, you need to get the string data out of bufferPtr. Fortunately, the Marshal class provides a number of methods to help you out. In this case, you use `PtrToStringAuto()`, which returns the desired message. If all goes well, you should see "Too many files opened for sharing." on the command line.

I realize that I glossed over some details with `FormatMessage()`—this method is very flexible so I'd suggest you read up on this method in the Windows Platform SDK for more information. Fortunately, if you're doing .NET development, you probably will call more managed methods than unmanaged, and even when you need to call unmanaged methods, most of them should be straightforward enough that you won't need to do pointer-to-string conversions on a regular basis.

Method Pointers

It's also possible to call managed methods via an unmanaged method pointer (typically done with delegates). Either `ldftn` or `ldvirtftn` can get the method pointer. As you saw with `call` and `callvirt`, `ldftn` can be used with virtual or nonvirtual methods, but `ldvirtftn` works with virtual methods only. Listing 3-2 demonstrates how you can get method pointers from `VirtualMethod()` and `NonVirtualMethod()` and invoke them.

Listing 3-2. Calling Methods via a Method Pointer

```
.locals init([0] native int nonVirtualFtnPtr,
    [1] native int virtualFtnPtr,
    [2] class SimpleType st)
// Invoke a non-virtual methods
// via function pointers.
newobj instance void
    SimpleType::.ctor()
stloc st

ldftn instance void
    SimpleType::NonVirtualMethod(int32)
stloc nonVirtualFtnPtr

ldloc st
ldc.i4 24
ldloc nonVirtualFtnPtr
calli instance void(int32)

// Invoke a virtual methods
// via function pointers.
```

```
ldloc st
ldvirtftn instance void
    SimpleType::VirtualMethod(int32)
stloc virtualFtnPtr

ldloc st
ldc.i4 24
ldloc virtualFtnPtr
calli instance void(int32)
```

With `ldvirtftn`, you need to push the object instance onto the stack before you get the method pointer; `ldftn` doesn't have this requirement.

Of course, once you have these pointers, you'd like to be able to call these methods. That's done with `calli`. `calli` works just like `call` or `callvirt`—you need to pass the type instance if the method is nonstatic, and then you push the arguments onto the stack. Finally, you push the method pointer onto the stack. The method descriptor after `calli` may look a little weird, but remember that by calling a method pointer you really don't care which type you call the method on. So long as the argument types and the return type match, you're good to go.[12] Note that `calli` can be used to call instance methods (both virtual and nonvirtual) and static methods. Also, `calli` is not a verifiable opcode in the first release of .NET.[13]

SOURCE CODE *The MethodTest.il file demonstrates how to call virtual and nonvirtual methods directly and through function pointers.*

Boxing, Unboxing, and Value Type Indirection

If you ever need to turn a value type into an object type and vice-versa, you use the box and unbox opcodes. Let's look at how box works with the int32 and Guid value types:

---

12. If you're calling an instance method via a function pointer, though, you need to make sure the correct instance reference is on the stack.

13. Section 3.20 of Partition III seems to suggest that this opcode *could* be verifiable, but for some reason, the first release considers it nonverifiable in all cases. This may change in the future.

```
.method public hidebysig instance void
    BoxIt() cil managed
{
    .maxstack  1
    .locals init ([0] int32 baseInt,
            [1] object intObj,
            [2] int32 dupInt,
            [3] valuetype [mscorlib]System.Guid baseGuid,
            [4] object guidObj,
            [5] valuetype [mscorlib]System.Guid dupGuid)
    // Set baseInt = 32.
    ldc.i4.s 32
    stloc.0
    // Box baseInt's value, and
    // set intObj = box.
    ldloc.0
    box [mscorlib]System.Int32
    stloc.1
    // Get a new Guid value,
    // and box that.
    call valuetype [mscorlib]System.Guid [mscorlib]System.Guid::NewGuid()
    stloc.3
    ldloc.3
    box [mscorlib]System.Guid
    stloc.s guidObj
```

In this code snippet (which I'll show you how to close off in a moment), you first put 32 into baseInt. You then box that value and store it in intObj. With a Guid, you need to call NewGuid() to get a Guid, but once that's stored in baseGuid, you box that value into guidObj. When you box a value type, all the runtime is doing is storing the value pushed onto the stack into an object along with the value type information specified in the token. Therefore, intObj "knows" that it has an int32 equal to 32, and guidObj "knows" it has some unique Guid value of type Guid.

This is important when you try to grab the value out of the box and put it into a value type—otherwise known as *unboxing*. This is done with unbox:

```
// Get the Int32 value out of intObj
ldloc.1
unbox [mscorlib]System.Int32
ldind.i4
stloc.2
// Get the Guid value out of intObj
ldloc.s guidObj
unbox [mscorlib]System.Guid
```

```
ldobj [mscorlib]System.Guid
stloc.s dupGuid
ret
}
```

When you include `unbox`, you push the object reference onto the stack that contains the boxed value. Next, you specify the type that you think the box contains. In your code, you've done it right in both cases, but if you had done something like this:

```
ldloc.1
unbox [mscorlib]System.Guid
```

you'd get an `InvalidCastException`.

The interesting part of the boxing/unboxing process is what `unbox` leaves on the stack: a managed pointer of the specified value type. Therefore, you need to dereference the pointer to get to the value, which is what `ldobj` and `ldind.i4` do. Note that `ldind.i4` and its related cousins[14] are in effect aliases to `ldobj`—they're just shorthand notations for the built-in value classes.

SOURCE CODE *The BoxingTest.il file demonstrates how boxing and unboxing works.*

Type Casting

Although it's desirable that you stick to type-safe code as often as possible, sometimes you run into situations where you need to cast a type. A good example of this is when you use the `Hashtable` class from `System.Collections`. You may have put a `String` into the hashtable via `Add()`, but when you want to bring it out, the return value of `Item` is an object. If you want to call a `String`-specific method (like `EndsWith()`), you need to cast the return value to a string. You can do this in CIL using either `isinst` or `castclass`.

---

14. See Section 3.42 of Partition III for all of the `ldind.xxx` opcodes—it's the same as `conv`.

To use isinst, you push the instance in question onto the stack. You then call isinit, giving it the name of a class. If the instance on the stack is an instance of the desired type, the instance is cast to the desired type. Otherwise, null is returned. Take a look at the following code snippet:

```
.locals init([0] [mscorlib]System.Collections.Hashtable ht)
newobj [mscorlib]System.Collections.Hashtable::.ctor()
stloc ht
ldloc ht
isinst [mscorlib]System.Object
pop
ldloc ht
isinst [mscorlib]System.String
```

The first isinst will push a type instance of System.Object that is cast from ht. The second call won't work, because Hashtable doesn't derive from String, so null will be on the stack.

The other way to do this is via castclass. castclass works just like isinst unless the target instance is not an instance of the desired type. You'll get an InvalidCastException in that case (this is really the only difference between the two opcodes). Let's modify the previous code snippet to use castclass:

```
.locals init([0] [mscorlib]System.Collections.Hashtable ht)
newobj [mscorlib]System.Collections.Hashtable::.ctor()
stloc ht
ldloc ht
castclass [mscorlib]System.Object
pop
ldloc ht
castclass [mscorlib]System.String
```

The first call will work, but the second one will fail.

Array Manipulation

CIL provides a couple of opcodes that make array creation and manipulation pretty easy to do. The first one is newarr, which allows you to create an array:

```
ldc.i4.s 100
newarr [mscorlib]System.Byte
ldc.i4.s 20
newarr SimpleType
```

The number pushed onto the stack before newarr is the number of elements that you want in the array. You specify the element's type via the token after newarr. newarr creates 0-based, one-dimensional arrays; to create multidimensional and/or nonzero-based arrays, you need to call CreateInstance() on the Array class.[15]

Once you have the array on the stack, you can get its length by using ldlen. This will push the length as a native unsigned integer, so you'll need to use conv.i4 to employ the value as a regular int32. You can also use ldelem and stelem to load and store array element values:

```
.locals init ([0] unsigned int8[] tempByteArray,
    [1] int32 arraySize)
// Create a 100-element byte array.
ldc.i4.s 100
newarr [mscorlib]System.Byte
stloc tempByteArray
// Get the length.
ldloc tempByteArray
ldlen
conv.i4
stloc arraySize
// Put the length into the third element.
ldloc tempByteArray
ldc.i4 2
ldloc arraySize
stelem.i1
// Load the third element's value.
ldloc tempByteArray
ldc.i4 2
ldelem.u1
```

You grab the array's length via ldlen and store that in arraySize. Next, you put that value into the third element of tempByteArray via stelem. Finally, you push that third value in tempByteArray onto the stack with ldelem.

There is also the ldelema opcode, which will load the element's address onto the stack:

```
ldloc tempByteArray
ldc.i4.0
ldelema [mscorlib]System.Byte
call instance string [mscorlib]System.Byte::ToString()
```

---

15. Note, though, that nonzero-based arrays are not CLS compliant.

SOURCE CODE *The ArrayTest.il file contains code that demonstrates how these array manipulation opcodes work.*

Memory Manipulation

When using value types, a couple of opcodes are available that allow you to initialize value types as well as copy a value type to another value type. Let's start by looking at two opcodes that are not verifiable, initblk and cpblk:

```
.class public sequential value ansi
    sealed beforefieldinit ThreeValues
{
    .field public int32 valueOne
    .field public float64 valueTwo
    .field public unsigned int8 valueThree
}

.class public beforefieldinit MemoryTest
    extends [mscorlib]System.Object
{
    .method private hidebysig static void
        Main(string[] args) cil managed
    {
        .entrypoint
        .maxstack 4
        .locals init ([0] valuetype ThreeValues baseThree,
            [1] valuetype ThreeValues targetThree,
            [2] valuetype ThreeValues safeThree,
            [3] valuetype ThreeValues safeCopyThree)

        //  Initialize baseThree via initblk
        ldloca baseThree
        ldc.i4 34
        sizeof ThreeValues
        initblk

        //   Set targetValue = baseThree
        //    via cpblk
        ldloca targetThree
        ldloca baseThree
        sizeof ThreeValues
        cpblk
```

initblk expects three values on the stack: an address to the target value type, the value to use to initialize the fields, and the size of the value type. cpblk needs the destination address, the source address, and the size of the value type. As you can see, you're pretty limited with initblk in terms of setting an initialization value. initblk just takes the second value on the stack and sets every byte value in the value type equal to that value. This is assuming that the size value equals the size of the value type, which is why I used the sizeof opcode, which calculates the size of the value type for you at runtime.

Another problem with these two opcodes is that they're not verifiable. The opcodes ldobj, stobj, and cpobj, shown in the following code example, allow you to move and copy initialized value types in a verifiable manner:

```
        // Now, let's do this "safer"
        // via ldobj and stobj
        ldloca safeThree
        ldloca baseThree
        ldobj ThreeValues
        stobj ThreeValues

        // A cpobj works just as well...
        ldloca safeCopyThree
        ldloca baseThree
        cpobj ThreeValues
        ret
    }
}
```

ldobj retrieves the value from the address on the stack and puts it onto the stack. stobj takes the value from the stack and sets the value type at the given address equal to this value. In the first set of opcodes in the preceding example, after ldobj is done, the only two values left on the stack are an address to safeThree and baseThree's value. cpobj achieves the same effect with one less opcode. It takes the value from the source value type (ldloca baseThree) and puts it into the destination value type (ldloca safeCopyThree).

SOURCE CODE *The MemoryTest.il file contains code that demonstrates these memory manipulation opcodes in action.*

String Manipulation

I'll finish this section with a quick discussion of an opcode that deals with strings. It's called ldstr, and it takes a string token and pushes the value onto the stack:

```
ldstr "Hello."
call void [mscorlib]System.Console::WriteLine(string)
```

The string "Hello" will be stored in the assembly's metadata. When this code is compiled, a token is specified instead of the literal string value (although ILDasm will show the string value for readability purposes).

You can create strings in other ways, but they're not as easy. Contrast ldstr with using the String type to create the same character stream as is shown in Listing 3-3.

Listing 3-3. Creating a String with a System.Char Array

```
.locals init ([0] char[] hello,
    [1] string sHello)
ldc.i4.5
newarr [mscorlib]System.Char
stloc.0
ldloc.0
ldc.i4.0
ldc.i4.s 72   // 'H'
stelem.i2
ldloc.0
ldc.i4.1
ldc.i4.s 101  // 'e'
stelem.i2
ldloc.0
ldc.i4.2
ldc.i4.s 108  // 'l'
stelem.i2
ldloc.0
ldc.i4.3
ldc.i4.s 108  // 'l'
stelem.i2
ldloc.0
ldc.i4.4
ldc.i4.s 111  // 'o'
stelem.i2
ldloc.0
newobj instance void [mscorlib]System.String::.ctor(char[])
stloc.1
```

It's nice that CIL provides an opcode to make this easy to do.

Controlling Code Flow

So far, the code snippets that I've shown in this chapter have all gone from start to finish without skipping over any of the codes in between. In this section, I'll show you how you can use opcodes to give you more control over the code flow in a method.

Let's start by looking at beq. This opcode looks at the two topmost stack values, and branches to the target if they are equal:

```
.class public beforefieldinit BranchTest
    extends [mscorlib]System.Object
{
    .method private hidebysig static void
        Main(string[] args) cil managed
    {
        .entrypoint
        .custom instance void
            [mscorlib]System.STAThreadAttribute::.ctor() =
            ( 01 00 00 00 )
        .maxstack 2
        .locals init ([0] int32 x)
        ldc.i4.3
        stloc.0
        ldc.i4.3
        ldloc.0
        beq are_equal
        ldstr "x is not 3."
        call void [mscorlib]System.Console::WriteLine(string)
        are_equal:  ret
    }
}
```

In this code, x is set to 3, and then that value is compared to 3. If they're equal, the code jumps to are_equal. In this case, nothing will be sent to the console; however, if your first instruction was this:

```
ldc.i4.2
```

you'd see "x is not 3" show up in the console window. You can also use the short form of beq, beq.s, but make sure that the size of the CIL code doesn't exceed the size of a signed 1-byte value.

Note that you don't have to specify a code label; you can use a byte offset if you'd like:

```
beq 10
```

However, I personally find it much easier to use a code label and let the compiler figure out the offset size.

A number of other branching instructions compare two values and branch depending on the result. They are bge (branch if greater than or equal to), bgt (branch if greater than), ble (branch if less than or equal to), and blt (branch if less than). In all four opcodes, the first value pushed is compared to the second to see if it satisfied the condition. For example, take a look at the following code snippet:

```
ldc.i4 5
ldc.i4 7
bgt it_is_greater
ldstr "5 is not greater than 7."
call void [mscorlib]System.Console::WriteLine(string)
ldc.i4 -3
ldc.i4 -3
ble it_is_less_than_or_equal
ldstr "-3 is not less than or equal to -3."
call void [mscorlib]System.Console::WriteLine(string)
it_is_less_than_or_equal: ret
it_is_greater: ret
```

The first case looks to see if 5 is greater than 7. It isn't, so the first WriteLine() call will occur. Next, the second case determines if –3 is less than or equal to –3. Of course, they're equal, so the second WriteLine() won't happen.

As with the comparison operators, bge, bgt, ble, and blt all have .un cousins, and all of the operators have short forms (for example, bge.un.s). Interestingly enough, there is an operator that is the opposite of beq, but it is only of the .un type: bne.un. It will break if the two integer values on the stack (evaluated as unsigned integers) or two F types are different.

There are two branch instructions that simply look at the value on the stack to determine if a branch should occur—brtrue and brfalse—and both have short-form variants. brtrue will branch if the value is not equal to 0 or is a nonnull value; brfalse is the opposite—it'll break if the value is 0 or a null reference:[16]

---

16. Also available are brinst, brnull, and brzero, but they're just aliases to brtrue and brfalse—see Section 3.17 of Partition III for more details.

```
ldnull
brfalse is_null
ldstr "No null reference detected."
call void [mscorlib]System.Console::WriteLine(string)
ret
is_null: ldstr "Null reference detected."
call void [mscorlib]System.Console::WriteLine(string)
ret
```

Because a null reference is pushed onto the stack, you'll get the "Null reference detected." message.

You can also unconditionally branch from the code flow via br.

```
// Opcodes go here…
br go_here_now
// More opcodes go here…
go_here_now:  ret
```

No matter what was on the stack before br, the method will exit.

Finally, the last branch-related opcode I'll discuss in this section is called switch. To use switch, you define a jump table; the branch will occur depending on the current value on the stack and the number of values in the jump table. An example will help show how this works:

```
.method private hidebysig void
    SwitchTest(int32 arg1) cil managed
{
    ldarg.1
    switch (is_zero_or_one,
        is_zero_or_one, no_match,
        no_match, no_match, is_five)

    br no_match
    is_zero_or_one: ldstr "x is 0 or 1."
    call void [mscorlib]System.Console::WriteLine(string)
    br.s end_method

    is_five:  ldstr "x is 5."
    call void [mscorlib]System.Console::WriteLine(string)
    br.s end_method

    no_match:  ldstr "x didn't meet a criteria."
    call void [mscorlib]System.Console::WriteLine(string)
    end_method:  ret
}
```

SwitchTest() takes an int32 as its only argument. You load its value onto the stack, and then you call switch. Your jump table has six targets for values 0 to 5 (switch only works with the stack value as unsigned). If arg1 is equal to 0 or 1, you branch to the is_zero_or_one label. If arg1 is 5, then you branch to is_five. Any other value will result in a branch to no_match. Note that you need to include a branch to no_match after switch to handle arg1 values that are not between 0 to 5 inclusive.

Now, you may be concerned that if you wanted to perform a switch on arg1 if it's equal to 0, 1, or 100, your jump table would get pretty large. If you follow the Partition document to the letter, then that would be the case, but you can play some games with switch to get around this:

```
.method private hidebysig void
    SwitchTest(int32 arg1) cil managed
{
    ldarg.1
    switch (is_zero_or_one,
        is_zero_or_one)
    ldarg.1
    ldc.i4 100
    beq.s is_one_hundred
    br.s no_match

    is_zero_or_one: ldstr "x is 0 or 1."
    call void [mscorlib]System.Console::WriteLine(string)
    br.s end_method

    is_one_hundred:  ldstr "x is 100."
    call void [mscorlib]System.Console::WriteLine(string)
    br.s end_method

    no_match:  ldstr "x didn't meet a criteria."
    call void [mscorlib]System.Console::WriteLine(string)
    end_method:  ret
}
```

As you can see, your jump table is only going to branch when arg1 is equal to 0 or 1. Note that when you don't have a match, you immediately take a look to see if the value is equal to 100. If it is, you use beq.s to tell the user you know arg1 is equal to 100. Keep this technique in mind when you need to use switch to keep the jump table size small.

SOURCE CODE *The BranchTest.il file contains code that demonstrates how the branch instructions work depending on what was passed to the program. It also shows how to manipulate arrays and call methods.*

Handling Exceptions

As you've seen with some of these opcodes, I've explicitly mentioned that they may throw exceptions (for example, conv.ovf.i4). In fact, the last source code example, BranchTest, will throw an IndexOutOfRangeException if nothing is passed on the command line. In this section, I'll show you how you can set up exception handlers to handle such errors gracefully.

Let's say you have a console application that takes an integer value as a command-line argument, like this:

```
ExceptionTest 1234
```

If no argument is given, the program will throw ArgumentException. Furthermore, the program will set its exit code to the given value. Since the exit code is an int32, if the value is too big, you'll get an OverflowException. Writing such a program in CIL is pretty easy given that you now know the proper opcodes—see Listing 3-4 for the implementation in CIL.

Listing 3-4. Checking Arguments in a Console Application

```
.class public beforefieldinit ExceptionTest
    extends [mscorlib]System.Object
{
    .method private hidebysig static void
        Main(string[] args) cil managed
    {
        .entrypoint
        .maxstack 2
        .locals init (int64 bigValue,
            int32 convertedValue)
        //  Set the locals to zero.
        ldc.i4.0
        conv.i8
        stloc.0
        ldc.i4.0
        stloc.1
```

```
        //  Check to see if we have at least
        //  one argument.
        ldarg.0
        ldlen
        conv.i4
        brtrue.s argument_given
        //  Throw an ArgumentException because
        //  nothing was passed.
        ldstr "No argument was passed."
        newobj instance void [mscorlib]System.ArgumentException::.ctor(string)
        throw
        //  Convert the given value to an int64.
        argument_given:  ldarg.0
        ldc.i4.0
        ldelem.ref
        call int64 [mscorlib]System.Int64::Parse(string)
        stloc.0
        //  Now try to convert that into an int32.
        ldloc.0
        conv.ovf.i4
        stloc.1
        //  Set the exit code and return.
        ldloc.1
        call void [mscorlib]System.Environment::set_ExitCode(int32)
        ret
    }
}
```

Note that I've introduced a new opcode: throw. This simply takes the current object on the stack and throws it.[17] Of course, you don't want to have these exceptions go unhandled; otherwise, you may get a nasty dialog box on the target machine like the one shown in Figure 3-2.[18]

---

17. Technically, the object to be thrown can be any object; it does not need to inherit from Exception. However, see Section 4.29 of Partition III to find out why you may not want to do this.

18. Of course, this dialog box may look different depending on the debuggers (if any) loaded on the target machine.

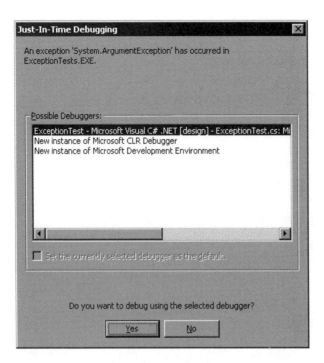

Figure 3-2. Unhandled exception

Therefore, let's add exception handling. The first thing to do is add a `.try` section around this code:

```
.maxstack 5
.locals init (int64 bigValue,
    int32 convertedValue,
    class [mscorlib]System.OverflowException oe,
    class [mscorlib]System.Exception e)
//  int initialization code goes here.
.try
{
    ldarg.0
    ldlen
    conv.i4
    brtrue.s argument_given
    //  CIL code goes here.
    call void [mscorlib]System.Environment::set_ExitCode(int32)
    leave method_exit
}
//  CIL code goes here.
method_exit: ret
```

The `.try` directive allows you to specify the code that will trap any thrown exceptions. `.try` also has another syntax that allows you to specify labels instead of a code block:

```
begin_try: ldarg.0
//  Main CIL code goes here.
end_try: call void [mscorlib]System.Environment::set_ExitCode(int32)
.try begin_try to end_try
```

If you use this syntax, the `.try` directive must come after the last opcode you want to protect.

Note that I don't use `ret` in the `.try` block; I use a new opcode, `leave`, which transfers control to another opcode (there's also `leave.s` for short jumps in code). In fact, you can't use any of the branch instructions (like `brtrue`) to get out of a `.try` block.

Now that you have your `.try` block in place, you need to catch the exception:

```
    leave method_exit
}
catch [mscorlib]System.OverflowException
{
    //  Report overflow error to the user.
    stloc.2
    ldstr "OverflowException caught:   "
    ldloc.2
    callvirt instance string [mscorlib]System.Exception::get_Message()
    call string [mscorlib]System.String::Concat(
        string, string)
    call void [mscorlib]System.Console::WriteLine(string)
    leave method_exit
}
```

You use the `catch` keyword, specifying the type of exception you want to catch. Note that if you want to rethrow the current exception, you use `rethrow`. It doesn't matter what is currently on the stack when you call `rethrow`; the runtime will simply throw the exception that caused the code to enter the current `catch` block.

If you have multiple `catch` blocks, the order in which they're given is important. For example, let's say you added this `catch` block after the previous one:

```
catch [mscorlib]System.Exception
{
    //  Exception code goes here.
}
```

Now, if you got an ArgumentException, the first catch block wouldn't see it, but the second one would. That's because ArgumentException does not inherit from OverflowException, but it does inherit from Exception. Conversely, if you switched your catch blocks around:

```
catch [mscorlib]System.Exception
{
    // Exception code goes here.
}
catch [mscorlib]System.OverflowException
{
    // Exception code goes here.
}
```

The first block would *always* get the thrown exceptions, because every exception inherits from Exception.

If you leave the code as-is, you've pretty much handled every exception that can be thrown at you. However, there are some additions that you can add to your exception handling toolkit. The first one you'll look at is the finally block. This block comes immediately after a .try block, and it will *always* run, even if an exception wasn't handled properly in the .try block. However, note the wording I just used: "comes immediately after." This does not mean you can do the following:

```
.try {}
finally {}
catch [mscorlib]System.Exception {}
```

You'll get an InvalidProgramException if you try this ordering. Therefore, you need to alter your code a bit to add the finally block—I'll sketch it out with the current exception structure:

```
.try
{
    .try
    {
        leave try_exit
    }
    catch [mscorlib]System.OverflowException
    {
        leave try_exit
    }
    catch [mscorlib]System.Exception
```

```
    {
        leave try_exit
    }
    try_exit: leave method_exit
}
finally
{
    // Finally-based code goes here.
    pop
    endfinally
}
method_exit: ret
```

You need to embed the current try-catch structure with another .try, and you also need to redirect the leave opcodes to branch to a place within the embedded .try block. Also, the last opcode that must occur within a finally block is endfinally.

You can also use a fault block. A fault block is similar to a finally block in that it will run if an unhandled exception occurs from the .try block. However, if the .try block is exited normally (via a leave opcode), then the fault block will *not* run. Modify your previous handler code structure to use a fault block:

```
.try
{
    .try
    {
        leave try_exit
    }
    catch [mscorlib]System.OverflowException
    {
        leave try_exit
    }
    try_exit: leave method_exit
}
fault
{
    // Fault-based code goes here.
    pop
    endfault
}
method_exit: ret
```

Notice that you removed the catch block for Exception. Therefore, if you get an exception other than OverflowException, the code in the fault block will run.

If no exceptions occur or an OverflowException occurs, the fault block code will not be executed.[19]

The last aspect that I'll cover regarding exception handling is filters and handlers. A filter/handler block pair is similar to a catch block in that it'll catch an exception. However, with a filter you can use variables to determine if the handler should run. For example, let's add a couple of variables to the .locals directive:[20]

```
.locals init (int64 bigValue,
    int32 convertedValue,
    int32 filterValue,
    class [mscorlib]System.OverflowException oe,
    class [mscorlib]System.Exception filterE,
    class [mscorlib]System.Exception e)
```

And let's initialize filterValue to 0:

```
ldc.i4.0
stloc filterValue
```

Now add a filter block to your structure. Rather than repeat the structure again, I'll just tell you that the following should appear right after the catch block for the OverflowException:

```
filter
{
    // This filter should run
    // if filterValue = 0
    pop
    ldloc filterValue
    ldc.i4.0
    beq enable_filter
    // Don't run the filter.
    disable_filter: ldc.i4.0
    br getout
    // If we got here, enable the filter.
    enable_filter: ldc.i4.1
    getout: endfilter
}
```

---

19. Note that endfinally and endfault are the same opcode—see Section 3.35 of Partition III.

20. By this time, some of the direct references to locals with ldloc and stloc will be off; the source code that you can download uses variable names instead of index values.

In the `filter` block, you're basically looking to see if `filterValue` is equal to 0. If it is, you push 1, or `exception_execute_handler`. This tells the runtime that you want to run your handler, which needs to be located immediately after the `filter` block:

```
{
    //  Report filtered overflow error to the user.
    castclass [mscorlib]System.Exception
    stloc filterE
    ldstr "Filtered Exception caught:  "
    ldloc filterE
    callvirt instance string [mscorlib]System.Exception::get_Message()
    call string [mscorlib]System.String::Concat(
        string, string)
    call void [mscorlib]System.Console::WriteLine(string)
    leave try_exit
}
```

If `filterValue` wasn't 0, you push 0, or `exception_continue_search`, onto the stack.

> **NOTE** *You may find it odd that there's a* `castclass` *in the filter handler. For some reason, the exception on the stack is typed as a* `System.Object`, *not as* `System.Exception`. *The code will run fine without* `castclass`, *but the assembly won't be verifiable without it, so that's why it's there.*

Now, in the `filter` block you need to manage your stack very carefully. The `filter` block requires that you have only one value on the stack when you leave: the `exception_XXX` value. That's why `pop` is in the block—you need to remove the exception that's on the stack when the filter is entered.

If you compile your IL file with `filterValue` set to 0 and run ExceptionTests without passing any arguments, the results should look like this:

```
Filtered Exception caught:  No argument was passed.
Press any key to continue...
```

If you set `filterValue` to any other value and run ExceptionTests the same way, the output will change:

```
Exception caught:  No argument was passed.
Type is System.ArgumentException
Press any key to continue...
```

Since the filter's criteria wasn't met, the exception trickled down to the last `catch` block. Of course, if an `OverflowException` occurred, the filter will never be reached.

 SOURCE CODE *The ExceptionTest.il file contains all of the code seen in this section.*

Opcode Miscellanea

To close out this chapter, I'll cover some issues and opcodes that didn't quite fit into the other sections, but that are also important and may lead you to further insights into .NET's inner workings.

Variable Argument Lists

As you saw in Chapter 2, you can define methods that take a variable number of arguments by using the `vararg` attribute:

```
.class public VariableArgumentTest
{
    .method public instance vararg
        string LotsOfArgs() {}
}
```

Of course, if someone calls this method from C#:

```
VariableArgumentTest vat = new VariableArgumentTest();
Console.WriteLine(vat.LotsOfArgs(__arglist(1, 2)));
Console.WriteLine(vat.LotsOfArgs(__arglist(1, 2, "Another one")));
Guid aGuid = Guid.NewGuid();
Console.WriteLine(vat.LotsOfArgs(__arglist(1.2, aGuid)));
```

how would you be able to pull these values out?

You would do it by using `arglist` in concert with a number of value types. `arglist` pushes an unmanaged pointer onto the stack that represents the variable number of arguments. Note that you should only use `arglist` if the method is marked with the `vararg` attribute.

Once you have this pointer (which is really a RuntimeArgumentHandle), you can use the ArgIterator structure to give you information about the arguments. You do this by iterating through the values via GetNextArg() (which returns a TypedReference instance), stopping when GetRemainingCount() returns 0. You can also determine the next argument's type via GetNextArgType(), which returns a RuntimeTypeHandle instance.

Let's see what the implementation code of LotsOfArgs() looks like—I'll focus on getting the ArgIterator instance set up correctly:

```
.method public instance vararg
    string LotsOfArgs()
{
    .maxstack  3
    .locals init ([0] valuetype [mscorlib]System.RuntimeArgumentHandle rah,
        [1] valuetype [mscorlib]System.RuntimeTypeHandle rth,
        [2] valuetype [mscorlib]System.ArgIterator ai,
        [3] typedref tr,
        [4] int32 argCount,
        [5] class [mscorlib]System.Text.StringBuilder sb)
    //  Initialize local variables.
    newobj instance void
        [mscorlib]System.Text.StringBuilder::.ctor()
    stloc.s sb
    ldc.i4.0
    stloc.s argCount
    //  Initialize the iterator with
    //  the arg. list handle.
    ldloca.s ai
    arglist
    call instance void
        [mscorlib]System.ArgIterator::.ctor(
        valuetype [mscorlib]System.RuntimeArgumentHandle)
    //  Lots of implementation code goes here…
    ret
}
```

This process is pretty easy—just load ai's address onto the stack, get the argument handle via arglist, and call ArgIterator's constructor. The source code contains the rest of the code necessary to enumerate through the arguments—specifically, it prints out the types of each argument.

SOURCE CODE *The VarArgTest.il file contains the* VariableArgumentTest *type so you can see how I implemented* LotsOfArgs(). *The VarArgTestClient project is a C# console application that uses the VarArgTest assembly.*

.maxstack Calculations

In the last chapter, I mentioned that you needed to make sure .maxstack was correct to avoid an exception at runtime. Of course, calculating this value isn't as easy as it looks. Take a look at this simple example:

```
ldc.i4.0  //  Stack size = 1
dup  //  Stack size = 2
stloc aVariable // Stack size = 1
```

As you see by the comments, it's easy to determine that .maxstack should be set to 2. However, when you add branch statements, you can't determine this as easily.

```
ldc.i4.0  //  Stack size = 1
ldloc aVariable  //  Stack size = 2
beq it_is_zero  //  Stack size = 0
ldc.i4.4  //  Stack size = 1
dup  //  Stack size = 2
dup  //  Stack size = 3
it_is_zero:  ret  // Stack size = 0 or 3
```

If aVariable is equal to 0, then the method will hit ret with nothing in the stack. If they're not equal, then there will be three values on the stack. Of course, it's easy to see once you make the calculation that .maxstack should be 3, but you can't do that until you check out each branch and determine which one will create the larger stack size.

Ultimately, there's no hard-and-fast way to make this calculation easy. It comes down to creating a stack size log throughout the method and using the largest value. And you have to get it right to ensure that you don't get any exceptions. For the most part, the default size of 8 should be sufficient for most methods, but if you have a lot of CIL in your method, you must check what the maximum number of values on the stack could be before you accept the default.

Pointer Prefixes

There are two prefixes that you should add to pointer-related opcodes under special circumstances. The first one is `unaligned.`:

```
ldloca someValueType
unaligned. 2
ldfld AValueType::AField
```

This opcode states that the following address may not fall on the natural alignment size.

The other prefix is `volatile.`:

```
ldloca someValueType
volatile.
ldfld AValueType::AField
```

This states that the value at the given address can be changed by another thread other than the current one. The runtime should always immediately retrieve or store the value from this address.

Note that these two prefixes can be used together:

```
ldloca someValueType
unaligned. 2
volatile.
ldfld AValueType::AField
```

These prefixes are used with the following opcodes: `ldind`, `stind`, `ldfld`, `stfld`, `ldobj`, `stobj`, `initblk`, or `cpblk`. `volatile.` can also be used with `ldsfld` and `stsfld`.

Method Jumps

Finally, I'll close this discussion of opcodes by looking at an opcode prefix called `tail.` and a new opcode called `jmp`. Although you probably won't use them or see them emitted from either VB .NET or C#, it's good to know how these work. Essentially, both are used to make a method call and to terminate the currently executing IL. Here's a simple code snippet showing how it works:

```
.class public beforefieldinit JumpTests
    extends [mscorlib]System.Object
{
```

```
.method public instance
    int32 GoSomewhereElseViaTail()
{
    ldarg.0
    tail.
    call instance int32 JumpTests::GoHere()
    ret
    //  Irrelevant code - it'll never be executed.
    ldc.i4.1
    ret
}

.method public instance
    int32 GoSomewhereElseViaJmp()
{
    jmp instance int32 JumpTests::GoHere()
    //  Irrelevant code - it'll never be executed.
    ldc.i4.1
    ret
}

.method public instance
    int32 GoHere()
{
    ldc.i4.7
    ret
}
}
```

With the tail. prefix, you must have a call, calli, or callvirt immediately after the prefix. Furthermore, the call must be followed by ret to make the code verifiable. You must push the arguments for the called method onto the stack; the stack must not contain any other values. Furthermore, tail. cannot be used to get out of exception blocks.

With jmp, you specify which method you wish to call. The stack must be completely cleaned out. jmp will take the current arguments and pass them on to the new method. As with tail., jmp can't be used to leave exception blocks.

Given that these two opcodes seem to produce the same results, what are the differences between the two? Here's a quick list:

- tail. is verifiable; jmp is not.

- It's possible to modify what is passed to the tail. call; with jmp, the target method gets what the current method gets.

SOURCE CODE *The JumpTest.il file contains the methods just shown so you can test them in your own client application to see their results. The JumpTestClient project is a C# console application that uses the JumpTest assembly.*

Conclusion

In this chapter, I covered a number of CIL opcodes. I went from the basics (stack manipulation) to operations to branch instruction. You learned how exception handling is added and the different permutations that can occur. In the next chapter, you get a chance to reinforce your knowledge of ilasm and CIL by creating a system entirely in CIL.

CHAPTER 4

ilasm and CIL in Practice

IN THIS CHAPTER, I'll review the concepts discussed in the last two chapters by creating a .NET system entirely in CIL. First, I'll cover what the system will do, and how it should work. Then, I'll walk you through creating the base types. Finally, I'll show you how to implement the GUI client that you'll use to test your component.

Generating Random Numbers

So far, I've gone over the ilasm directives and CIL opcodes from a functional standpoint. That is, I've talked about how they work, usually in the context of a small code snippet. However, I've found that more pieces of the puzzle fall into place when I try to build something that's more practical than a straightforward example, and you might feel the same. Therefore, I'm going to demonstrate how you create a component that generates random integer numbers. The client will be able to specify a range that the random numbers will fall between along with the number of random numbers desired, and the component will return these random values in three different ways:[1]

- As an array that contains all of the numbers

- Via a delegate

- Via an event based on that delegate

This system should allow you to review pretty much everything that I've covered so far in this book without getting too bogged down in the details of a complex design.

---

1. You may have noticed that I hinted at this example with previous code samples in Chapter 2; this section just formalizes the design.

121

Designing the Essentials

Now, creating random numbers isn't hard. .NET provides a couple of predefined types that you can use: System.Security.Cryptography.RNGCryptoServiceProvider and System.Random. For the purposes of this example, you'll go with System.Random, as it's a bit easier to use. The bigger issue is designing your system from an external view first so your coding will be focused on implementing these types.

You need a type that is the central point for specifying ranges and providing random values. You'll call this type RandomValues. It will have two private fields, m_MaxValue and m_MinValue, which will allow you to store the range the user provides. They will default to 100 and 0, respectively. You'll provide a custom constructor that the user can use to set the range when the instance is made. Furthermore, you'll have two properties, Max and Min, with which the user can adjust the range as needed.

You'll also need a delegate so you can call back to the client, informing them of new random values. You'll call this delegate RandomDelegate. The delegate's method should take only one parameter, an int32.

Finally, you'll create three methods to generate the random values: Generate(), GenerateViaDelegate(), and GenerateViaEvent(). Generate() will return an array of type int32. GenerateViaDelegate() will take a RandomDelegate type to notify the client of a new value, whereas GenerateViaEvent() will fire a defined event, NewRandom. Each method will take an argument that specifies the number of random numbers RandomValues should generate.

To get a visual feel for the design, look at the UML diagram in Figure 4-1.

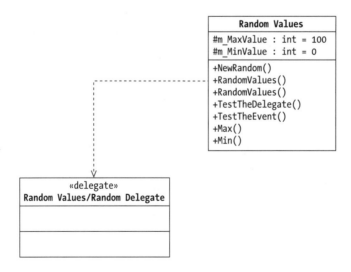

Figure 4-1. UML diagram of RandomValues types

This diagram isn't complete, but it shows the basic structure of the design. The coding goal is that if a VB.NET developer wanted to use this component, he could do this:

```
Dim randomNumbers As RandomValues = _
    New RandomValues(1, 100)
Dim results() As Integer =  randomNumbers.Generate(50)
```

Or, if a C# developer wanted to get the values using events, she could write the code like this:

```
private void OnNewRandomNumber(int NewNumber) {}
//…
RandomValues randomNumbers = new RandomValues(1, 100);
randomNumbers.NewRandom +=
    new RandomValues.RandomDelegate(this.OnNewRandomNumber);
randomNumbers.GenerateViaEvent(50);
randomNumbers.NewRandom -=
    new RandomValues.RandomDelegate(this.OnNewRandomNumber);
```

Implementing the Essentials

You have the blueprint, so let's create the assembly structure. I'll go over the types individually, as they each have their own subtleties.

Stubbing Out the Delegate

You'll begin with the basics. Define the assembly-based directives and RandomDelegate:

```
.assembly extern mscorlib {}

.assembly RIG
{
    .hash algorithm 0x00008004
    .ver 1:0:0:0
}

.module RIG.dll

.namespace RIG
{ //  Type definitions go here…}
```

This is the easy part. You've defined your assembly,[2] module, and namespace names. Now comes the fun part. Let's define the RandomValues and RandomDelegate types:

```
.class public beforefieldinit RandomValues
    extends [mscorlib]System.Object
{
    .class sealed nested public RandomDelegate
        extends [mscorlib]System.MulticastDelegate
    {
        .method public hidebysig specialname rtspecialname
            instance void .ctor(object Instance,
            native int Target) runtime managed
        {}
        .method public hidebysig virtual instance void
            Invoke(int32 NewRandomValue) runtime managed
        {}
        .method public hidebysig newslot virtual
            instance class [mscorlib]System.IAsyncResult
            BeginInvoke(int32 NewRandomValue,
            class [mscorlib]System.AsyncCallback callback,
            object Instance) runtime managed
        {}
        .method public hidebysig newslot virtual
            instance void EndInvoke(
            class [mscorlib]System.IAsyncResult result)
            runtime managed
        {}
    }
    // More RandomValues information
    // (e.g. fields, methods) goes here…
}
```

I had you make RandomDelegate a nested type of RandomValues because I think it makes sense to have the delegate associated with the type that uses it. Remember that RandomDelegate's methods will have no implementation—they're created by the runtime.

---

2.   By the way, RIG stands for Random Integer Generator.

Field Definitions

Now let's define the fields:

```
.field private static literal string ERROR_RANGE =
    "MinValue must be smaller than MaxValue."
.field family int32 m_MaxValue
.field family int32 m_MinValue
.field private class RIG.RandomValues/RandomDelegate m_NewRandom
```

The ERROR_RANGE constant will be used when you check for the given minimum and maximum values and throw exceptions when needed. m_NewRandom will be used by RandomValues to store the delegates when clients add and remove their request to receive the event. Note that the "/" (slash) character between RandomValues and RandomDelegate is not a typo. Whenever you use a nested type, you use a "/" instead of the expected "." (dot). This notation makes the nested class relationship explicit in the declaration.

Event Methods

Okay, on to the methods. Start by implementing the methods that the client will use to add and remove event notifications as shown in Listing 4-1.

Listing 4-1. Adding Event Notifications

```
.method public hidebysig specialname
    static void addNewRandom(
    class RIG.RandomValues/RandomDelegate DelegateToAdd)
    cil managed synchronized
{
    .maxstack 2
    .locals init (class RIG.RandomValues/RandomDelegate temp)
    ldarg.0
    ldfld
        class RIG.RandomValues/RandomDelegate
        RIG.RandomValues::NewRandom
    ldarg.0
    call class [mscorlib]System.Delegate
        [mscorlib]System.Delegate::Combine(
        class [mscorlib]System.Delegate,
        class [mscorlib]System.Delegate)
    castclass RIG.RandomValues/RandomDelegate
```

```
        stloc.0
        ldarg.0
        ldloc.0
        stfld class RIG.RandomValues/RandomDelegate
            RIG.RandomValues::NewRandom
        ret
    }


.method public hidebysig specialname
    static void removeNewRandom(
    class RIG.RandomValues/RandomDelegate DelegateToRemove)
    cil managed synchronized
{
    .maxstack 2
    .locals init (class RIG.RandomValues/RandomDelegate temp)
    ldarg.0
    ldfld
        class RIG.RandomValues/RandomDelegate
        RIG.RandomValues::NewRandom
    ldarg.1
    call class [mscorlib]System.Delegate
        [mscorlib]System.Delegate::Remove(
        class [mscorlib]System.Delegate,
        class [mscorlib]System.Delegate)
    castclass RIG.RandomValues/RandomDelegate
    stloc.0
    ldarg.0
    ldloc.0
    stfld class RIG.RandomValues/RandomDelegate
        RIG.RandomValues::NewRandom
    ret
}


.event RIG.RandomValues/RandomDelegate NewRandom
{
    .addon instance void RIG.RandomValues::addNewRandom(
        class RIG.RandomValues/RandomDelegate)
    .removeon instance void RIG.RandomValues::removeNewRandom(
        class RIG.RandomValues/RandomDelegate)
}
```

addNewRandom() takes a RandomDelegate as its only argument. It then uses the static method Combine() to essentially add the two delegates together. That's why I had you include the private RandomDelegate field NewRandom—when this method is called, the field is loaded via `ldsfld`, and its current invocation list is appended with whatever is in `DelegateToAdd`. The return type of `Combine()` is simply `Delegate`, so you need to `castclass` the result so you can store the new list in `NewRandom`. `removeNewRandom()` basically does the reverse—it calls `Remove()` instead of `Combine()` to get rid of a delegate call or set of invocation calls. The `.event` directive states which two methods are the ones that clients can use to set up an event notification.

Constructors

The next set of methods I'll cover are the constructors, which are shown in Listing 4-2. Actually, I'll only show the custom constructor that takes two arguments, as both constructors are similar in implementation:

Listing 4-2. Creating Constructors

```
.method public hidebysig specialname rtspecialname
    instance void .ctor( int32 MinValue, int32 MaxValue) cil managed
{
    .maxstack  2
    //  Set the initial values for
    //  m_MaxValue (100) and
    //  m_MinValue (0).
    ldarg.0
    ldc.i4.s 100
    stfld int32 DelegatesAndEvents.RandomValues::m_MaxValue
    ldarg.0
    ldc.i4.0
    stfld int32 DelegatesAndEvents.RandomValues::m_MinValue
    //  Call the base constructor.
    ldarg.0
    call instance void [mscorlib]System.Object::.ctor()
    //  Make sure min is smaller than max!
    ldarg.1
    ldarg.2
    blt.s Values_Are_OK
    ldstr "MinValue must be smaller than MaxValue."
    newobj instance void [mscorlib]System.ArgumentException::.ctor(string)
    throw
    Values_Are_OK:
    ldarg.0
    ldarg.1
    stfld int32 DelegatesAndEvents.RandomValues::m_MinValue
    ldarg.0
```

```
    ldarg.2
    stfld int32 DelegatesAndEvents.RandomValues::m_MaxValue
    ret
}
```

This is pretty basic stuff, but there's one piece that I need to cover in detail. The first six opcodes initialize your private fields, and then you call the base constructor (these first eight opcodes are exactly the same in the default constructor). Next, you check to see if MinValue is less than MaxValue via blt.s. If they are, then you reset the m_MinValue and m_MaxValue to the given values. However, if they're not, you throw an ArgumentException.

Creating the Properties

Before you move on to the heart of RandomValues, let's get the two properties in the CIL stream. I'll show how Max is implemented, as Min is virtually identical to Max:

```
.method public hidebysig specialname instance int32
    get_Max() cil managed
{
    .maxstack 1
    ldarg.0
    ldfld int32 RIG.RandomValues::m_MaxValue
    ret
}

.method public hidebysig specialname instance void
    set_Max(int32 NewValue) cil managed
{
    .maxstack  2
    ldarg.1
    ldarg.0
    ldfld int32 RIG.RandomValues::m_MinValue
    bgt.s Values_Are_OK
    ldstr "MinValue must be smaller than MaxValue."
    newobj instance void
        [mscorlib]System.ArgumentException::.ctor(string)
    throw
    Values_Are_OK:
    ldarg.0
    ldarg.1
    stfld int32 RIG.RandomValues::m_MaxValue
    ret
}
```

```
.property instance int32 Max()
{
    .get instance int32
        RIG.RandomValues::get_Max()
    .set instance void
        RIG.RandomValues::set_Max(int32)
}
```

This code is pretty simple. get_Max() retrieves the value from m_MaxValue, and set_Max() changes m_MaxValue so long as the given value NewValue is larger than m_MinValue. The Min-related methods work exactly the same, except in set_Min(), the given value must be greater than m_MinValue.

Implementing Generate()

Now you can move on to the fun stuff. Start by implementing Generate(), which is shown in Listing 4-3.

Listing 4-3. Returning Random Values

```
.method public hidebysig instance int32[]
        Generate(int32 RandomCount) cil managed
{
    .maxstack 3
    .locals init (int32[] retVal,
        class [mscorlib]System.Random rng,
        int32 newRandomValue, int32 x)
    // Create an array
    // with the size given.
    ldarg.1  // load RandonCount onto stack
    conv.ovf.u4  // Convert it to an unsigned int32
    newarr [mscorlib]System.Int32
    stloc.0 // store the array in retVal
    // Create the random number generator.
    newobj instance void [mscorlib]System.Random::.ctor()
    stloc.1
    // Initialize x and newRandomValue.
    ldc.i4.0
    stloc.2 // push 0 into newRandomValue
    ldc.i4.0
    stloc.3 // push 0 into x
```

```
// Start generating values.
br.s Is_Array_Full
Get_New_Random:
// Make sure the new value
// is between the min. and max.
ldloc.1  // load rng
ldarg.0  // load this pointer
ldfld int32 RIG.RandomValues::m_MinValue
ldarg.0
ldfld int32 RIG.RandomValues::m_MaxValue
callvirt instance int32
    [mscorlib]System.Random::Next(int32, int32)
stloc.2  // store new value in newRandomValue variable
// Put the value into the array
// at the correct location.
ldloc.0  // array
ldloc.3  // x
ldloc.2  // new value
stelem.i4
// Increment the count.
ldloc.3
ldc.i4.1
add
stloc.3
Is_Array_Full:
// Do we have enough values?
ldloc.3
ldarg.1
blt.s Get_New_Random
// Push retVal onto the stack.
ldloc.0
ret
}
```

The first thing you do is create an array, retVal, of type Int32 that will store your random values. RandomCount tells you how many values the client wants. Next, you enter a loop governed by x that generates all of the random values via Next() on a Random instance (stored in rng). Note that you use m_MixValue and m_MaxValue when you call Next() to ensure the new random value is within the client's desired boundaries. Each new value is put into the array via stelem.i4. Once the array is full (checked when x is greater than or equal to RandomCount via blt.s), you push the array onto the stack, and return.

Implementing *GenerateViaDelegate()*

The next method to implement is GenerateViaDelegate(), shown in Listing 4-4.

Listing 4-4. Using Delegates to Broadcast Random Values

```
.method public hidebysig
    instance void GenerateViaDelegate(
    class RIG.RandomValues/RandomDelegate Proc,
    int32 RandomCount) cil managed
{
    .maxstack 3
    .locals init (class [mscorlib]System.Random rng,
        int32 newRandomValue, int32 x)
    // Create the random number generator.
    newobj instance void
        [mscorlib]System.Random::.ctor()
    stloc.0
    // Initialize x and newRandomValue.
    ldc.i4.0
    stloc.1
    ldc.i4.0
    stloc.2
    // Start generating values.
    br.s Are_We_Done
Keep_Going:
    // Make sure the new value
    // is between the min. and max.
    ldloc.0
    ldarg.0
    ldfld int32 RIG.RandomValues::m_MinValue
    ldarg.0
    ldfld int32 RIG.RandomValues::m_MaxValue
    callvirt instance int32
        [mscorlib]System.Random::Next(int32, int32)
    stloc.1
    // Invoke the delegate, passing the new
    // random value.
    ldarg.1  // pull the Proc address onto the stack
    ldloc.1  // the new random value
    callvirt instance void
        RIG.RandomValues/RandomDelegate::Invoke(int32)
```

```
// Increment the count.
ldloc.2
ldc.i4.1
add
stloc.2
Are_We_Done:
// Did we generate enough values?
ldloc.2
ldarg.2
blt.s Keep_Going
ret
}
```

The implementation is virtually identical to Generate(), except in this case, you pass newRandomValue to the given delegate when you call Invoke().

Implementing GenerateViaEvent()

There's little difference between GenerateViaEvent() and GenerateViaDelegate(), other than GenerateViaEvent() doesn't need to take a RandomDelegate as an argument. In fact, I'll only show you the CIL where the code varies between the two. The following code snippet in GenerateViaEvent() replaces the three lines of code in GenerateViaDelegate() where the delegate is invoked:

```
.method public hidebysig instance void
    GenerateViaEvent(int32 RandomCount) cil managed
{
    // CIl code goes here..
    // Raise the event, passing it
    // the new random value.
    ldarg.0
    ldfld class RIG.RandomValues/RandomDelegate
        RIG.RandomValues::NewRandom
    ldloc.1
    callvirt instance void
        RIG.RandomValues/RandomDelegate::Invoke(int32)
    // More CIl code goes here..
    ret
}
```

With GenerateViaEvent(), you pass the random values to the NewRandom event (which is really just a RandomDelegate delegate), calling Invoke() to let all clients know that a new value has been created.

Generating the RIG Assembly

That's it! If you run ilasm on the IL file:

```
ilasm RIG.il /dll
```

you should get a RIG.dll file.

 SOURCE CODE *The RIG.il file contains all of the code discussed so far in this chapter.*

Designing the Test Harness

Now that you have your RIG.dll, how do you know that it works correctly? You need some way to interact with it to verify that you get expected behavior. In this section, I'll go over a GUI design that you'll implement. This GUI will allow you to test all three GenerateXXX() methods and display exception information if errors occur. Figure 4-2 shows what this window should look like when you're done.

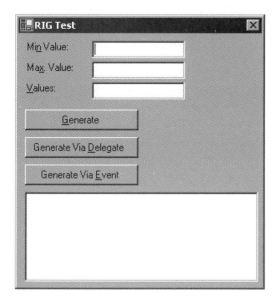

Figure 4-2. GUI design

The first two text boxes allow the user to pick the range for the random values, and the third text box designates how many values should be generated. Each button corresponds to one of the GenerateXXX() methods.

Implementing the Test Harness

Now, implementing a .NET GUI in CIL isn't hard, but it is rather tedious. Let's go through each part in detail.

Referencing Assemblies for UI Design

To start, your RIGTestClient.il file needs to include a couple of new assemblies:

```
.assembly extern System.Windows.Forms
{
    .publickeytoken = (B7 7A 5C 56 19 34 E0 89)
    .ver 1:0:3300:0
}
.assembly extern System
{
    .publickeytoken = (B7 7A 5C 56 19 34 E0 89)
    .ver 1:0:3300:0
}
.assembly extern System.Drawing
{
    .publickeytoken = (B0 3F 5F 7F 11 D5 0A 3A)
    .ver 1:0:3300:0
}
.assembly extern RIG {}
.subsystem 2
```

Each of these assemblies are needed to define base classes for components (System), create windows and UI components (System.Windows.Forms), and control component positioning (System.Drawing). You also need to reference your random number generator assembly, and since this is a GUI program, you need to set the .subsystem directive appropriately.

Defining UI Components

Next, you must create a class that extends the Form type. Within this class, you define your UI components (for example, text boxes) as fields so you can control them throughout the life of the form:

```
.class public beforefieldinit frmMain
    extends [System.Windows.Forms]System.Windows.Forms.Form
{
    .field private class
        [System.Windows.Forms]System.Windows.Forms.Button btnGenerate
    .field private class
        [System.Windows.Forms]System.Windows.Forms.Button btnGenerateDelegate
    .field private class
        [System.Windows.Forms]System.Windows.Forms.Button btnGenerateEvent
    .field private class
        [System.Windows.Forms]System.Windows.Forms.Label lblMax
    .field private class
        [System.Windows.Forms]System.Windows.Forms.Label lblMin
    .field private class
        [System.Windows.Forms]System.Windows.Forms.Label lblValues
    .field private class
        [System.Windows.Forms]System.Windows.Forms.ListBox lstResults
    .field private class
        [System.Windows.Forms]System.Windows.Forms.TextBox txtMax
    .field private class
        [System.Windows.Forms]System.Windows.Forms.TextBox txtMin
    .field private class
        [System.Windows.Forms]System.Windows.Forms.TextBox txtValueCount
    //  …
}
```

You can probably guess by the field names which component relates to the screen shown in Figure 4-2.

Initializing the Form

When the test program starts up, you need to display the window with all of the components set up correctly. Let's start by looking at the constructor for frmMain, which is called by the entry point:

```
.method private hidebysig static void Main() cil managed
{
    .entrypoint
    .custom instance void
        [mscorlib]System.STAThreadAttribute::.ctor() = ( 01 00 00 00 )
    .maxstack 1
    newobj instance void RIGTestClient.frmMain::.ctor()
    call void
        [System.Windows.Forms]System.Windows.Forms.Application::Run(
        class [System.Windows.Forms]System.Windows.Forms.Form)
    ret
}
.method public hidebysig specialname rtspecialname instance
    void .ctor() cil managed
{
    .maxstack 2
    ldarg.0
    call instance void [System.Windows.Forms]System.Windows.Forms.Form::.ctor()
    ldarg.0
    call instance void RIGTestClient.frmMain::SetupForm()
    ret
}
```

Main() creates a new instance of frmMain. I'll get back to the constructor in a moment, but take a look at the CIL code after the frmMain instance is made. Application.Run() is a method that will display the given form and also set up event handlers necessary to ensure proper teardown of the window. You could do this all yourself, but I'll let Run() take care of that grunge in this example.

Now, in frmMain's constructor, you call SetupForm(). This is a method that does a lot of component initialization, like setting a label's text value or the position of a button (as the following code snippet demonstrates):

```
.method private hidebysig instance void
    SetupForm() cil managed
{
    .maxstack  4
    .locals init (class
```

```
    [System.Windows.Forms]System.Windows.Forms.Control[] V_0)
ldarg.0
ldfld class
    [System.Windows.Forms]System.Windows.Forms.Button
    RIGTestClient.frmMain::btnGenerate
ldc.i4.8    ldc.i4.s 88
newobj instance void
    [System.Drawing]System.Drawing.Point::.ctor(    int32, int32)
callvirt instance void
    [System.Windows.Forms]System.Windows.Forms.Control::set_Location(
    valuetype [System.Drawing]System.Drawing.Point)
//  Other component initialization goes here…
}
```

The 8 and 88 values are passed to a Point reference, which is in turn passed to the Location property (set_Location()). This property defines the upper-left location of the control.

I won't show you all of the code here as that would take up too much space (and most of it is pretty dry and not much to look at), but I'll cover a couple of interesting lines of CIL code contained within SetupForm(). First, you'll note that after all of the component objects are created and the references are stored in their proper field locations, there's this piece of code:

```
ldarg.0
call instance void
    [System.Windows.Forms]System.Windows.Forms.Control::SuspendLayout()
```

Whenever you want to set a number of properties on contained controls or the window itself, you should use SuspendLayout(), as this prevents a bunch of Layout() events from firing. To resume Layout() event firings, call ResumeLayout() (which I do near the end SetupForm()). Technically, you don't have to do this—I tested my code and it works just fine without the calls—but I think it's good coding practice to use for most UI component modifications scenarios.

The other interesting code snippet occurs when you attach component events to your own methods:

```
ldarg.0
ldfld class [System.Windows.Forms]System.Windows.Forms.Button
    RIGTestClient.frmMain::btnGenerate
ldarg.0
ldftn instance void RIGTestClient.frmMain::btnGenerate_Click(
    object, class [mscorlib]System.EventArgs)
```

```
newobj instance void
    [mscorlib]System.EventHandler::.ctor(object, native int)
callvirt instance void
    [System.Windows.Forms]System.Windows.Forms.Control::add_Click(
    class [mscorlib]System.EventHandler)
```

To set up your event handlers, you need to pass a method pointer to an EventHandler instance. In this case, you want to have btnGenerate_Click() invoked whenever btnGenerate is clicked. Therefore, you use ldftn to push the method pointer onto the stack, and pass that to EventHandler's constructor as a native int. The EventHandler instance is then passed to the control's add_Click() method to complete the hook.

Calling Generate()

The form initialization code is set up. Let's start looking at the test methods—you'll begin by calling Generate(). It's pretty lengthy and there's a fair amount of code that is duplicated in the other two test methods, so I'll cover everything in this section in small sections. First, here's the method initialization and list cleanup code:

```
.method private hidebysig instance void
    btnGenerate_Click(object sender, class [mscorlib]System.EventArgs e)
    cil managed
{
    .maxstack 3
    .locals init (class [RIG]RIG.RandomValues rv,
        int32[] randomValues,
        int32 x,
        class [mscorlib]System.Exception ex)
    .try
    {
        ldarg.0
        ldfld class [System.Windows.Forms]
            System.Windows.Forms.ListBox
            RIGTestClient.frmMain::lstResults
        callvirt instance class
            [System.Windows.Forms]
            System.Windows.Forms.ListBox/ObjectCollection
            [System.Windows.Forms]
            System.Windows.Forms.ListBox::get_Items()
        callvirt instance void
            [System.Windows.Forms]
            System.Windows.Forms.ListBox/ObjectCollection::Clear()
```

You set up a try block to handle any exceptions that may occur within btnGenerate_Click()—you'll see the catch block later on in this section. You then clear any items within lstResults by calling Clear(). Note that this method exists on the ObjectCollection reference defined by the Items property, so you first need to get that reference on the stack via a callvirt on get_Items().

Next, you need to convert the range values in the text boxes:

```
ldarg.0
ldfld class [System.Windows.Forms]
    System.Windows.Forms.TextBox
    RIGTestClient.frmMain::txtMin
callvirt instance string
    [System.Windows.Forms]
    System.Windows.Forms.Control::get_Text()
call int32 [mscorlib]System.Int32::Parse(string)
ldarg.0
ldfld class [System.Windows.Forms]
    System.Windows.Forms.TextBox
    RIGTestClient.frmMain::txtMax
callvirt instance string
    [System.Windows.Forms]
    System.Windows.Forms.Control::get_Text()
call int32 [mscorlib]System.Int32::Parse(string)
```

Of course, if the user enters a value like "5tg6ji" in one of the text boxes, you'll get an exception, but your try block will trap it and send it to the catch block.

Now that you have your range, you can create a RandomValues instance, convert the value in txtValueCount, and call Generate():

```
newobj instance void
    [RIG]RIG.RandomValues::.ctor(int32, int32)
stloc.0
ldloc.0
ldarg.0
ldfld class [System.Windows.Forms]
    System.Windows.Forms.TextBox
    RIGTestClient.frmMain::txtValueCount
callvirt instance string
    [System.Windows.Forms]
    System.Windows.Forms.Control::get_Text()
call int32 [mscorlib]System.Int32::Parse(string)
callvirt instance int32[]
    [RIG]RIG.RandomValues::Generate(int32)
stloc.1
```

Note that the previous CIL leaves the converted range values on the stack, so you can call `.ctor()` knowing that the correct values will be transferred.

Once you have the values, you need to add them to the list box. This implementation is given in Listing 4-5.

Listing 4-5. Adding Random Values to a ListBox Control

```
ldc.i4.0
stloc.2
br.s Are_We_Done

Display_Value:
ldarg.0
ldfld class [System.Windows.Forms]
    System.Windows.Forms.ListBox
    RIGTestClient.frmMain::lstResults
callvirt instance class
    [System.Windows.Forms]
    System.Windows.Forms.ListBox/ObjectCollection
    [System.Windows.Forms]
    System.Windows.Forms.ListBox::get_Items()
ldloc.1
ldloc.2
ldelema [mscorlib]System.Int32  // push the elements address onto the stack
call instance string [mscorlib]System.Int32::ToString()
callvirt instance int32
    [System.Windows.Forms]
    System.Windows.Forms.ListBox/ObjectCollection::Add(object)
pop
ldloc.2
ldc.i4.1
add
stloc.2
Are_We_Done:
ldloc.2
ldloc.1
ldlen
conv.i4
blt.s Display_Value
leave.s End_Method
}
```

Recall that `ldelema` will push the element's address onto the stack, so you can call `ToString()` to push the string representation of the value onto the stack.

The last piece of code is the catch block:

```
catch [mscorlib]System.Exception
{
    //  Show the exception information to the screen.
    stloc.3
    ldloc.3
    callvirt instance string
        [mscorlib]System.Exception::get_Message()
    ldloc.3
    callvirt instance string [mscorlib]System.Exception::ToString()
    call string [mscorlib]System.String::Concat(string, string)
    call valuetype
        [System.Windows.Forms]
        System.Windows.Forms.DialogResult
        [System.Windows.Forms]
        System.Windows.Forms.MessageBox::Show(string)
    pop
    leave.s End_Method
}
End_Method: ret
}
```

You use MessageBox to display the exception information—I'll show what the message box look like later on when you compile the assembly.

Calling GenerateViaDelegate()

Most of the code in btnGenerateDelegate_Click() is similar to btnGenerate_Click() (such as that for parsing the range values), so I won't show that again. Listing 4-6 shows the code that sets up the delegate and calls GenerateViaDelegate().

Listing 4-6. Getting Random Values via a Delegate

```
.method private hidebysig instance void
    btnGenerateDelegate_Click(
    object sender, class [mscorlib]System.EventArgs e)
    cil managed
{
    .maxstack  4
    .locals init (class [RIG]RIG.RandomValues rv,
        class [mscorlib]System.Exception ex)
    .try
    {
```

```
                    //  Other CIL code goes here…
                    newobj instance void
                        [RIG]RIG.RandomValues::.ctor(int32, int32)
                    stloc.0
                    ldloc.0
                    ldarg.0
                    ldftn instance void
                            RIGTestClient.frmMain::OnNewRandomNumber(int32)
                    newobj instance void
                    [RIG]RIG.RandomValues/RandomDelegate::.ctor(
                        object, native int)
                    ldarg.0
                    ldfld class [System.Windows.Forms]
                        System.Windows.Forms.TextBox
                        RIGTestClient.frmMain::txtValueCount
                    callvirt instance string
                        [System.Windows.Forms]
                        System.Windows.Forms.Control::get_Text()
                    call int32 [mscorlib]System.Int32::Parse(string)
                    callvirt instance void
                        [RIG]
                        RIG.RandomValues::GenerateViaDelegate(
                    class [RIG]RIG.RandomValues/RandomDelegate, int32)
                    leave.s End_Method
                }
                catch [mscorlib]System.Exception
                { //  Handling code goes here… }
                End_Method:   ret
            }
```

OnNewRandomNumber() is an instance method that is used when the delegate is invoked within GenerateViaDelegate()—that's why its address is retrieved via ldftn to pass it into the RandomDelegate instance. Here's what this method looks like:

```
.method public hidebysig instance void
    OnNewRandomNumber(int32 NewNumber) cil managed
{
    .maxstack 2
    //  Add the new value to the results list.
    ldarg.0
    ldfld class [System.Windows.Forms]
        System.Windows.Forms.ListBox
        RIGTestClient.frmMain::lstResults
```

```
    callvirt instance class
        [System.Windows.Forms]
        System.Windows.Forms.ListBox/ObjectCollection
        [System.Windows.Forms]
        System.Windows.Forms.ListBox::get_Items()
    ldarga.s NewNumber
    call instance string [mscorlib]System.Int32::ToString()
    callvirt instance int32
        [System.Windows.Forms]
        System.Windows.Forms.ListBox/ObjectCollection::Add(
        object)
    pop
    ret
}
```

This is similar to the code you saw in btnGenerate_Click() when you displayed the results to lstResults.

Calling GenerateViaEvent()

Finally, Listing 4-7 shows the code that tests GenerateViaEvent(). As I did in the previous section, I'll only show the code that's essential to making this test.

Listing 4-7. Receiving Random Values with an Event

```
.method private hidebysig instance void
    btnGenerateEvent_Click(object sender,
    class [mscorlib]System.EventArgs e) cil managed
{
    .maxstack 4
    .locals init (class [RIG]RIG.RandomValues rv,
        class [mscorlib]System.Exception ex)
    .try
    {
        newobj instance void [RIG]RIG.RandomValues::.ctor(int32, int32)
        stloc.0
        ldloc.0
        ldarg.0
        ldftn instance void
            RIGTestClient.frmMain::OnNewRandomNumber(int32)
        newobj instance void
            [RIG]RIG.RandomValues/RandomDelegate::.ctor(
            object, native int)
```

```
            callvirt instance void
                [RIG]RIG.RandomValues::addNewRandom(
                class[RIG]RIG.RandomValues/RandomDelegate)
            ldloc.0
            ldarg.0
            ldfld class [System.Windows.Forms]
                System.Windows.Forms.TextBox
                RIGTestClient.frmMain::txtValueCount
            callvirt instance string
                [System.Windows.Forms]
                System.Windows.Forms.Control::get_Text()
            call int32 [mscorlib]System.Int32::Parse(string)
            callvirt instance void [RIG]
                RIG.RandomValues::GenerateViaEvent(int32)
            ldloc.0
            ldarg.0
            ldftn instance void
                RIGTestClient.frmMain::OnNewRandomNumber(int32)
            newobj instance void
                [RIG]RIG.RandomValues/RandomDelegate::.ctor(
                object, native int)
            callvirt instance void
                [RIG]RIG.RandomValues::removeNewRandom(
                class [RIG]RIG.RandomValues/RandomDelegate)
            leave.s End_Method
        }
        catch [mscorlib]System.Exception
        { //  Handling code goes here… }
        End_Method:   ret
    }
```

The first thing you need to do is hook the event. Do this by getting OnNewRandomNumber()'s address via ldftn, and passing it into a RandomDelegate instance. Next, call addNewRandom() to complete the hook. After you call GenerateViaEvent(), reverse the event hook by calling removeNewRandom().

Generating the RIGTestClient Assembly

That's it for the UI code—if you run ilasm on the IL file:

```
ilasm RIGTestClient.il
```

you should get a RIGTestClient.exe file. Feel free to run the application and test out some scenarios. For example, Figure 4-3 shows what the window looks like after the Generate button is pressed.

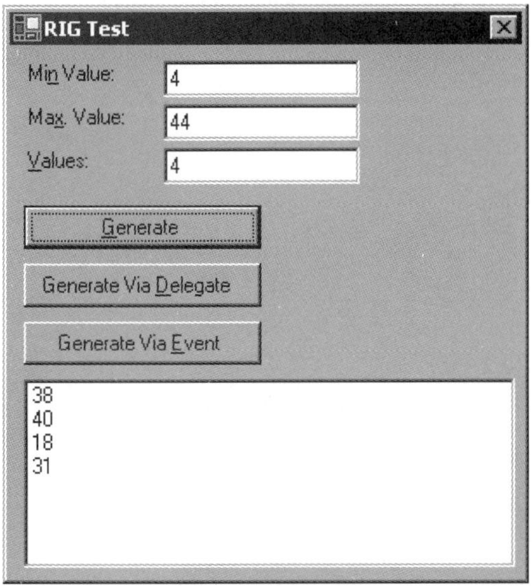
RIG Test
Min Value:
4
Max. Value:
44
Values:
4
Generate
Generate Via Delegate
Generate Via Event
38
40
18
31

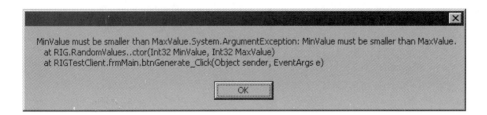

Figure 4-3. Generate() results

Of course, if you enter incorrect values in the text boxes, you'll get a message box informing you of your mistake. Figure 4-4 shows what happens if you enter a minimum value of "4", but a maximum value of "1".

MinValue must be smaller than MaxValue.System.ArgumentException: MinValue must be smaller than MaxValue.
at RIG.RandomValues..ctor(Int32 MinValue, Int32 MaxValue)
at RIGTestClient.frmMain.btnGenerate_Click(Object sender, EventArgs e)
OK

Figure 4-4. Invalid range

Figure 4-5 demonstrates the exception generated (which is caught in the `catch` blocks of each button's `Click()` event implementation code) if the text box contains a noninteger value (like "ff").

Figure 4-5. Formatting exception

Also, make sure you have RIG.dll in the same directory as RIGTestClient.exe; otherwise, you'll get a nasty dialog box when you try to create a RandomValues instance as Figure 4-6 demonstrates.

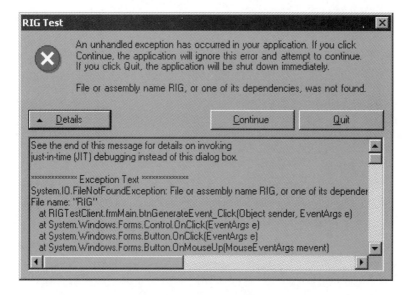

Figure 4-6. Assembly cannot be located.

 SOURCE CODE *The RIGTestClient.il file contains all of the UI code.*

Conclusion

In this chapter, I walked you through a complete .NET system written entirely in CIL. You created a server-side component that generated random values and returned the results via arrays, delegates, and events. You also created a test client that allowed you to ensure that the component's code behavior was correct. In the next chapter, you'll look at how you can debug your CIL-based assemblies.

CHAPTER 5

Debugging CIL

In this chapter, I'll cover how you can debug your CIL-based applications. I'll demonstrate how you can create debug builds of your assemblies, the tools that you can use to debug them, and how to get them running in the debugger.

Debug Builds

Up to this point, I've been showing you directives and opcodes along with source code examples that you can compile on your own machine. My hope is that when you compile my code, nothing crashes and everything works out. However, we all know the real world doesn't work like that—humans are fallible and coding errors occur. Therefore, you need to be able to debug your CIL-based assemblies.

However, if you've tried to open up a file that contains your CIL code in VS .NET and debug an assembly, you found out that it just doesn't work. Fortunately, there are a couple of tools that you can use to help you find out where these bugs are occurring. Before you start to use these tools, though, you need to create one important file—the debug file.

Let's say that you have the following type defined in a console application:

```
.class public beforefieldinit BadConsole
    extends [mscorlib]System.Object
{
    .method private hidebysig static void
        Main(string[] args) cil managed
    {
        .entrypoint
        .maxstack  2
        .locals init ([0] int32 x)
        //  Set x = 0.
        ldc.i4.0
        stloc.0
        //  Get the next argument
        //  if there's another one.
        br.s Are_We_Done
        Get_Next: ldarg.1
        ldloc.0
        ldelem.ref
        call void [mscorlib]System.Console::WriteLine(string)
```

```
        //  Increment x.
        ldloc.0
        ldc.i4.1
        add
        stloc.0
        Are_We_Done: ldloc.0
        ldarg.0
        ldlen
        conv.i4
        blt.s Get_Next
        ret
    }
}
```

If you compiled the IL file, it would be successful.[1] However, running it at the command line like this:

```
BadConsole print my arguments
```

would produce the unwelcome dialog box shown in Figure 5-1.

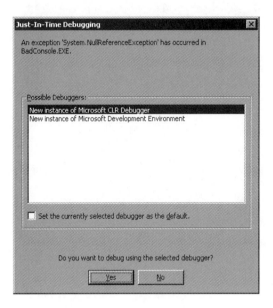

Figure 5-1. Invalid program exception

---

1.   This is assuming you had the correct assembly references that I didn't show in the code snippet.

This doesn't help much. You have no idea where the problem is—the message includes no line numbers, no variable names, not even an address location. And even if your machine has a couple of debuggers set up, it's more than likely that the assembly will be located on a client's box that doesn't have a debugger. The end result will probably be a justifiable complaint from your customers who are wondering why you'd ever ship them a program that doesn't work.

However, before you devolve into doing a bunch of `Console.WriteLine()` statements at each line of code to figure out what's going wrong,[2] there's an alternative. The first step in tracking the problem down is creating the program debug database file (.pdb). This is done by using the /debug switch at ilasm's command line:

```
ilasm /debug BadConsole.il
```

You'll notice that when you do this, a BadConsole.pdb file will show up in the same directory with the assembly. This file contains all of the symbols necessary for a debugger to load the assembly along with the source code so you can step through each line of code.

The Command-Line Tool: cordbg.exe

Now that you have your PDB file, you can debug your application. Two debugging tools come with .NET:

- cordbg.exe: A command-line tool

- dbgclr.exe: A GUI-based tool

In this section, I'll cover the first one. If you want to follow along, compile the BadConsole.il file with the /debug switch.

cordbg Basics

Let's start by going through the basic motions of cordbg. To use this tool, open up a console window, navigate to the directory that contains BadConsole.exe, and enter the following:

```
cordbg BadConsole print my args
```

---

2.   And do you *really* want to do that in CIL?

The strings after BadConsole are there to pass in arguments to your application. Note that you must pass any relevant arguments to the debugged application first. You can pass in cordbg commands as well, but they must be prefixed with the "!" (exclamation point) character.

Figure 5-2 shows what the console should look like if cordbg was able to load your assembly.

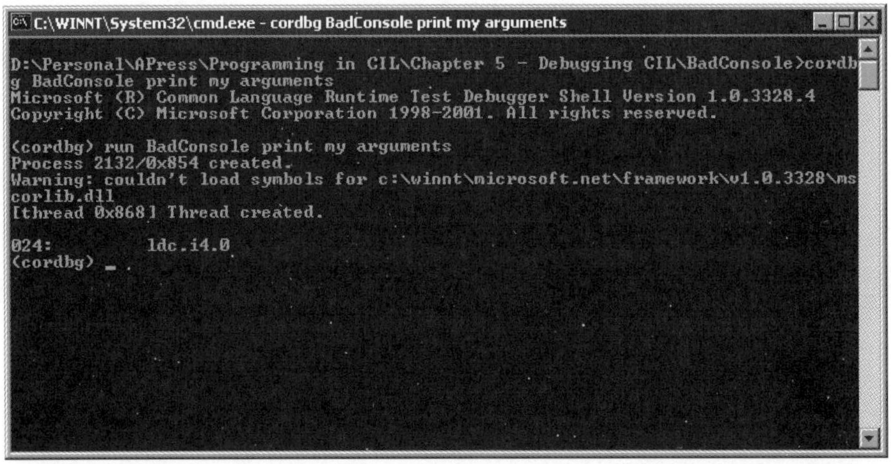

Figure 5-2. Launching cordbg

Don't worry about the warning message; so long as you get the (cordbg) prompt and the first opcode in your Main() method is showing up, you're okay.[3]

Now that you're running in the debugger, you'd like to be able to determine where the problem is. First, type **sh**ow—this command will show source code lines before and after the current code line. You can also vary the number of displayed lines by giving a code line value after show—here's what the output looks like when show 3 is used:

```
(cordbg) show 3
021:           .maxstack  2
022:           .locals init ([0] int32 x)
023:           // Set x = 0.
024:*          ldc.i4.0
025:           stloc.0
026:           // Get the next argument
027:           // if there's another one.
```

---

3. For more information on getting these symbol files for system executables, see
   ms-help://MS.NETFrameworkSDK/vsdebug/html/vxtskInstallingDebugSymbols.htm.

If you look at line 24, you'll see an asterisk—this denotes which line of code is the current line.

Note that each cordbg command has an abbreviated version for reduced typing. For example, you can type sh 3 instead of show 3 to get the same effect. I'll use the full command string in this chapter, as it's easier to figure out what each command does that way; however, when I introduce a new cordbg command, I'll bold the minimal set of characters that are necessary for the command in case you want to use the shortcut version.[4]

Before you start moving through your code, let's take a look at the values of your local variables. You do this with the **p**rint command:

```
(cordbg) print
args=(0x00c098d0) array with dims=[3]
x=0x00000000
$thread=(null)
```

You can also specify a particular variable to display:

```
(cordbg) print x
x=0x00000000
```

If you want to display an array's argument, you must use a simple expression:

```
(cordbg) print args[1]
args[1]=(0x00c09908) "my"
```

You can also change the value of a variable with **s**et:

```
(cordbg) print x
x=0x00000000
(cordbg) set x 0x3
x=0x00000003
(cordbg) print x
x=0x00000003
```

Since your locals look good right now, let's not change any of the variable's values. Let's move to the next line of code to see if you run into a problem. There are a number of ways to step through code in cordbg:

---

4. While I won't show any multithreaded assemblies in this chapter, you can prefix most of the cordbg commands with an asterisk (*) to apply them to every thread in the assembly.

- **n**ext [*count*]: Steps though the code (stepping over method calls) to the next source line if *count* isn't specified; otherwise, cordbg steps *count* code lines.

- **so** [*count*]: Same as next [*count*].

- **s**tep [*count*]: Steps though the code (stepping into method calls) to the next source line if *count* isn't specified; otherwise, cordbg steps *count* code lines.

- **si** [*count*]: Same as step [*count*].

- **in** [*count*]: Same as step [*count*].

- **ns**ingle [*count*]: Steps through the code (skipping method calls) to the next instruction if *count* isn't specified; otherwise, cordbg steps *count* instructions.

- **ss**ingle [*count*]: Steps through the code (stepping into method calls) to the next instruction if *count* isn't specified; otherwise, cordbg steps *count* instructions.

- **o**ut [*count*]: Steps out of the current method if *count* isn't specified; otherwise, cordbg steps out *count* methods.

- **setip** *line number*: Sets the next code line to execute, which is specified by *line number*.

Let's start with the simple process of going to the next line of code, which can be done with **n**ext. If you do this and then enter show 3, you should see the following output:

```
(cordbg) next
025:            stloc.0
(cordbg) show 3
022:            .locals init ([0] int32 x)
023:            //  Set x = 0.
024:            ldc.i4.0
025:*           stloc.0
026:            //  Get the next argument
027:            //  if there's another one.
028:            br.s Are_We_Done
```

Well, at least you know that ldc.i4.0 wasn't the culprit. You need to issue more next commands before you find your bug. To cut to the chase, you need to get line 32 to be the current code line to see the exception. Once you're there, issue another next command:

```
(cordbg) next
First chance exception generated: (0x00c09944) <System.NullReferenceException>
Unhandled exception generated: (0x00c09944) <System.NullReferenceException>
  _className=<null>
  _exceptionMethod=<null>
  _exceptionMethodString=<null>
  _message=(0x00c099cc) "Object reference not set to an instance of an object."
  _innerException=<null>
  _helpURL=<null>
  _stackTrace=(0x00c09a48) array with dims=[12]
  _stackTraceString=<null>
  _remoteStackTraceString=<null>
  _remoteStackIndex=0x00000000
  _HResult=0x80004003
  _source=<null>
  _xptrs=0x0012f3d0
  _xcode=0xc0000005
032:            ldelem.ref
```

You now know the line where the error occurs, but you don't necessarily know why. However, at least you're closer to solving this dilemma. Apparently, ldelem.ref is trying to get an array element, but it's failing. Well, you know that ldelem.ref requires two pieces of information on the stack: the array reference and the array index value. If you look at the two lines of CIL code before it:

```
ldarg.1
ldloc.0
```

you can finally see the problem. ldarg.1 doesn't exist! Remember, Main() is a static method, so args is at index value 0.

Watching Register Values and Native Instructions

One interesting aspect of cordbg is that you can actually see the native instructions that the runtime emits from your CIL code. Let's get out of the debugger by entering **ex**it or **q**uit, and restart the debugger for BadConsole[5] using the same command line arguments as before. Use step to walk through the code until you get to the invalid ldarg.1 instruction. Next, enter **dis**assemble:

```
(cordbg) disassemble 7
  [0008] push        ebx
  [0009] mov         ebx,ecx
  [000b] xor         esi,esi
  [000d] xor         edi,edi
  [000f] mov         esi,edi
  [0011] nop
  [0012] jmp         00000032
 *[0014] mov         edi,esi
  [0016] mov         dword ptr [ebp-10h],esi
  [0019] mov         eax,dword ptr [ebp-10h]
  [001c] cmp         eax,dword ptr [edi+4]
  [001f] jb          00000009
  [0021] xor         ecx,ecx
  [0023] call        7637E067
  [0028] mov         edi,dword ptr [edi+eax*4+0Ch]
```

Now, I'm not going to cover x86 instructions in this book in any great detail.[6] However, I want to get you a little comfortable working at this level in case you ever need to do some power debugging to figure out if something is terribly wrong with the JITter.[7] Plus, it's interesting to see how ldarg.1 causes a NullPointerException in this case.

---

5. Note that if you want to stop the current debugging session, but you don't want to leave cordbg, enter kill.

6. Interested readers can download the three volumes of Intel's *Architecture Software Developer's Manual* at http://developer.intel.com/design/pentium4/manuals/.

7. A scenario that's *highly* unlikely, but you never know. . . .

Before moving to the next native instruction set, let's take a snapshot of the register values by issuing the **reg**isters command:

```
(cordbg) registers
Thread 0x12c:
EIP = 02e8c394 ESP = 0012f8a8 EBP = 0012f8c8 EAX = 0037539b ECX = 00c098d0
EDX = 00000004 EBX = 00c098d0 ESI = 00000000 EDI = 00000003
ST0 = -1.#IND ST1 = -1.#IND ST2 = -1.#IND ST3 = -1.#IND ST4 = -1.#IND
ST5 = -1.#IND ST6 = -1.#IND ST7 = -1.#IND
EFL = 0293 CS = 001b DS = 0023 ES = 0023 FS = 0038
GS = 0000 SS = 0023 CY = 1 PE = 0 AC = 1
ZR = 0 PL = 1 EI = 1 UP = 0
Dr0 = 00200020 Dr1 = 003c0020 Dr2 = 0063002f
Dr3 = 00730061 Dr6 = 00000005 Dr7 = 00000000
ControlWord = ffff027f StatusWord = ffff0120 TagWord = ffffffff
ErrorOffset = 791f7e0c ErrorSelector = 0119001b DataOffset = 0012ec98
DataSelector = ffff0023 Cr0NpxState = 00000000
```

This may look like a bunch of junk if you've never looked as assembly code before, and that's perfectly fine.[8] Although I encourage you to learn what these register values are used for, I only want you to use registers in this case to help you figure out what's getting messed up by taking snapshots of the register values after each native instruction set.

Now, type **ss**ingle and then show 1:

```
(cordbg) ssingle
[0016] mov          dword ptr [ebp-10h],esi
(cordbg) show 1
029:          Get_Next: ldarg.1
030:*          ldloc.0
031:
```

You'll notice that you moved one CIL instruction for that mov x86 instruction. Now enter registers; I'll only display the registry value that changed, edi:

```
(cordbg) registers
EDI = 00000000
```

---

8.   Your values will probably be completely different from mine. That's OK—as I discuss specific register values, just focus on the register label itself and don't try to compare your results with mine.

Again, issue ssingle and then registers. You'll notice that nothing changed. This is because you're taking the value in esi, and putting it in the memory location pointed at by ebp with an offset value of 16 (0x10, or 10h). Let's grab the value out of ebp and see what it is, because you know the next instruction will put it into eax so you can see if the **du**mp command works:

```
(cordbg) dump 0x0012f8b8 4
12f8b8 00000000
```

The dump command takes an address value, and returns the information in memory located at that address. You can follow that address value with the number of bytes you want to display. In this case, I show 4 bytes. The SDK doesn't specify what the default value will be if you don't give the byte size, but in my experience I've always seen 128 bytes if I only give the address value. As you can see, if you take the value in ebp, subtract it by 0x10, and get the memory result, you'll get the same value as esi.

Okay, let's move to the next native instruction:

```
(cordbg) disassemble
[001c] cmp         eax,dword ptr [edi+4]
(cordbg) show 1
031:
032:*      ldelem.ref
033:       call void [mscorlib]System.Console::WriteLine(string)
```

Notice that ldelem.ref takes more than one instruction. Take care if you're trying to match up x86 instructions to CIL instructions; there may not be a one-to-one mapping, so you'll need to issue a bunch of disassemble-show pairs to figure out the instruction relationships. Also, if you look at eax, it's now equal to esi:

```
(cordbg) registers
EAX = 00000000
```

Now issue ssingle again. Yikes! You should get an exception. But why did you get it? Let's take a look at the native instruction that causes the error:

```
[001c] cmp         eax,dword ptr [edi+4]
```

cmp acts just like CIL's cmp instruction. However, take a look at what's in edi. It's 0x00000000. If you try to dump that with a positive offset of 4, here's what you get:

```
(cordbg) dump 0x00000004 4
Couldn't read the asked-for memory
```

Oops. That's not a good sign—you can't access memory at that address. The runtime ends up interpreting this as a NullPointerException, and you're toast.

Setting Breakpoints

Now, you may have been getting tired of entering next all the time to get to the invalid line of code in BadConsole. Fortunately, cordbg lets you define breakpoints in your code via the **b**reak command. If you start a new cordbg session for BadConsole and enter the command break 029, you'll see the following:

```
(cordbg) break 029
Breakpoint #1 has bound to D:\Personal\APress\Programming in CIL\
    Chapter 5 - Debugging CIL\BadConsole\BadConsole.exe.
#1      D:\Personal\APress\Programming in CIL\Chapter 5 - Debugging CIL\
    BadConsole\BadConsole.il:29    Main+0x4(il) [active]
```

By specifying the line number of the currently executing code, cordbg puts a breakpoint at that line. Now, if you enter **g**o (or **con**t):

```
(cordbg) go
break at #1    D:\Personal\APress\Programming in CIL\Chapter 5 - Debugging CIL\
    BadConsole\BadConsole.il:29    Main+0x4(il) [active]
029:        Get_Next: ldarg.1
```

you'll notice that you stop at your breakpoint.

If you want a list of breakpoints currently defined in your application, just enter break:

```
(cordbg) break
#1      D:\Personal\APress\Programming in CIL\Chapter 5 - Debugging CIL\
    BadConsole\BadConsole.il:29    Main+0x4(il) [active]
```

Each breakpoint is given an identifier which you can specify to remove them (I'll show you how to do this in a moment). Unfortunately, these breakpoints don't persist if you get out of the cordbg session completely. However, if you kill an assembly and then rerun the same assembly under the same cordbg session, the breakpoints will remain.

If you want to remove a breakpoint, enter **rem**ove, giving the appropriate breakpoint ID:

```
(cordbg) remove 1
(cordbg) break
(cordbg)
```

In this case, you only had one breakpoint, so a subsequent break command lists nothing.

You can also specify a breakpoint in a method from a class via an offset like this:

```
(cordbg) break BadConsole::Main:4
#8      <UnknownModule>!BadConsole::Main:4        [unbound]
```

Note that if the class is currently loaded by the debugger, the breakpoint will be unbound. Therefore, you should use this syntax before you load the assembly. Once the assembly is loaded in the debugger, your breakpoint will become active, and the debugger will stop on that breakpoint. If you want to get a list of currently loaded classes so you can avoid creating a breakpoint that won't work anyway in the current session, enter list cl.

 NOTE *The* list *command can also be used to list loaded modules* (list mod) *and global functions* (list fu). *Note that these lists can get very long, so make sure your console's vertical screen buffer size is large enough so you can scroll the list.*

Modes

cordbg has a number of modes that you can turn on and off via the mode command. For example, run cordbg without specifying BadConsole on the command line. Once cordbg is up, enter the following command:

```
(cordbg) mode AppDomainLoads 1
AppDomain and Assembly load events are displayed
(cordbg) run BadConsole
Process 2128/0x850 created.
Appdomain #1, DefaultDomain -- Created
Assembly 0x00084bcc, c:\winnt\microsoft.net\framework\v1.0.3328\mscorlib.dll --
Loaded
        in appdomain #1, DefaultDomain
Warning: couldn't load symbols for c:\winnt\microsoft.net\framework\v1.0.3328\ms
corlib.dll
[thread 0x84c] Thread created.
Assembly 0x0009f7d4, D:\Personal\APress\Programming in CIL\Chapter 5 - Debugging
 CIL\BadConsole\BadConsole.exe -- Loaded
        in appdomain #1, BadConsole
024:        ldc.i4.0
```

The AppDomainLoads mode allows you to see when a new application domain or assembly has been loaded. When you start BadConsole, these events are displayed.

Table 5-1 lists all of the modes available in cordbg and what they do.

Table 5-1. cordbg Modes

ARGUMENT	DESCRIPTION
AppDomainLoads	Displays application domain and assembly load events
ClassLoads	Displays class load events
DumpMemoryInBytes	Displays memory contents as bytes or DWORDS
EnhanceDiag	Displays enhanced diagnostic information
HexDisplay	Displays numbers in hexadecimal or decimal format
ILNatPrint	Displays offsets in Microsoft intermediate language (MSIL) or native-relative language, or both
ISAll	Steps through all interceptors
ISClinit	Steps through class initializers
ISExceptF	Steps through exception filters
ISInt	Steps through user interceptors
ISPolicy	Steps through context policies
ISSec	Steps through security interceptors
JitOptimizations	Specifies whether JIT compilation generates code that is easier to debug
LoggingMessages	Displays managed code log messages
ModuleLoads	Displays module load events
SeparateConsole	Specifies whether the process being debugged gets its own console
ShowArgs	Displays method arguments in the stack trace
ShowModules	Displays module names in the stack trace
ShowStaticsOnPrint	Displays static fields for objects
ShowSuperClassOnPrint	Displays contents of base class for objects
USAll	Steps through all unmapped stop locations
USEpi	Steps through method epilogs
USPro	Steps through method prologs
USUnmanaged	Steps through unmanaged code

Note that if you change a mode value in a cordbg session, that value will remain the same the next time you run cordbg.

Recording and Using cordbg Scripts

The cordbg tool has more commands than what I've talked about in this chapter; I only cover those commands that I think will help you solve the majority of the problems you'll run into as a CIL programmer. One thing you may notice, though, when you use cordbg is that it gets rather tedious typing in the commands, even if you use the short versions. There is a way to set up some primitive scripts for cordbg so you can record your actions and repeat them later for your benefit.

If you're currently in the debugger, you can use the > command with a file as its argument to specify where you want the command tracing to go:

```
(cordbg) > BadConsoleCordbgRun.txt
```

Now, every command you enter will be sent to this file. When you're done recording your commands, just issue > without a filename:

```
(cordbg) >
```

You can open the text file to modify it if you want to remove or add cordbg commands. Here's a dump of a script file I've included with the downloaded code:

```
break BadConsole::Main:6
run BadConsole print my args
go
show 5
disassembly 5
...
kill
quit
```

In fact, since these script files are nothing but text files, you can create a cordbg script file without having to be in cordbg to record your commands. Once you're comfortable with the commands, you should be able to create these script files on your own, external to cordbg.

When you're happy with the script file, you can execute the commands in cordbg via the < command:

```
(cordbg) < BadConsoleCordbgRun.txt
```

You can take this one step further. By passing your script file as a command list to cordbg and redirecting the output to a text file, your input commands will be echoed out to the text file, along with all of the output normally generated by cordbg:

```
D:\BadConsole>cordbg !< BadConsoleCordbgRun.txt > Output.txt
```

Once the script session is done, Output.txt will contain the results of your cordbg commands. This is a very handy feature, especially if you have to map native instructions to CIL code or you have to do memory dumps after each line of code is run. You can automate everything and look at the results at your leisure.

The GUI Tool: dbgclr.exe

The other debugging tool that comes with .NET is dbgclr.exe, which uses a Windows interface to allow you to control the debugging process. Figure 5-3 shows what the tool looks like when you launch it.

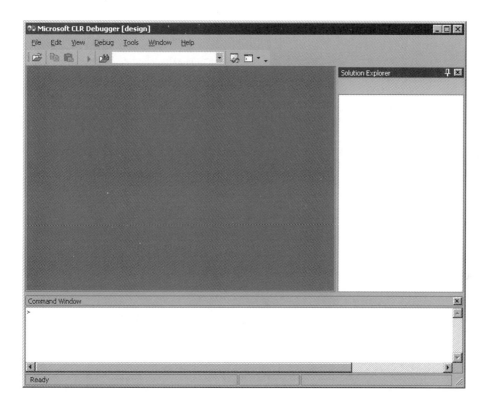

Figure 5-3. Launching dbgclr

Let's see what you need to do to debug BadConsole. First, select File ➤ Open ➤ File (or Ctrl-O) and select BadConsole.il. Now, you need to select the program you want to debug that relates to this source code. Select Debug ➤ Program To Debug. Figure 5-4 shows you the dialog box that is displayed.

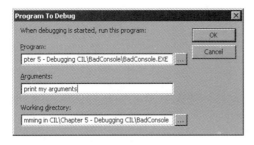

Figure 5-4. Selecting the program to debug

If you are following along with this example, enterBadConsole.exe as the target assembly, as I've done in Figure 5-4, and set the command-line parameters that you need to pass into your code.[9]

Now that you have the essentials defined, set some breakpoints so you can stop the program at ideal locations. Figure 5-5 shows you where I've set three breakpoints in BadConsole.il.

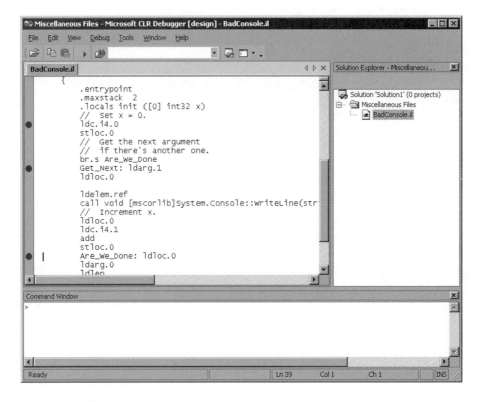

Figure 5-5. Adding breakpoints

---

9. You may not have noticed yet, but if you don't pass in any arguments to BadConsole, you don't get an exception.

Let's get this assembly up and running. Press F5 or select Debug ➤ Start—either way, if everything is right, the program should stop at the first breakpoint, as is shown in Figure 5-6.

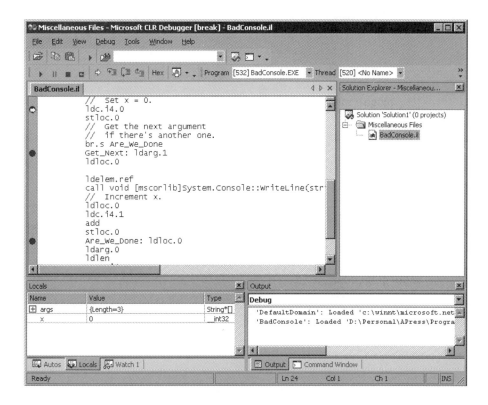

Figure 5-6. First breakpoint

Debugging Windows

Notice that in the lower-left corner you get all of the arguments and the local variables displayed in the Locals window. If you want to change a value, double-click the appropriate Value cell.

Now, this is not the only debugging window that you can use. If you go to Debug ➤ Windows, you'll see a listing of a bunch of useful windows that you can use. Table 5-2 lists all of the choices along with a brief description of what they do.

Table 5-2. Debug Windows

MENU OPTION	HOT KEY COMBINATION	DESCRIPTION
Breakpoints	Ctrl-Alt-B	Allows you to set breakpoints in your code
Running Documents	Ctrl-Alt-N	Displays all running documents
Watch	Ctrl-Alt-W, 1-4	Sets watch conditions on variables
Autos	Ctrl-Alt-V, A	Displays variables in the current statement
Locals	Ctrl-Alt-V, L	Shows the values of local variables
This	Ctrl-Alt-V, T	Displays information about the this pointer (if applicable)
Immediate	Ctrl-Alt-I	Allows the user to enter expressions
Call Stack	Ctrl-Alt-C	Displays the current call stack
Threads	Ctrl-Alt-H	Displays information on all running threads
Modules	Ctrl-Alt-U	Shows all loaded modules
Memory	Ctrl-Alt-M, 1-4	Retrieves memory information via address values
Disassembly	Ctrl-Alt-D	Displays native instructions
Registers	Ctrl-Alt-G	Displays registry values

Let's look at a couple of these in detail.

The Breakpoints Window

This window shows any breakpoints that are currently defined, as demonstrated in Figure 5-7.

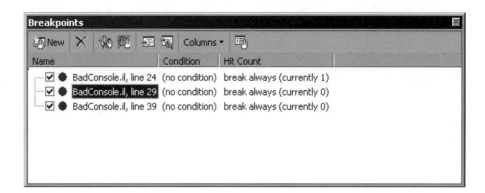

Figure 5-7. Breakpoints window

If you want to create a new breakpoint, right-click anywhere within the window, and select New Breakpoint (this can also be done by selecting Debug ➤ New Breakpoint or pressing Ctrl-B). You'll see a dialog box like the one in Figure 5-8 appear.

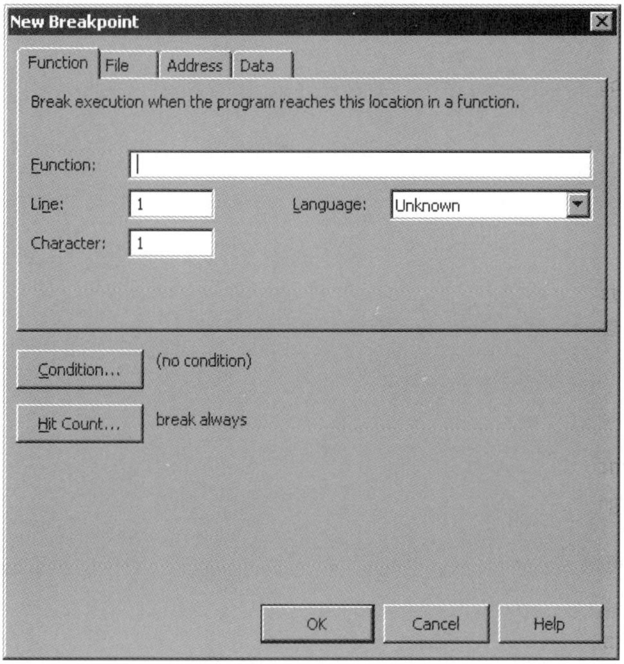

Figure 5-8. Defining a new breakpoint

As this figure shows, you can define where the breakpoint occurs four different ways:

- By a line location in a function

- By a line location in a file

- By a memory address

- By a change in a variable's data value

In all four cases, you can also refine the breakpoint's execution conditionally via the Condition button and/or its hit count via the Hit Count button. The Breakpoint Condition dialog box is shown in Figure 5-9.

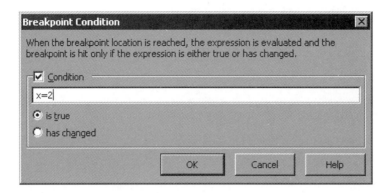

Figure 5-9. Breakpoint Condition dialog box

When the breakpoint is hit, it will look at the given expression and break if the condition is satisfied and the is true option is selected, or if the condition isn't true and the has changed option is selected.

The other way to control the breakpoint is via the Breakpoint Hit Count dialog box as shown in Figure 5-10.

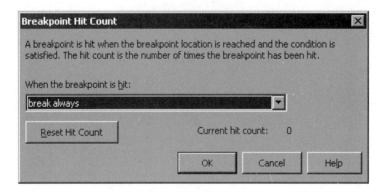

Figure 5-10. Breakpoint Hit Count dialog box

Each time the breakpoint is hit, the debugger will look to see if the current hit count satisfies one of these four conditions:

- Always break

- Break if the count is equal to a given number

- Break if the count is greater than or equal to a given number

- Break if the count is a multiple of a given number

In the last three cases, a text box will be displayed to the right of the combo box so you can define the hit count criteria.

Once you've defined a breakpoint, click the OK button. You can always modify the breakpoint's properties by right-clicking it and selecting Properties from the context menu.

The Disassembly Window

The Disassembly window shows you the native instructions relative to the CIL code as illustrated in Figure 5-11.

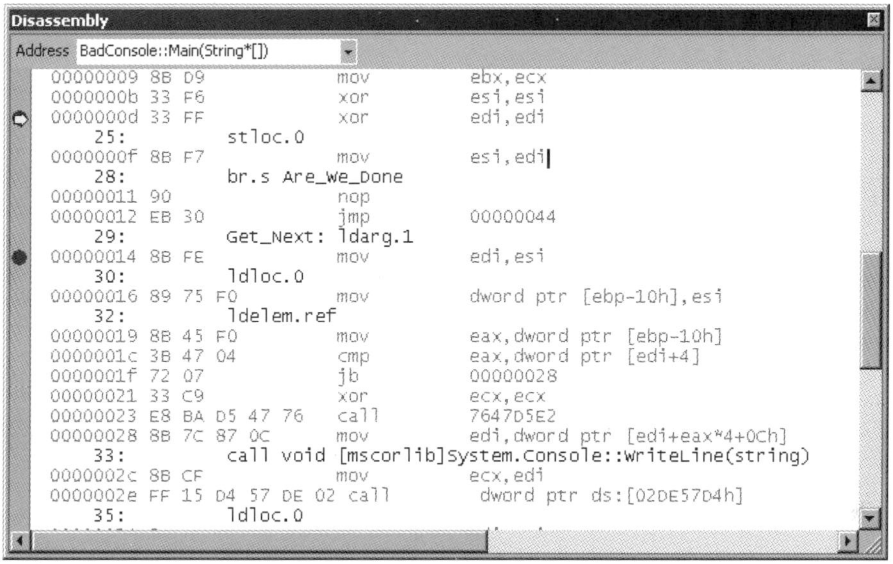

Figure 5-11. Disassembly window

What's really nice about this window is that it embeds the native instructions *with* the CIL code. No more creating disassemble/show command pairs as you had to do in cordbg! You can also set breakpoints on the native instruction—if you do, you'll notice that a similar breakpoint shows up in the main code window.

Furthermore, you can tailor the disassembly information displayed by right-clicking the window and selecting one of the six Show options. In Figure 5-11, I'm showing everything: the instruction address, the code bytes, the source code, and so on. It's interesting to see the number of instructions and native byte size of each CIL opcode.

The Registers Window

The Registers window, shown in Figure 5-12, displays the current state of the registers.

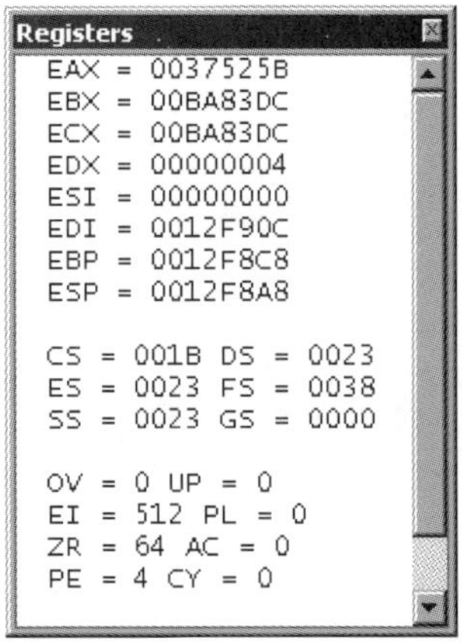

```
Registers                          ☒
     EAX = 0037525B                 ▲
     EBX = 00BA83DC
     ECX = 00BA83DC
     EDX = 00000004
     ESI = 00000000
     EDI = 0012F90C
     EBP = 0012F8C8
     ESP = 0012F8A8

     CS = 001B DS = 0023
     ES = 0023 FS = 0038
     SS = 0023 GS = 0000

     OV = 0 UP = 0
     EI = 512 PL = 0
     ZR = 64 AC = 0
     PE = 4 CY = 0              ▼
```

Figure 5-12. Registers window

By right-clicking the window and choosing from the various context menu options, you can selectively show the CPU registers, the CPU segments, and/or the flag values. You'll notice that as you step through your code (either CIL or native), the register(s) that just changed will turn red in color.

Saving the Solution

There's more to dbgclr than I can show; as I did with cordbg, I just wanted you to become familiar with the essentials. Feel free to step through BadConsole in dbgclr and see what you think of the GUI environment compared to cordbg. However, note that once you're done debugging, you can save the setup as a solution, which you can bring up later on by selecting File ➤ Open Solution.

Actually, saving your setup is not so straightforward. There's no Save Solution menu option anywhere within dbgclr. The only way I've been able to save a solution is if I first pick the assembly to debug, and *then* open its associated CIL file. When I exit, dbgclr asks me if I would like to save my solution. Although it's nice that you can persist your setup, I hope its access to the user is improved in a future version.

SOURCE CODE *The BadConsole folder contains the BadConsole.il file, the BadConsoleCordbgRun.txt script file, and the dbgclr-related solution files for BadConsole.*

Debugger Differences

Ultimately, I think developers should always try new tools, but they should also feel comfortable with the tools they use. I personally gravitate toward GUI-based tools, so dbgclr is my CIL debugger of choice. That doesn't mean I think cordbg is terrible; in fact, I think there are advantages to both tools:

- cordbg lets you run scripts; there's no direct way to do this in dbgclr.

- dbgclr lets you see the native instructions with the CIL in the Disassembly window; there's nothing like this in cordbg.

- You can get the source code for cordbg—it's in %Program Files%\Microsoft Visual Studio .NET\FrameworkSDK\Tool Developers Guide\Samples\debugger. There's no source code for dbgclr.

- dbgclr can display a much broader set of information than what cordbg can at one time.

Again, try both tools out, and pick the one that you feel works best for you.

Debugging In-Process Assemblies

So far, I've been using EXEs as the assembly type in the debugging tools. However, the story changes a little bit when you need to debug a DLL. In this section, I'll show you how you can get your .NET DLLs loaded in a debugger.

DLLs in dbgclr

I'll start with dbgclr this time, as I think it's easier to demonstrate what you need to do in the DLL with dbgclr. Let's start by looking at a class that's compiled in a DLL—Listing 5-1 shows the code.

Listing 5-1. Creating a DLL Assembly

```
.module BadInProcAssembly.dll
.class public beforefieldinit BadClass
    extends [mscorlib]System.Object
{
    .method public hidebysig specialname rtspecialname
        instance void .ctor() cil managed
    {
        .maxstack  1
        ldarg.0
        call instance void [mscorlib]System.Object::.ctor()
        ret
    }

    .method public hidebysig instance int32
        BadDivide(int32 Arg) cil managed
    {
        .maxstack 2
        ldarg.1
        ldc.i4.0
        div
        ret
    }

    .method public hidebysig instance int32
        ReturnArg(int32 Arg) cil managed
    {
        .maxstack 1
        ldloc.0
        ret
    }
}
```

The errors are pretty easy to spot. BadDivide() will always throw a
DivideByZeroException because of ldc.i4.0. ReturnArg() should return the
value in Arg, but it tries to return the this reference. This will result in an
InvalidProgramException.

Now, let's write a test console executable called BadInProcCaller, which is
shown in Listing 5-2, to see what these methods will do.

Listing 5-2. Using a DLL-Based Assembly

```
.method private hidebysig static void
    Main(string[] args) cil managed
{
    .entrypoint
    .maxstack 3
    .locals init (int32 x,
        class [BadInProcAssembly]BadClass bc,
        int32 retVal)
    //  Set x = 3
    ldc.i4.3
    stloc.0
    //  Create a new BadClass.
    newobj instance void [BadInProcAssembly]BadClass::.ctor()
    stloc.1

    //  Call BadDivide.
    ldloc.1
    ldloc.0
    call instance int32 [BadInProcAssembly]BadClass::BadDivide(int32)
    pop

    //  Call ReturnArg.
    ldloc.1
    ldloc.0
    call instance int32 [BadInProcAssembly]BadClass::ReturnArg(int32)
    stloc.2

    //  Print the value.
    ldloca.s 2
    call instance string [mscorlib]System.Int32::ToString()
    call void [mscorlib]System.Console::WriteLine(string)
    ret
}
```

Next, compile both assemblies with debug information:

```
ilasm BadInProcAssembly.il /dll /debug
ilasm BadInProcCaller.il /debug
```

If you run BadInProcCaller, you'll get the dialog box shown in Figure 5-1, stating that a DivideByZeroException has occurred. If you click the Yes button, you'll jump right to the div instruction in BadDivide().

Well, the debugger got into the DLL just fine, so what's the difference between this and an EXE? The only problem is that it took an exception to get the debugger in place. It would be nice to have everything set up in dbgclr first, have the calling program run, and then catch the invocation of BadDivide() *before* the exception occurs. Here's how you do this in dbgclr.[10] First, you need to change your client's Main() code a little bit:

```
.locals init (int32 x,
    class [BadInProcAssembly]BadClass bc,
    int32 retVal)

// Wait for the user.
ldstr "Press any key to continue..."
call void [mscorlib]System.Console::WriteLine(string)
call string [mscorlib]System.Console::ReadLine()
pop

// Set x = 3
```

You'll see why you need this hesitation in a moment.

Now fire up dbgclr, load BadInProcAssembly.il, and set a breakpoint on ldarg.1 in BadDivide(). However, don't use the Program To Debug dialog box, as shown in Figure 5-4 earlier. Instead, this time run BadInProcCaller first, but *don't* press any key to continue. Once the program is running, select Tools ➤ Debug Processes (Ctrl-Alt-P). You should see the window shown in Figure 5-13.

Highlight BadInProcCaller.exe as you see I've done in Figure 5-13, and click the Attach button. You'll notice that dbgclr is now ready to debug BadInProcAssembly.il. Once you close this dialog box and press the Enter key for BadInProcCaller, you'll notice that the focus shifts back to dbgclr, and the breakpoint has been hit.

---

10. Readers who have done any MTS/COM+ development will be familiar with the technique I'm about to show.

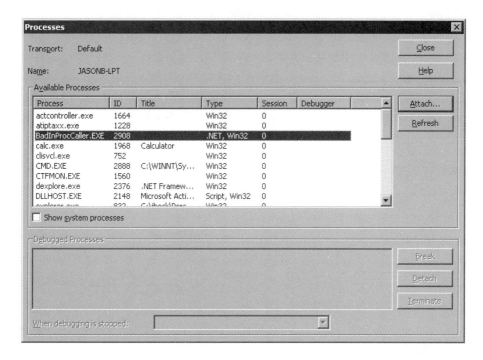

Figure 5-13. Debug Processes window

There's another way to get the DLL's code loaded in dbgclr. In `BadDivide()`, all you need to do is add one new CIL opcode:

```
.method public hidebysig instance int32
    BadDivide(int32 Arg) cil managed
{
    .maxstack 2
    break
    ldarg.1
    ldc.i4.0
    div
    ret
}
```

`break` is an opcode that tells the runtime you want the program's execution to stop right where it's at.[11] Now, if you recompile BadInProcAssembly.il and run BadInProcCaller, you'll see that you get a message box informing you of an exception, but note that the exception message is "Launch for user." If you jump into the debugger, you'll see that the code is stopped on the CIL opcode right after `break` (`ldarg.1`).

---

11. `break` isn't limited to in-proc assemblies; it'll work the same in any kind of assembly.

DLLs in cordbg

Getting a program to break in cordbg basically requires the same kind of techniques as you would use for dbgclr. Before delving into this discussion, make sure you've compiled BadInProcAssembly without the break opcode in BadDivide().

Now, run cordbg, but before you start to debug BadInProcCaller, set a breakpoint where BadDivide() is called:

```
(cordbg) break BadInProcCaller::Main:0x1A
(cordbg) run BadInProcCaller
(cordbg) go
```

I've eliminated cordbg's output in this text, but the result of these commands should be that you end up at the call to BadDivide(). If you issue the step command at this point, you'll jump into BadDivide().

Although this gets the job done, you can also set the breakpoint in BadClass before BadInProcCaller is run:

```
(cordbg) break BadClass::BadDivide
(cordbg) run BadInProcCaller
(cordbg) go
```

Of course, using the break opcode in BadDivide will get the job done as well.

 SOURCE CODE *The InProcDebugging folder contains both the BadInProcAssembly.il and BadInProcCaller.il files.*

Registry Control

You've seen that if you have a .NET assembly that throws an unhandled exception, you'll get a dialog box that asks you if you want to debug the offending assembly. However, you may have noticed that you can't select cordbg as one of the debugging options. If you really like cordbg and you want to use it as the default debugging process, you can do so with a couple of Registry changes.

> **CAUTION** *This should be standard practice, but whenever you make any change to the Registry, always back it up in case you accidentally delete all of the CLSIDs under HKEY_CLASSES_ROOT.*

To start, open up regedit (or whatever tool you use to traverse the Registry) and go to HKEY_LOCAL_MACHINE\Software\Microsoft\.NETFramework\. You should see something like what is shown in Figure 5-14.

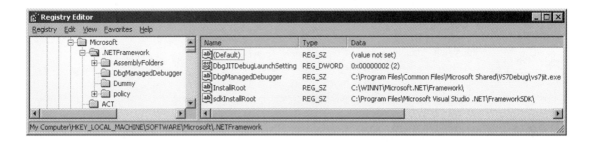

Figure 5-14. Default .NET debugging setup

The DbgJITDebugLaunchSetting key can be one of three values. If it's 0 and a .NET assembly creates an unhandled exception, a message box will be displayed as shown in Figure 5-15.

Figure 5-15. CLR Debugging Services message box

Clicking the OK button will create a stack dump; clicking Cancel will attach the assembly to the default debugger. If it's 1, nothing will be displayed to the user; the program will get a stack dump of the error and the assembly will terminate. If it's 2, control will automatically be passed to the default debugger.

The DbgManagedDebugger key defines the default debugger mentioned for values 0 and 2. Notice it's not cordbg or dbgclr but vs7jit.exe that is defined. This isn't a debugger by itself; it simply manages the debuggers that you can attach to. However, as you've seen, this doesn't include cordbg.

To use cordbg as your default debugger, change DbgManagedDebugger as follows:

```
C:\Program Files\Microsoft Visual Studio .NET\FrameworkSDK\Bin\cordbg.exe !a %d
```

If you looked at what vs7jit.exe was being passed on the command line, you would've seen "PID %D". The runtime is passing the process ID to vs7jit, so I just used that to pass the attach command to cordbg. Try it out—if you set DbgJITDebugLaunchSetting to 0 and run BadInProcCaller, you'll see that cordbg is launched with the correct process attached.

Verifying Assemblies

Although a debugger is a great tool to have around, it's even better if you can prevent errors from showing up in a released system. You've probably noticed by now that the ilasm compiler doesn't always catch your CIL coding errors. It'll definitely bark when you've typed an incorrect CIL code (like ldardg, which doesn't exist), but if you try to use an argument that doesn't exist (like ldarg.2 when the static method takes no arguments), ilasm will happily generate the assembly.

Sometimes, though, the error is so bad that you can't even debug the program. Take a look at the class shown in Listing 5-3.

Listing 5-3. Creating Types for Verification Testing

```
.class public beforefieldinit VerifyTest
    extends [mscorlib]System.Object
{
    .method private hidebysig static void
        Main(string[] args) cil managed
    {
        .entrypoint
        //  This should be 3.
        .maxstack 1
        break
        ldc.i4.0
        ldc.i4.1
        ldc.i4.2
        call void VerifyTest::AddArguments(int32, int32, int32)
```

```
        call instance string [mscorlib]System.Int33::ToString()
        call void [mscorlib]System.Console::WriteLine(string)
        ret
    }

    .method private hidebysig static int32
        AddArguments(int32 X, int32 Y, int32 Z)
    {
        .maxstack 2
        ldarg.0
        ldarg.1
        add
        ldarg.3
        add
        ret
    }
}
```

If you examine the code carefully, you'll notice a couple of errors right away. For example, Int33 is not a valid type in mscorlib, and there is no fourth argument in AddArguments() (that is, ldarg.3 should be ldarg.2). But an even more insidious problem exists—the value for .maxstack in Main(). In this case, you can tell that the value should be 3, but in more complex examples it's not always this easy to tell. Unfortunately, having the wrong value for .maxstack can lead to development horrors, because you won't be able to debug the program.

To see this for yourself, compile the class in a file called PEVerifyTest.il, and run the program. You'll get an error message, stating that an InvalidProgramException has occurred, but if you try to debug the program, it won't be able to load your code into the debugger, even if you created the PDB file. Ouch! Even with a break opcode in Main(), you can't get into your code in the debugger. If a program generates an InvalidProgramException, you're sunk.[12]

Fortunately, there's a tool called PEVerify that comes with .NET that helps you diagnose these annoying CIL bugs. PEVerify makes sure that an assembly follows all of the metadata and instructions verification rules specified in the Partition documents.[13] Therefore, use PEVerify on your assembly and see what happens:

---

12. The debugger will tell you which method the InvalidProgramException happened in, but that's it.

13. See Section 21 of Partition II for metadata validation rules. Each CIL opcode in Partition III has a section that discusses the verifiability rules.

```
D:\PEVerifyTest>peverify PEVerifyTest.exe /md /il
Microsoft (R) .NET Framework PE Verifier  Version 1.0.3328.4
Copyright (C) Microsoft Corporation 1998-2001. All rights reserved.
[IL]: Error:
    [d:\peverifytest\peverifytest.exe : VerifyTest::Main] [offset 0x00000002]
    [opcode    ldc.i4.1] Stack overflow.
[IL]: Error: [d:\peverifytest\peverifytest.exe : VerifyTest::Main]
    [HRESULT 0x80004005] -    Unspecified error
[IL]: Error: [d:\peverifytest\peverifytest.exe : VerifyTest::AddArguments]
    [offset 0x00000003]
    [opcode ldarg.3]
    [argument #0x00000003] Unrecognized argument number.
[IL]: Error: [d:\peverifytest\peverifytest.exe : VerifyTest::AddArguments]
    [HRESULT 0x80004005] -
    Unspecified error
4 Errors Verifying PEVerifyTest.exe
```

The /md and /il options force PEVerify to check both metadata and instructions. If you don't specify either one, PEVerify will check both unless it finds a metadata error—then it won't check the instructions for potential violations.

As you can see, you have four errors. The first error specifies that the second statement in Main() is incorrect—it results in a stack overflow. The offset value tells you how many bytes you must traverse in the method to find the error. Sure enough, that's where the stack would overflow because you've just pushed a second value onto the stack, and .maxstack is 1. In this case, the error isn't with the CIL itself; all PEVerify will tell you is where an error will occur. The third error tells you that you're not using a valid argument index in AddArguments(). Again, using the offset given, you'll find that ldarg.3 is not correct. It should be ldarg.2.

Now, the other two errors don't really tell you much, so let's fix these two problems, recompile, and run PEVerify:

```
D:\PEVerifyTest>peverify PEVerifyTest.exe /md /il
Microsoft (R) .NET Framework PE Verifier  Version 1.0.3328.4
Copyright (C) Microsoft Corporation 1998-2001. All rights reserved.
[IL]: Error: [d:\peverifytest\peverifytest.exe : VerifyTest::Main]
    [offset 0x00000004]
    [opcode call] [token  0x0A000003] Unable to resolve token.
[IL]: Error: [d:\peverifytest\peverifytest.exe : VerifyTest::Main]
    [HRESULT 0x80004005] -    Unspecified error
2 Errors Verifying PEVerifyTest.exe
```

The second error is still unknown, but now you know a little more about the first error. If you move to the code under scrutiny, you'll see that the return value to AddArguments() is wrong; it should be an int32.

Recompile and run PEVerify again:

```
D:\PEVerifyTest>peverify PEVerifyTest.exe /md /il
Microsoft (R) .NET Framework PE Verifier  Version 1.0.3328.4
Copyright (C) Microsoft Corporation 1998-2001. All rights reserved.
[IL]: Error: [d:\peverifytest\peverifytest.exe : VerifyTest::Main]
    [offset 0x00000009]
    [opcode call] [found Int32] [expected address of Int32]
    Unexpected type on the stack.
1 Errors Verifying PEVerifyTest.exe
```

Hmmm . . . I have to admit I didn't expect this one. The problem is AddArguments() puts an int32 onto the stack, but ToString() wants a reference to an int32. So you need to change the code a bit to use ldloca instead:

```
.method private hidebysig static void
    Main(string[] args) cil managed
{
    .entrypoint
    .locals init (int32 retVal)
    .maxstack 3
    break
    ldc.i4.0
    ldc.i4.1
    ldc.i4.2
    call int32 VerifyTest::AddArguments(int32, int32, int32)
    stloc.0
    ldloca 0
    call instance string [mscorlib]System.Int32::ToString()
    call void [mscorlib]System.Console::WriteLine(string)
    ret
}
```

This should do it:

```
D:\PEVerifyTest>peverify PEVerifyTest.exe /md /il
Microsoft (R) .NET Framework PE Verifier  Version 1.0.3328.4
Copyright (C) Microsoft Corporation 1998-2001. All rights reserved.
All Classes and Methods in PEVerifyTest.exe Verified
```

Now, if you run PEVerifyTest, the debugging dialog box will come up, but that's because break is still in Main(). If you ignore the breakpoint, you'll see that Main() prints 3 (0+1+2).

SOURCE CODE *The PEVerifyTest folder contains the PEVerifyTest.il.*

Debugging Compiled Programs

To close out this session on debuggers, I'd like to show you how you can debug precompiled assemblies.

Let's say you purchased an assembly called BadDivider.dll[14] to handle all of your integral dividing needs.[15] To see how it works, you write a little test program called TestDivider.il:

```
.method private hidebysig static void
    Main(string[] args) cil managed
{
    .entrypoint
    .maxstack 3
    .locals init (class [BadDivider]Divider d,
        int32 retVal)
    // Create a new Divider.
    newobj instance void [BadDivider]Divider::.ctor()
    stloc.0

    // Call Divide.
    ldloc.0
    ldc.i4 25
    ldc.i4 5
    call instance int32 [BadDivider]Divider::Divide(int32, int32)
    stloc.1

    // Print the value.
    ldloca 1
    call instance string [mscorlib]System.Int32::ToString()
    call void [mscorlib]System.Console::WriteLine(string)
    ret
}
```

---

14. This assembly (but not its source code) is included with the book's downloadable code.

15. Of course, this is a very contrived case, as there's no reason to buy such a trivial component, but it's not the capabilities of the assembly that matter in this case.

If you run this assembly, you would expect to see 5 (25/5) as the output. But watch what happens:

```
C:\BadDivider>TestDivider
488024
```

What? This is not what you expect at all—it's completely wrong. Unfortunately, as you try to get a hold of technical support, you realize that the company has gone out of business, and you're on your own. Even worse, you recommended to your superiors that this assembly was critical to the success of your project, and the due date is tomorrow. What are you going to do?[16]

Fortunately, knowing what you now know about CIL and the debuggers, you can get around this problem. First, open up a command window, go to the directory that contains BadDivider.dll, and enter the following at the command line:

```
ildasm BadDivider.dll /output:BD.il
```

Rename the current assembly name so you don't lose it:

```
ren BadDivider.dll BackupBadDivider.dll
```

Now open up BD.il, and change the code for `Divide()` from this:

```
.method public hidebysig instance int32
    Divide(int32 X,
    int32 Y) cil managed
{
    // Code size       4 (0x4)
    .maxstack  2
    IL_0000:  ldarg.0
    IL_0001:  ldarg.1
    IL_0002:  div
    IL_0003:  ret
} // end of method Divider::Divide
```

---

16. You could run PEVerify and tell the company that they released an assembly with two IL errors, but since there's no way to get a hold of the vendor in this fictitious case, it doesn't matter (although it helps you to run PEVerify so you can glean more information on BadDivider's problems).

to this:

```
.method public hidebysig instance int32
    Divide(int32 X,
    int32 Y) cil managed
{
    // Code size       4 (0x4)
    .maxstack  2
    break
    IL_0000:  ldarg.0
    IL_0001:  ldarg.1
    IL_0002:  div
    IL_0003:  ret
} // end of method Divider::Divide
```

I realize you may have already seen the erroneous code, but let's keep going for demonstration's sake. Save the changes and recompile, making sure you create the PDB file:

```
ilasm BD.il /dll /output:BadDivider.dll /debug
```

Now you can see why you needed to rename the original DLL. To avoid recompiling the client TestDivider, you create the new assembly with the same name as the purchased assembly.

To see why I had you do all of this, run TestDivider. The program will break when Divide() is invoked; Figure 5-16 shows what dbgclr looks like when break is hit.

From here, you can probably look at the CIL and determine that you've made an indexing mistake with your arguments. You're actually going to load the address value to the this reference with ldarg.0, and you're going to divide it by the first argument (ldarg.1) instead of the second argument (ldarg.2), which isn't what it should do. However, even if you didn't see this right away, if you look at the x86 disassembly, you'll see that there's an idiv opcode that will do the integral divide for you. If you trace back in the assembly, you'll figure out that esi is set right after the ldarg.0 command—this value is eventually stored in eax. That's what causes the incorrect result.

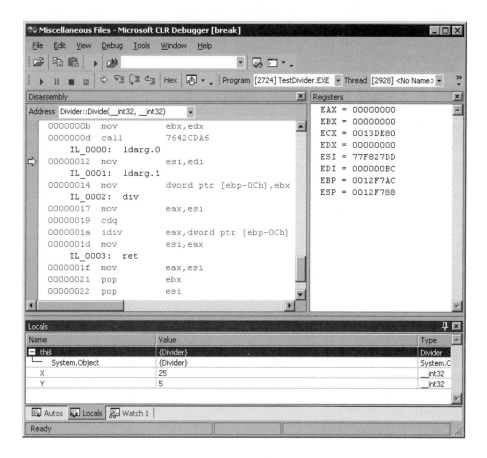

Figure 5-16. BadDivider in debug mode

Now that you know what the problem is, you can easily correct it:

```
.method public hidebysig instance int32
    Divide(int32 X,
    int32 Y) cil managed
{
    // Code size       4 (0x4)
    .maxstack  2
    break
    IL_0000:  ldarg.1
    IL_0001:  ldarg.2
    IL_0002:  div
    IL_0003:  ret
} // end of method Divider::Divide
```

Note that I didn't remove break just yet. You should test the change first in the debugger to see if you get the correct behavior. Once you test it and recompile BadDivider.dll with BD.il without break, TestDivider should work as expected:

```
C:\BadDivider>TestDivider
5
```

Pretty interesting, isn't it? You reverse-engineered a third-party component and plugged it back in without the client knowing any better.

Preventing Recompilation

On the one hand, having the ability to change a compiled assembly like this has its benefits. I remember a situation where I was using a third-party grid control in my Visual Basic application. I had UI logic that ran when the user moved from one cell to another so I could update total values on the form. However, when I updated the control, the new version of that code wouldn't fire anymore. The problem came down to the event code—to update the totals, it locked the grid so it could scroll through the values without having the grid physically scroll in the UI. In the new version, this didn't work anymore; the control's internals changed without any warning.

Of course, it took two support calls before the company that produced this control finally believed me. This translated into some lost time and dollars for the client, as I had to scramble to come up with a workaround. Now, I can decompile the assembly, put a breakpoint in the method, and fix it.

This isn't a very elegant solution in some situations. If the component vendor is not going out of business, you may not want to kludge a solution and effectively make two versions of the same assembly. What happens when the next release occurs? Will you want to maintain your patched version? If you have no hope of getting any technical support, at least you can internally maintain the assembly for a while. And if you do find a bug, you may be able to find the fix for the vendor using ildasm and ilasm in concert like I did in the last section.[17]

But the other side of the coin to this issue is the assembly vendors. Suddenly, there's a very easy way to see how their components work. Depending on what the assembly does, you may not want a user to redistribute your many hours of R&D as a hacked assembly that leaves no traces that you were the owner. Even worse, there's the possibility that users will start making changes to the assembly, which would lead to upgrade nightmares. Let's go over some potential solutions to this problem.

---

17. Whether they reimburse you financially for your heroic efforts is another story.

Native Image Generation

One technique you may try is to create a native image of your assembly. This is done via the ngen tool, which comes with .NET. This tool doesn't work with CIL source files, rather it takes a .NET assembly and transforms it into a native assembly. For example, you can create a native image of BadDivider.dll as follows:

```
ngen BadDivider.dll
```

The tool creates a native image of the assembly, but it puts the result into the Native Image Cache (or NIC). You can see what's in the cache by using the /show argument with ngen:

```
ngen /show
```

Unfortunately, the results aren't what you might expect. The problem is that you still need the original assembly for the client code to run properly. ngen essentially creates native implementations of your methods, but the metadata is contained in the original assembly. If you try to run TestDivider.exe after you performed an ngen operation on BadDivider.dll and deleted (or renamed) BadDivider.dll, TestDivider will throw a `FileNotFoundException`. The runtime will always load the CIL-based assembly, but it's smart enough to use the native implementations if they exist in the NIC.

Therefore, you can't distribute a native image without the regular assembly. Someone will always be able to reengineer the assembly like I did before, and if you rename the resulting assembly and target the client to use this new assembly, you can prevent the runtime from using the native implementations.

Strong-Naming the Assembly

Another possible diversion is strong-naming your assembly. Giving your assembly a strong name basically states that you are the one who generated this assembly. You can generate a key pair via the sn tool, and then you pass that key file into ilasm via the /key option:

```
C:\>sn -k MyKeys.snk
C:\>ilasm BadInProcAssembly.il /dll /debug /key:MyKeys.snk
```

What's nice about this feature is that you can set up security policies to grant permissions to specific assemblies based on that strong name. As long as the private key hasn't been compromised, you can be assured that the signature is unique. In fact, it's possible to set up a permission structure with assemblies that can't run at all if they don't have a strong name. Furthermore, if you are the owner of strong-named assembly, you can write code that limits the clients that can use its types via the caller's strong names.

Unfortunately, whatever policy you decide to set up, the end result is that a person will still be able to decompile and recompile your assembly, but he or she will not be able to sign the assembly with that strong name. The best you can do with strong-naming your assembly is to prevent others from reverse-engineering your code and reapplying your brand to it.

Web Services

If your clients have high-speed Internet access, another option available is to make them Web services. Clients can access the assembly's functionality, but they can't get the physical assembly itself. Also, if a bug did occur in your assembly, fixing the offending code means that all clients get the fix at one time.

Of course, there may be situations in which this is not feasible. For example, if you were writing a high-powered graphics engine to compete with DirectX, you probably don't want the method invocations to occur over HTTP. However, if you know that you must protect your resources, then keeping them off the client's machine may be the safest way to do so.

Obfuscation

There's one last option on your plate, and it's called *obfuscation*. This is basically a technique in which a tool will take input, like source code or a PE file, and create output that makes it very difficult for reverse-engineering tools to discover what the executable is doing. However, it will not change the expected behavior of the code, and it may make loading times quicker. Out of all the options available, this one covers all of the bases, and I think it's the best measure you can take to protecting your investment. Remember, though, that obfuscation is not a guarantee. Someone with enough perseverance may figure out ways to get around an obfuscator in the future.

You can purchase third-party tools to perform this function for you. However, let's see what obfuscators do in more detail so you have a better understanding of how they work.[18]

---

18. Full coverage of how obfuscators work is beyond the scope of one chapter. I strongly suggest reading the paper "Java Control Flow Obfuscation," which can be downloaded at http://www.cs.auckland.ac.nz/research/theses/1998/low_douglas_thesis1998.pdf, for detailed coverage on this topic.

NOTE *If you're interesting in using an obfuscator, please check out the following sites for obfuscators that were available at the time of this book's writing:* http://www.wiseowl.com *(Demeanor for .NET),* http://preemptive.com/dotfuscator *(Dotfuscator for Microsoft .NET),* http://www.remotesoft.com/salamander/obfuscator.html *(Salamander .NET Obfuscator), and* http://www.lesser-software.com *(LSW DotNet-IL-Obfuscator). Dan Appleman also has an e-book on obfuscators entitled* **Obfuscating .NET: Protecting Your Code from Prying Eyes**—*you can find more information (along with a link to his open-source QND-Obfuscator) at* http://www.desaware.com/EBook4L2.htm.

Symbol Obfuscation

Let's return to the BadDivider example I used before, but this time I'll show the class definition as well:

```
.class public beforefieldinit Divider
    extends [mscorlib]System.Object
{
    .method public hidebysig instance int32
        Divide(int32 X, int32 Y) cil managed
    {
// …
    }
}
```

As this class is public, it's accessible by code that references the assembly that Divider is a part of. Now, if you made this type internal, it would not be accessible to a client like TestDivider. But that doesn't protect it; via ILDasm anyone could still see it, and given its name along with its method name, someone who is decompiling your code may decide to focus their efforts upon this class. That's because the class name has some semantic meaning. If you saw a class in BadDivider's assembly called Logger, you probably wouldn't give it much thought, as it's likely used for debugging purposes that don't have much to do with the technical problem of dividing two integer values.

Now, I don't know of an obfuscator that could change method names to make them "semantically unappealing," but they can do something like this:

```
internal class 29700584-AA62-4a12-A93A-DDFA90936E75
{
    public int 722982AF-32F0-47cd-BFE7-66007C435768(int32 X, int32 Y)
    {
        //…
    }
}
```

These are invalid C# class and method names, so don't try to mimic this code in that language. I'm only illustrating the point that the semantic meaning behind the class is completely gone. Furthermore, the class and method names are invalid, so a reverse-engineering tool could not blindly take a discovered name and insert it into a generated C# code stream because it wouldn't work. But these names are perfectly valid from a CIL perspective:

```
.class internal auto ansi beforefieldinit
    '29700584-AA62-4a12-A93A-DDFA90936E75'
    extends [mscorlib]System.Object
{
    .method public hidebysig instance int32
            '722982AF-32F0-47cd-BFE7-66007C435768'
            (int32 X, int32 Y) cil managed
    {
        // Do our secret "dividing" here…
    }
}
```

Note that an obfuscator will only do this to features that are not accessible outside of the assembly. Therefore, if you wanted to protect your dividing secrets, you'd need to make an inaccessible type that Divider would call to handle the division. The obfuscator wouldn't touch Divider, so high-level language clients could still access the functionality. Also, a good obfuscator will use smaller mangled names than GUIDs—in fact, it will create names that are invalid in most .NET languages and are smaller than the original names, improving load times in the process.

NOTE *In fact, some obfuscators will use language keyword names, like* class *or* If, *to confuse decompilers. And one obfuscator, Demeanor for .NET, will name virtually all of the classes and their method's local variables with the **same** name. Due to the way metadata is handled, this is perfectly valid, and makes the job for a reverse-engineering tool much harder.*

Code Obfuscation

Symbol obfuscation by itself is not enough. Most decompilers will simply keep an internal list of discovered names and emit their own generic yet valid names (like local1 or class1). Although these names aren't very helpful, they are valid and can be used in most any .NET language. However, the real key for any obfuscator is to alter the implementation such that it trips up a reverse-engineering tool without affecting the intended goals of the implementation.

There are a number of techniques that obfuscators can use to confuse a decompiler, such as moving implementations into separate threads or adding dead code. One approach, called *opaque predicates*, is particularly effective because it adds code that requires dynamic analysis of the original code, which is computationally expensive.

For example, adding opaque predicates to `Divide()` may look something like this after it's been reverse-engineered:[19]

```
public int Divide(int X, int Y)
{
    Node c = new Node();
    Node d = c.Create();
    if(c == d)
    {
        return this / X;
    }
    else
    {
        return 8;
    }
}
```

NOTE *Remember that your code is buggy—it's trying to divide the instance reference by X. I know it looks odd, but a reverse-engineering tool would probably output what was there.*

Don't worry about what Node looks like. The point is that the inserted code has affected the "look" of the code, but it will not affect the *intent* of the code. That's because you know that the c and d variables will always be equal, so your original code will run. However, someone who is reverse-engineering the code now has to worry about the two Node variables and what they are doing.[20] The more predicates that are added, the worse it gets for the decompiler.

---

19. Note that an obfuscator can work at either the source-code or assembly level. I'm only showing the example in C# as it's easier to follow than CIL.

20. And, chances are Node's name would've been obfuscated as well, which makes the job of reading the reverse-engineered code much more difficult.

Unfortunately, a drawback with code obfuscation is that it will bloat the original code base. The degree of the bloat will vary depending on the techniques used, so a good obfuscation tool should allow you to determine which methods to target for obfuscation due to their implementation-sensitive nature. Although decompilers may be able to decompile some methods, they will have a much harder time with the methods you've obfuscated.

SOURCE CODE *The BadDivider folder contains the BadDivider.dll (but not the source code!) along with TestDivider.il.*

Conclusion

In this chapter, you saw how you can debug your CIL-based assemblies. I went over cordbg and dbgclr, discussing the necessary commands and windows to use the tools effectively. I also covered a number of tools and techniques to help create correct assemblies and to reverse-engineer defective assemblies. In the next chapter, you'll gain insight into CIL programming techniques by observing the VB .NET and C# compilers as well as what can and can't be done in these languages.

CHAPTER 6

.NET Languages and CIL

In this chapter, I'll walk through a number of code snippets written in various .NET languages and demonstrate what the differences are in their assemblies. I'll compare and contrast debug and release builds. You'll get a chance to look at how different language constructs are translated into CIL by the different compilers. I'll show you how a piece of code in one language may not create the output you expect. As you'll see throughout this chapter, what you code is not always what you get. By knowing CIL, you'll be able to figure out what's really going on.

Debug and Release Builds

To start, let's take a look at a small piece of code that's implemented in a couple of .NET languages and see what the CIL looks like. You'll build the code in both debug and release modes to find out how the CIL changes between the modes. Here's what the general flow of the code is doing in all of the implementations:

1. Gets the type of the current instance and stores it in a local variable called someType.

2. Gets the name of the type via the Name property, and stores it in a string called typeName.

3. If name is equal to "SimpleCode", does the following:

   • Declares an integer and call it i.

   • Creates a boolean called yes and set it to true.

   • Returns yes.

4. Returns a false value.

The C# Implementation

Here's what the pseudocode looks like in C#:

```
public bool TestForTypeName()
{
    Type someType = this.GetType();
    String typeName = someType.Name;

    if(true == typeName.Equals("SimpleCode"))
    {
        int i;
        bool yes = true;
        return yes;
    }
    return false;
}
```

Although the code follows the requirements to the letter, you as a developer may be squirming at three parts of the code:

- There's no reason to create i; it's a waste of space.

- The yes variable really isn't needed as you could simply return true.

- The someType variable really isn't needed either as it's never used after Name is called.

I don't know how many times I've seen dead code or code that could be optimized make it into the compilation process of a production system. This is usually due to a combination of a couple of issues—for example, the code has been updated by a number of developers, and with large functions it's not always obvious where the dead code lies.[1] In any event, let's see what C#'s compiler does with this method.

Listing 6-1 shows what the resulting CIL looks like if you compile TestForTypeName() in debug mode.

---

1. Technically, the C# compiler will tell you if a variable is not being used as is the case with i, but it won't be able to make the optimization with someType.

Listing 6-1. C# Compilation Results in Debug Mode

```
.method public hidebysig instance bool  TestForTypeName() cil managed
{
  // Code size       42 (0x2a)
  .maxstack  2
  .locals init ([0] class [mscorlib]System.Type someType,
           [1] string typeName,
           [2] int32 i,
           [3] bool yes,
           [4] bool CS$00000003$00000000)
  IL_0000:  ldarg.0
  IL_0001:  callinstance class [mscorlib]System.Type
    [mscorlib]System.Object::GetType()
  IL_0006:  stloc.0
  IL_0007:  ldloc.0
  IL_0008:  callvirt    instance string
    [mscorlib]System.Reflection.MemberInfo::get_Name()
  IL_000d:  stloc.1
  IL_000e:  ldloc.1
  IL_0414f:  ldstr       "SimpleCode"
  IL_0014:  callvirt    instance bool [mscorlib]System.String::Equals(string)
  IL_0019:  brfalse.s  IL_0022
  IL_001b:  ldc.i4.1
  IL_001c:  stloc.3
  IL_001d:  ldloc.3
  IL_001e:  stloc.s     CS$00000003$00000000
  IL_0020:  br.s        IL_0027
  IL_0022:  ldc.i4.0
  IL_0023:  stloc.s     CS$00000003$00000000
  IL_0025:  br.s        IL_0027
  IL_0027:  ldloc.s     CS$00000003$00000000
  IL_0029:  ret
} // end of method SimpleCode::TestForTypeName
```

Let me draw your attention to a couple of interesting things about the results. First, you'll see that all of the code has been translated into CIL and included in the assembly—that is, the C# compiler made no optimizations whatsoever. The other interesting aspect about the debug build is the fifth local variable, CS$00000003$00000000. It's not a variable you create in your code; the C# compiler creates this variable to make the debugging process "friendlier." To see what I mean by this statement, here are the last few lines of CIL with the C# code inlined:

```
//000022:          return yes;
  IL_001d:  ldloc.3
  IL_001e:  stloc.s     CS$00000003$00000000
  IL_0020:  br.s        IL_0027
//000023:      }
//000024:
//000025:      return false;
  IL_0022:  ldc.i4.0
  IL_0023:  stloc.s     CS$00000003$00000000
  IL_0025:  br.s        IL_0027
//000026:      }
  IL_0027:  ldloc.s     CS$00000003$00000000
  IL_0029:  ret
} // end of method SimpleCode::TestForTypeName
```

You'll notice that when each `return` statement is reached in C# code, there's no corresponding `ret` opcode. Instead, the return value is stored in CS$00000003$00000000, and then an unconditional branch occurs (`br.s`). This branch is made to the end of the method ("}"), where the value is finally returned.

Before I show why this has an advantage during debugging, let's tell the compiler to turn optimizations on for the debug build. You do this in VS .NET by right-clicking the project node in the Solutions Explorer window and selecting the Properties menu option. Select the Build node underneath Configuration Properties and set the Optimize Code property to true (see Figure 6-1 for details).

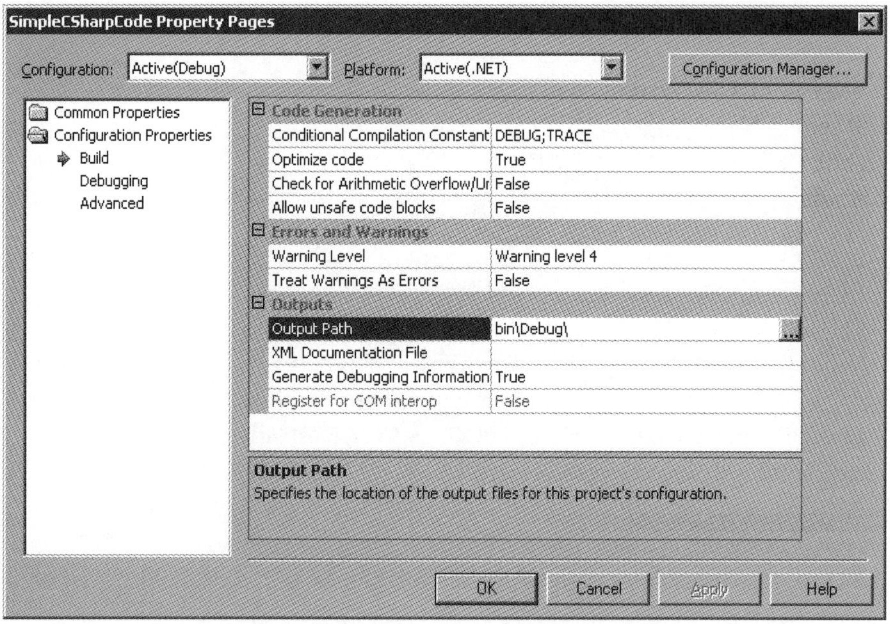

Figure 6-1. Project properties

When you recompile the code, the CIL will look like the code in Listing 6-2.

Listing 6-2. C# Compilation Results in Debug Mode with Optimizations

```
.method public hidebysig instance bool  TestForTypeName() cil managed
{
  // Code size       33 (0x21)
  .maxstack  2
  .locals init ([0] class [mscorlib]System.Type someType,
           [1] string typeName,
           [2] bool yes)
  IL_0000:  ldarg.0
  IL_0001:  call        instance class [mscorlib]System.Type
    [mscorlib]System.Object::GetType()
  IL_0006:  stloc.0
  IL_0007:  ldloc.0
  IL_0008:  callvirt    instance string
    [mscorlib]System.Reflection.MemberInfo::get_Name()
  IL_000d:  stloc.1
  IL_000e:  ldloc.1
  IL_000f:  ldstr       "SimpleCode"
  IL_0014:  callvirt    instance bool [mscorlib]System.String::Equals(string)
  IL_0019:  brfalse.s  IL_001f
  IL_001b:  ldc.i4.1
  IL_001c:  stloc.2
  IL_001d:  ldloc.2
  IL_001e:  ret
  IL_001f:  ldc.i4.0
  IL_0020:  ret
} // end of method SimpleCode::TestForTypeName
```

You can see that i is no longer declared as a local, and there's no temporary return value listed either. If you step through this optimized code in the debugger, you'll see that i doesn't show up in the Locals window as a local variable. You'll also notice that when you hit a return statement, you immediately jump out of the method, rather than go to the end.

If you're in debug mode, I'd strongly suggest not optimizing your build because of the changes that happen at the CIL level, especially when it comes to exiting a method. The reason is it gives you is a chance to see what the last value is before the method is finished. In the case of TestForTypeName(), it's not a big deal, because you can see in the code that you'll return a true or a false. This becomes a nice feature to have when you perform a calculation in the return statement.

To see why this feature is desirable, take a look at the following code:

```
public int IncrementIntValue()
{
    int i = 0;
    return i++;
}
```

If you turn on optimizations in debug mode, you'll end up never seeing what the value is for i unless you're in the calling method. If you want to see what i is before the method exits, just leave optimizations off.[2]

Now, when you compile the application in release mode, there's no debug file created, but the results are the same as before from a CIL perspective. The only difference is that the local variable names are mangled. Here's a snippet from TestForTypeName() in release mode with optimizations on:

```
.method public hidebysig instance bool
  TestForTypeName() cil managed
{
  // Code size        33 (0x21)
  .maxstack  2
  .locals init (class [mscorlib]System.Type V_0,
          string V_1,
          bool V_2)
```

The names you gave the variables are no longer there. This makes it a little harder to follow the code, as good variable names will give hints to people when they analyze decompiled code; they also make the symbol sizes smaller in the metadata, but they don't affect your code in any way.

The VB .NET Implementation

Now let's look at the method in VB .NET:

```
Public Function TestForTypeName() As Boolean
    Dim someType As Type = Me.GetType()
    Dim typeName As String = someType.Name

    If True = typeName.Equals("SimpleCode") Then
        Dim i As Integer
        Dim yes As Boolean = True
        Return yes
    End If

    Return False
End Function
```

---

2. In this case, it's easy to see that i will be 1 when the method is finished, but in more complex cases it may be nice to see the value before the method exits.

VB .NET is similar to C# in that the CIL results are the same in both debug and release mode if optimizations are turned on (except for the variable name mangling). Note that in VB .NET the project properties window looks a little different from the C# project properties window, as it relates to optimization configuration. You can turn them on and off by going to the Optimizations node under Configuration Properties and selecting Enable optimizations as Figure 6-2 shows.

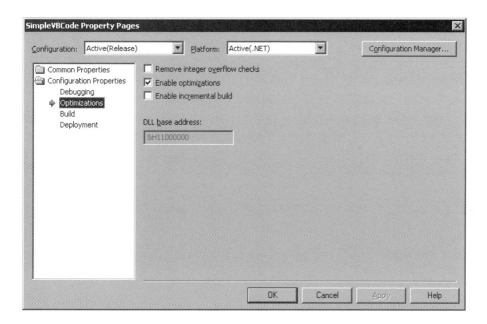

Figure 6-2. Project properties in VB .NET

There are some differences, though, between debug and release builds with optimizations off, as well as how VB .NET implements the code compared to C#. Listing 6-3 shows the CIL code in release mode with no optimizations.

Listing 6-3. VB .NET Compilation Results in Release Mode with Optimizations

```
//  VB .NET Release - no optimizations
.method public instance bool  TestForTypeName() cil managed
{
  // Code size       42 (0x2a)
  .maxstack  3
```

```
        .locals init (class [mscorlib]System.Type V_0,
                bool V_1,
                string V_2,
                int32 V_3,
                bool V_4)
    IL_0000:  ldarg.0
    IL_0001:  callvirt    instance class [mscorlib]System.Type
        [mscorlib]System.Object::GetType()
    IL_0006:  stloc.0
    IL_0007:  ldloc.0
    IL_0008:  callvirt    instance string
        [mscorlib]System.Reflection.MemberInfo::get_Name()
    IL_000d:  stloc.2
    IL_000e:  ldc.i4.1
    IL_000f:  ldloc.2
    IL_0010:  ldstr       "SimpleCode"
    IL_0015:  callvirt    instance bool
        [mscorlib]System.String::Equals(string)
    IL_001a:  bne.un.s    IL_0024
    IL_001c:  ldc.i4.1
    IL_001d:  stloc.s     V_4
    IL_001f:  ldloc.s     V_4
    IL_0021:  stloc.1
    IL_0022:  br.s        IL_0028
    IL_0024:  ldc.i4.0
    IL_0025:  stloc.1
    IL_0026:  br.s        IL_0028
    IL_0028:  ldloc.1
    IL_0029:  ret
} // end of method SimpleCode::TestForTypeName
```

Notice that VB .NET does not create a dummy variable to store the return value; rather, it creates a variable (V_1) with the same type as the return type. This lets the VB .NET developer use the method name as the return value. It's more prevalent if you look at the debug build shown in Listing 6-4.

Listing 6-4. VB .NET Compilation Results in Debug Mode

```
.method public instance bool  TestForTypeName() cil managed
{
  // Code size       44 (0x2c)
  .maxstack  3
```

```
    .locals init ([0] class [mscorlib]System.Type someType,
             [1] bool TestForTypeName,
             [2] string typeName,
             [3] int32 i,
             [4] bool yes)
  IL_0000:  nop
  IL_0001:  ldarg.0
  IL_0002:  callvirt   instance class [mscorlib]System.Type
    [mscorlib]System.Object::GetType()
  IL_0007:  stloc.0
  IL_0008:  ldloc.0
  IL_0009:  callvirt   instance string
    [mscorlib]System.Reflection.MemberInfo::get_Name()
  IL_000e:  stloc.2
  IL_000f:  ldc.i4.1
  IL_0010:  ldloc.2
  IL_0011:  ldstr      "SimpleCode"
  IL_0016:  callvirt   instance bool [mscorlib]System.String::Equals(string)
  IL_001b:  bne.un.s   IL_0025
  IL_001d:  ldc.i4.1
  IL_001e:  stloc.s    yes
  IL_0020:  ldloc.s    yes
  IL_0022:  stloc.1
  IL_0023:  br.s       IL_002a
  IL_0025:  nop
  IL_0026:  ldc.i4.0
  IL_0027:  stloc.1
  IL_0028:  br.s       IL_002a
  IL_002a:  ldloc.1
  IL_002b:  ret
} // end of method SimpleCode::TestForTypeName
```

As you can see, the local variable at index position 1 is named
TestForTypeName. This is the variable that's set if you do something like this in code:

```
TestForTypeName = True
```

You'll also note that VB .NET includes some nop opcodes in the CIL stream.
The reason it does this is to include all of the VB .NET code it can into the debugging experience. For example, here's the CIL code inlined with the VB .NET code:

```
// Source File 'D:\Personal\APress\Programming in CIL\
// Chapter 6 - dotNET Languages and CIL\SimpleVBCode\SimpleVBCode.vb'
//000009:        Public Function TestForTypeName() As Boolean
```

```
  IL_0000:  nop
//000010:                 Dim someType As Type = Me.GetType()
  IL_0001:  ldarg.0
  IL_0002:  callvirt    instance class [mscorlib]System.Type
    [mscorlib]System.Object::GetType()
  IL_0007:  stloc.0
```

Compare that code to the CIL code from C#:

```
// Source File 'D:\Personal\APress\Programming in CIL\
// Chapter 6 - dotNET Languages and CIL\
// SimpleCSharpCode\SimpleCSharpCode.cs'
//000018:  Type someType = this.GetType();
  IL_0000:  ldarg.0
  IL_0001:  call        instance class [mscorlib]System.Type
    [mscorlib]System.Object::GetType()
  IL_0006:  stloc.0
```

If you've ever debugged a program in C#, try setting a breakpoint on the method declaration. Even though VS .NET puts the breakpoint on that line of code, you'll see that the breakpoint is pushed down to the first line of executable code when you start up the debugger. However, in VB .NET, it's different. You can set a breakpoint on the method declaration and it won't move. By putting nop opcodes into the CIL stream, VB .NET's compiler can bind these "do-nothing" lines of code to the debug version of the assembly.

The Component Pascal Implementation

The last high-level language implementation I'll show you is Component Pascal (CP):

```
MODULE SimpleCPCode;
    IMPORT System := mscorlib_System, CPmain, Console;

    TYPE SimpleCode* = POINTER TO EXTENSIBLE RECORD
        (System.Object) END;

    PROCEDURE (this : SimpleCode) TestForTypeName*() :
        BOOLEAN, NEW, EXTENSIBLE;
```

```
        VAR someType : System.Type;
            typeName : System.String;
            i : INTEGER;
            yes : BOOLEAN;
    BEGIN
        someType := this.GetType();
        typeName := someType.get_Name();
        IF (typeName.Equals(MKSTR("SimpleCode"))) THEN
            yes := TRUE;
            RETURN yes;
        END;
        RETURN FALSE;
    END TestForTypeName;
END SimpleCPCode.
```

As far as I can tell from the CP docs, there's no debug or release build available, so you'll only be seeing one CIL implementation, which is shown in Listing 6-5.

Listing 6-5. Component Pascal Compilation Results

```
.method public newslot virtual instance bool
        TestForTypeName() cil managed
{
  // Code size        41 (0x29)
  .maxstack  8
  .locals init ([0] class [mscorlib]System.Type someType,
           [1] string typeName,
           [2] int32 i,
           [3] bool yes)
  IL_0000:  ldarg.0
  IL_0001:  call
    instance class [mscorlib]System.Type object::GetType()
  IL_0006:  stloc.0
  IL_0007:  ldloc.0
  IL_0008:  callvirt
    instance string [mscorlib]System.Reflection.MemberInfo::get_Name()
  IL_000d:  stloc.1
  IL_000e:  ldloc.1
  IL_000f:  ldstr      "SimpleCode"
  IL_0014:  call       string [RTS]CP_rts::mkStr(char[])
  IL_0019:  call       instance bool string::Equals(string)
  IL_001e:  brfalse    IL_0027
  IL_0023:  ldc.i4.1
```

```
IL_0024:  stloc.3
IL_0025:  ldloc.3
IL_0026:  ret
IL_0027:  ldc.i4.0
IL_0028:  ret
} // end of method SimpleCode::TestForTypeName
```

There really isn't anything interesting with this code except the call to MKSTR(), which originates from CP's runtime assembly (RTS). This is necessary because CP needs to resolve the call to Equals() since it's overloaded by System.String.[3] Because the "SimpleCode" literal could be a String or an Object, CP's compiler can't resolve the call on its own. Note that I could've made a separate String variable to make the call unambiguous:

```
VAR targetName : System.String;
targetName := "SimpleCode";
IF (typeName.Equals(targetName)) THEN
```

Commentary

In all three cases, the implementations are pretty similar, but with some slight differences. C#'s compiler is pretty aggressive in eliminating dead code in comparison to the other two languages.[4] However, there are some optimizations that we as humans can see that the compilers can't. For example, we all know there's no reason to create a Type reference to get its name—here's how they could all be optimized:

```
//  C# code
String typeName = this.GetType().Name;
'  VB .NET code
Dim typeName As String = Me.GetType().Name
(*  CP Code *)
typeName := this.GetType().get_Name();
```

---

3. Later on, I'll demonstrate a more convoluted example with overridden and overloaded methods.

4. For a listing of the optimizations that C#'s compiler will perform, please read the section "Optimizations" in Chapter 36 of Eric Gunnerson's book, *A Programmer's Introduction to C#, Second Edition* (Apress, 2001).

However, it's interesting to see what the compilers do with this optimization. Here's the CIL for all three languages:

```
//  C# and CP CIL
IL_0001:  call  instance class
  [mscorlib]System.Type [mscorlib]System.Object::GetType()
IL_0006:  callvirt instance string
  [mscorlib]System.Reflection.MemberInfo::get_Name()
//  VB .NET CIL
IL_0001:  callvirt instance class
  [mscorlib]System.Type [mscorlib]System.Object::GetType()
IL_0006:  callvirt instance string
  [mscorlib]System.Reflection.MemberInfo::get_Name()
```

Both C# and CP call GetType() with call, whereas VB .NET calls it with callvirt. This is a nonvirtual method, and calling nonvirtual methods with callvirt is legal, but why is VB .NET the only language to emit a callvirt? It's being more cautious than the other two compilers. callvirt will always check to see that the instance reference is the first argument on the stack—if it's null, it throws a NullReferenceException. call won't do this. At the end of the day, they're both legitimate choices. If the reference were null, VB .NET would throw the exception before the method is called. In the other two languages, the error wouldn't occur until the reference was accessed (if at all).

SOURCE CODE *The SimpleVBCode, SimpleCSharpCode, and SimpleCPCode projects contain the code written in the different languages discussed in this section.*

Language Constructs

In this section, I'll dive into specific language keywords and constructs and what the generated CIL looks like. It's interesting to see what the compilers are doing with your favorite (or not-so-favorite) language's keywords—in some cases, it might make you question whether you should ever use a certain construct at all.

VB .NET's With Statement

Let's start with an easy one. VB .NET has a With statement that allows you to reference an object's members without redundant typing of the object's variable name.

For example, here's a piece of code that prints out the contents of an `Atom` instance:

```
Function PrintAtom(ByVal TargetAtom As Atom)
    Console.WriteLine("Atom name is " & TargetAtom.Name)
    Console.WriteLine("Atom symbol is " & TargetAtom.Symbol)
    Console.WriteLine("Number of protons and electrons:  " & _
        TargetAtom.Electrons)
    Console.WriteLine("Number of neutrons:  " & _
        TargetAtom.Nucleus.Neutrons.Length)
End Function
```

By using `With`, you eliminate the need to type `TargetAtom` whenever you access its property values:

```
Function WithPrintAtom(ByVal TargetAtom As Atom)
    With TargetAtom
        Console.WriteLine("Atom name is " & .Name)
        Console.WriteLine("Atom symbol is " & .Symbol)
        Console.WriteLine("Number of protons and electrons:  " & .Electrons)
        Console.WriteLine("Number of neutrons:  " & .Nucleus.Neutrons.Length)
    End With
End Function
```

Note that `With` only works on objects, so you can't use `With` on `Console` to make the `WriteLine()` calls smaller from a typing perspective.

When you're accessing a number of a particular object's properties and methods, `With` is a nice piece of syntactic sugar to make the code a bit cleaner. In fact, it's so nice that when I wear my C# hat I wish it had a similar construct. The only way to get close to faking it is to set a variable with a very short name (like x) equal to the object reference in question:

```
Atom PrintAtom(Atom TargetAtom)
{
    Atom x = TargetAtom;
    Console.WriteLine("Atom name is " + x.Name);
    // etc.
}
```

What's interesting is that VB .NET is doing the same thing behind the scenes. Let's take a look at some of the CIL produced by these two methods. Here's the first two `WriteLine()` calls in `PrintAtom()`:

```
.method public static object  PrintAtom(
  class WithTest.WithTest/Atom TargetAtom) cil managed
{
  // Code size       106 (0x6a)
  .maxstack  2
  .locals init (object V_0)
  IL_0000:  ldstr       "Atom name is "
  IL_0005:  ldarg.0
  IL_0006:  callvirt    instance string WithTest.WithTest/Atom::get_Name()
  IL_000b:  call        string [mscorlib]System.String::Concat(string,
                                                               string)
  IL_0010:  call        void [mscorlib]System.Console::WriteLine(string)
  IL_0015:  ldstr       "Atom symbol is "
  IL_001a:  ldarg.0
  IL_001b:  callvirt    instance string WithTest.WithTest/Atom::get_Symbol()
  IL_0020:  call        string [mscorlib]System.String::Concat(string,
                                                               string)
  IL_0025:  call        void [mscorlib]System.Console::WriteLine(string)
```

As expected, TargetAtom is loaded each time information is needed out of it (ldarg.0). Now look at the same code in WithPrintAtom():

```
.method public static object  WithPrintAtom
  (class WithTest.WithTest/Atom TargetAtom) cil managed
{
  // Code size       110 (0x6e)
  .maxstack  2
  .locals init (object V_0,
          class WithTest.WithTest/Atom V_1)
  IL_0000:  ldarg.0
  IL_0001:  stloc.1
  IL_0002:  ldstr       "Atom name is "
  IL_0007:  ldloc.1
  IL_0008:  callvirt    instance string WithTest.WithTest/Atom::get_Name()
  IL_000d:  call        string [mscorlib]System.String::Concat(string,
                                                               string)
  IL_0012:  call        void [mscorlib]System.Console::WriteLine(string)
  IL_0017:  ldstr       "Atom symbol is "
  IL_001c:  ldloc.1
  IL_001d:  callvirt    instance string WithTest.WithTest/Atom::get_Symbol()
  IL_0022:  call        string [mscorlib]System.String::Concat(string,
                                                               string)
  IL_0027:  call        void [mscorlib]System.Console::WriteLine(string)
```

In this case, the compiler created a local variable of type Atom and set it equal to TargetAtom (ldarg.0 and stloc.1). Then, whenever TargetAtom is needed, VB .NET actually loads the local variable (ldloc.1) and not the original variable.

This may seem a bit odd at first glance. Why create the dummy variable? In this case, there's not much of a difference between a local variable and a method argument. However, the reasoning behind this process becomes clearer when you start calling properties or methods as part of the With statement. Take a look at the following code:

```
With TargetAtom.Symbol
    Console.WriteLine("Atom object information:  " & .ToString)
End With
```

It's possible that the value returned from Symbol would change if you loaded TargetAtom onto the stack to get its value to implement the With statement. The way With works is that the value used when the With block is entered doesn't change throughout the block.[5] So the compiler doesn't have much of a choice but to cache the value once and then use that value throughout the lifetime of the With block.

SOURCE CODE *The WithTest project contains the methods discussed in this section.*

Implementing Interface Methods

As you have seen, .NET allows you to create interfaces that classes can implement. Furthermore, it's possible to specify which method on which interface your class is implementing.[6] However, the way that this is done varies between languages.

---

5. See Section 8.4 of the Visual Basic Language Specification of the .NET SDK.

6. This isn't possible with ATL out of the box; see http://www.sellsbrothers.com/tools/default.aspx for a workaround to this problem if you run into it and you're still coding COM servers in ATL.

Consider the following set of interface definitions:

```
namespace DriveInterfaces
{
    public interface IGolfer
    {
        string Drive();
    }

    public interface IStockCarRacer
    {
        string Drive();
    }

    public interface ISundayDriver
    {
        string Drive();
    }
}
```

Now, let's say I need to model two different classes: a person who is a stock car racer and a golfer, and another person who's a bad automobile driver as well as a bad golfer. Therefore, the way the first person drives the stock car is different than the way she drives a golf ball; the second person is lousy at both activities. Listing 6-6 shows how this is implemented in C#.

Listing 6-6. Interface Implementation in C#

```
public class StockCarGolfer : IStockCarRacer, IGolfer
{
    public StockCarGolfer() {}

    string IStockCarRacer.Drive()
    {
        return "Without rubbing you ain't got racing!";
    }

    string IGolfer.Drive()
    {
        return "350 yards right down the middle of the fairway...";
    }
}

public class BadDriver : ISundayDriver, IGolfer
{
```

```
    public BadDriver() {}

    string ISundayDriver.Drive()
    {
        return this.Drive();
    }

    string IGolfer.Drive()
    {
        return this.Drive();
    }

    private string Drive()
    {
        return "I'm a bad driver no matter what I do.";
    }
}
```

In C#, interface methods can be overridden by adding methods to the class that match the interface's methods. In this case, you can't add a method called Drive() because each interface defines the exact same method. Therefore, C# allows you to define which interface method you're implementing by explicitly stating the method along with the interface name (string IGolfer.Drive(), for example). This is known as *explicit interface inheritance*, and the resulting CIL looks like this:

```
.method private hidebysig newslot final virtual
        instance string  DriveInterfaces.IGolfer.Drive() cil managed
{
  .override [DriveInterfaces]DriveInterfaces.IGolfer::Drive
  // Code size       7 (0x7)
  .maxstack  1
  IL_0000:  ldarg.0
  IL_0001:  call        instance string CSharpDrivers.BadDriver::Drive()
  IL_0006:  ret
} // end of method BadDriver::DriveInterfaces.IGolfer.Drive
```

Note that the method name includes the interface name along with the interface's assembly name. The method is private, so you can't access the method from outside the class, nor can you access the method from within the class:

```
// This works
this.Drive();
// This doesn't
this.DriveInterfaces.IGolfer.Drive();
```

The technique works well if the methods don't share implementations, as is the case with StockCarGolfer. However, you'll note that in BadDriver, both methods call the same implementation. In C#, there's no way to state that a method implements more than one interface method. With VB .NET, though, you have more flexibility in terms of how you implement the interface's methods. Listing 6-7 shows the implementation of the two classes in VB .NET.

Listing 6-7. Interface Implementation in VB .NET

```
Public Class StockCarGolfer
    Implements IStockCarRacer, IGolfer

    Public Sub New()
    End Sub

    Private Function StockCarDrive() As String _
        Implements IStockCarRacer.Drive

        Return "Without rubbing you ain't got racing!"
    End Function

    Public Function GolfDrive() As String _
        Implements IGolfer.Drive

        Return "350 yards right down the middle of the fairway..."
    End Function
End Class

Public Class BadDriver
    Implements ISundayDriver, IGolfer

    Public Sub New()
    End Sub

    Public Function Drive() As String _
        Implements ISundayDriver.Drive, IGolfer.Drive

        Return "I'm a bad driver no matter what I do."
    End Function
End Class
```

With the `Implements` keyword you can specify which methods will be implemented by the current method. In this case, the implementation of `Drive()` in `BadDriver` looks like this in CIL:

```
.method public newslot final virtual instance string
        Drive() cil managed
{
  .override [DriveInterfaces]DriveInterfaces.ISundayDriver::Drive
  .override [DriveInterfaces]DriveInterfaces.IGolfer::Drive
  // Code size       6 (0x6)
  .maxstack  1
  .locals init (string V_0)
  IL_0000:  ldstr      "I'm a bad driver no matter what I do."
  IL_0005:  ret
} // end of method BadDriver::Drive
```

Note that the method is also declared as `public`, so it's possible to use the method as a client of `BadDriver` as well as from within the type:

```
'  External
Dim bd As BadDriver = new BadDriver
bd.Drive
'  Internal
Me.Drive()
```

Oberon has the same abilities that VB .NET does when it comes to implementing interface methods . . . or so the documentation says. However, the results are quite striking. Listing 6-8 shows the same two types defined in Oberon.

Listing 6-8. Interface Implementation in Oberon

```
MODULE OberonDrivers;
    TYPE StockCarGolfer* = OBJECT
        IMPLEMENTS DriveInterfaces.IStockCarRacer, DriveInterfaces.IGolfer;
        PROCEDURE StockCarDrive() : System.String
            IMPLEMENTS DriveInterfaces.IStockCarRacer.Drive;

        BEGIN
            RETURN "Without rubbing you ain't got racing!";
        END StockCarDrive;
        PROCEDURE GolfDrive*() : System.String
            IMPLEMENTS DriveInterfaces.IGolfer.Drive;
```

```
        BEGIN
            RETURN "350 yards right down the middle of the fairway...";
        END GolfDrive;
    END StockCarGolfer;
    TYPE BadDriver* = OBJECT
        IMPLEMENTS DriveInterfaces.ISundayDriver, DriveInterfaces.IGolfer;
        PROCEDURE SundayDrive() : System.String
            IMPLEMENTS DriveInterfaces.ISundayDriver.Drive;

        BEGIN
            RETURN "I'm a bad driver no matter what I do.";
        END SundayDrive;
        PROCEDURE GolferDrive() : System.String
            IMPLEMENTS DriveInterfaces.IGolfer.Drive;

        BEGIN
            RETURN "I'm a bad driver no matter what I do.";
        END GolferDrive;
    END BadDriver;
END OberonDrivers.
```

You'll be able to compile the code, but if you try to use them in another application, you'll be in for a rude shock. Here's a piece of test code that I created in C# to see what would happen with these types:

```
StockCarGolfer scg = new StockCarGolfer();
IStockCarRacer ISCGStock = scg;
Console.WriteLine("Calling Drive() on StockCarGolfer via IStockCarRacer = " +
    ISCGStock.Drive());
IGolfer ISCGGolf = scg;
Console.WriteLine("Calling Drive() on StockCarGolfer via IGolfer = " +
    ISCGGolf.Drive());
Console.WriteLine("Calling GolfDrive() on StockCarGolfer = " +
    scg.GolfDrive());
Console.WriteLine("Calling StockCarDrive() on StockCarGolfer = " +
    scg.StockCarDrive());
```

I had similar code for BadDriver, but it doesn't pay to show it, because the test code won't execute. When I ran this code, I got a TypeLoadException. The reason becomes clear when you look at the type's methods in ILDasm:

```
.method public final virtual instance string
        StockCarDrive() cil managed
{
```

```
// Code size       6 (0x6)
.maxstack  11
IL_0000:  ldstr      "Without rubbing you ain't got racing!"
IL_0005:  ret
} // end of method StockCarGolfer::StockCarDrive
```

Because no .override directive is present, the runtime can't determine that you're actually trying to override Drive() from IStockCarDriver, so it gives up.[7] In fact, PEVerify doesn't like this assembly either:

```
peverify /il /md OberonDrivers.dll

Microsoft (R) .NET Framework PE Verifier  Version 1.0.3705.0
Copyright (C) Microsoft Corporation 1998-2001. All rights reserved.

[IL]: Error:  [token  0x02000002] Type load failed.
[IL]: Error:  [token  0x02000003] Type load failed.
2 Errors Verifying OberonDrivers.dll
```

I think this is an excellent example of verifying assemblies that you receive from vendors. In this case, if I ran PEVerify on OberonDrivers.dll, I would've seen a problem before I spent the time to create a test harness.[8]

SOURCE CODE *The DriveInterfaces project contains the interface definitions, and the CSharpDrivers, VBDrivers, and OberonDrivers projects contain the implementations of these interfaces.*

On Error Resume Next, or How to Create a Lot of CIL

If you'd ever programmed in VB before .NET, you know that error handling was pretty rudimentary. You had to use the goto statement and then you usually jumped to a label:

---

7. The reason this worked with the Oberon example in Chapter 1 is because the interface and class methods matched, so the runtime was able to determine that the interface was implemented correctly.

8. I think that most vendors will do this before they publish their assemblies. However, it doesn't hurt to do a quick check on them before you use them—the time it takes to run PEVerify on an assembly relative to the time it may take to figure out why something isn't working as expected is worth it in my book.

```
Sub GotoErrorHandling(ByVal X As Integer, ByVal Y As Integer)
    On Error GoTo ErrorHandler

    Dim Z As Integer
    Z = X \ Y

    Exit Sub

ErrorHandler:

End Sub
```

This syntax is still preserved in VB .NET, but VB .NET also allows you to handle exceptions via the Try-Catch-End Try blocks:

```
Sub NewErrorHandling(ByVal X As Integer, ByVal Y As Integer)
    Try
        Dim Z As Integer
        Z = X \ Y
    Catch e As Exception

    End Try
End Sub
```

Of course, you can simply ignore errors if you want:

```
Sub NoErrorHandling(ByVal X As Integer, ByVal Y As Integer)
    Dim Z As Integer
    Z = X \ Y
End Sub
```

However, if a DivideByZeroException occurs, you're sunk, unless somewhere up the call stack a method will catch the exception. To allow code to execute without letting an exception trickle up the stack, you can use On Error Resume Next:

```
Sub ResumeNextErrorHandling(ByVal X As Integer, ByVal Y As Integer)
    On Error Resume Next
    Dim Z As Integer
    Z = X \ Y
End Sub
```

Although you may be tempted to use `On Error Resume Next`,[9] I would strongly recommend another approach. For one, you may be suppressing exceptions that simply should not be suppressed. If you're trying to open a file and the runtime won't let you for security reasons, it's far better to catch that exception than it is to have your file processing code continue. The other reason is the code bloat that happens, even with two lines of VB .NET code, as just demonstrated. Let's look at each method in detail to see what's going on. First, take a look at NoErrorHandling():

```
.method public static void  NoErrorHandling(int32 X,
                                            int32 Y) cil managed
{
  // Code size       5 (0x5)
  .maxstack  2
  .locals init (int32 V_0)
  IL_0000:  ldarg.0
  IL_0001:  ldarg.1
  IL_0002:  div
  IL_0003:  stloc.0
  IL_0004:  ret
} // end of method ErrorResumeNext::NoErrorHandling
```

Nothing surprising here—the two arguments are loaded and then X is divided by Y. Now let's look at the new, modern way of handling exceptions in VB .NET with NewErrorHandling():

```
.method public static void  NewErrorHandling(int32 X,
                                             int32 Y) cil managed
{
  // Code size       21 (0x15)
  .maxstack  2
  .locals init (int32 V_0,
          class [mscorlib]System.Exception V_1)
  .try
  {
    IL_0000:  ldarg.0
    IL_0001:  ldarg.1
    IL_0002:  div
    IL_0003:  stloc.0
    IL_0004:  leave.s    IL_0014
  }  // end .try
  catch [mscorlib]System.Exception
```

---

9. I have to admit, I've used it on VB projects in the past, primarily in the error handling code itself. But I've made a resolution to never use this feature as long as I live, especially after seeing what happens when it's used!

```
{
    IL_0006:  dup
    IL_0007:  call void [Microsoft.VisualBasic]
      Microsoft.VisualBasic.CompilerServices.ProjectData::SetProjectError(
      class [mscorlib]System.Exception)
    IL_000c:  stloc.1
    IL_000d:  call void [Microsoft.VisualBasic]
      Microsoft.VisualBasic.CompilerServices.ProjectData::ClearProjectError()
    IL_0012:  leave.s    IL_0014
  }  // end handler
  IL_0014:  ret
} // end of method ErrorResumeNext::NewErrorHandling
```

You've seen .try blocks in CIL before, but the code that was added to the catch block wasn't expected. SetProjectError() and ClearProjectError() are methods that are used by the VB .NET runtime (Microsoft.VisualBasic.dll) to set the current exception object (Err) because you don't have to specify an exception variable in the catch statement as I am doing. This is a holdover from pre-.NET VB syntax in which a global exception object was available; in VB .NET, the Err object is still available and can be used in the exception handler to catch the (probable) DivideByZeroException.

Let's move on to GotoErrorHandler(), which is shown in Listing 6-9.

Listing 6-9. "On Error Goto" Results in CIL

```
.method public static void  GotoErrorHandling(int32 X,
                                              int32 Y) cil managed
{
  // Code size       84 (0x54)
  .maxstack  2
  .locals init (int32 V_0,
           class [mscorlib]System.Exception V_1,
           int32 V_2,
           int32 V_3)
  IL_0000:  call       void [Microsoft.VisualBasic]
    Microsoft.VisualBasic.CompilerServices.ProjectData::ClearProjectError()
  IL_0005:  ldc.i4.1
  IL_0006:  stloc.3
  IL_0007:  ldarg.0
  IL_0008:  ldarg.1
  IL_0009:  div
  IL_000a:  stloc.0
  IL_000b:  leave.s    IL_004b
  IL_000d:  leave.s    IL_004b
```

```
IL_000f:  isinst     [mscorlib]System.Exception
IL_0014:  brfalse.s  IL_001f
IL_0016:  ldloc.3
IL_0017:  brfalse.s  IL_001f
IL_0019:  ldloc.2
IL_001a:  brtrue.s   IL_001f
IL_001c:  ldc.i4.1
IL_001d:  br.s       IL_0020
IL_001f:  ldc.i4.0
IL_0020:  endfilter
IL_0022:  castclass  [mscorlib]System.Exception
IL_0027:  dup
IL_0028:  call       void [Microsoft.VisualBasic]
  Microsoft.VisualBasic.CompilerServices.ProjectData::SetProjectError(
  class [mscorlib]System.Exception)
IL_002d:  stloc.1
IL_002e:  ldloc.2
IL_002f:  brfalse.s  IL_0033
IL_0031:  leave.s    IL_004b
IL_0033:  ldc.i4.m1
IL_0034:  stloc.2
IL_0035:  ldloc.3
IL_0036:  switch     (
                      IL_0045,
                      IL_0047)
IL_0043:  leave.s    IL_0049
IL_0045:  leave.s    IL_0049
IL_0047:  leave.s    IL_000d
IL_0049:  rethrow
IL_004b:  ldloc.2
.try IL_0000 to IL_000f filter IL_000f handler IL_0022 to IL_004b
IL_004c:  brfalse.s  IL_0053
IL_004e:  call       void [Microsoft.VisualBasic]
  Microsoft.VisualBasic.CompilerServices.ProjectData::ClearProjectError()
IL_0053:  ret
} // end of method ErrorResumeNext::GotoErrorHandling
```

Basically, VB .NET's compiler adds a .try block with a filter block to implement the jump to the ErrorHandler label when an exception occurs. The exception code that VB .NET emits is pretty interesting to trace. The filter starts at IL_000f. If the thrown object is an Exception type (which it always should be), then V_3's value is loaded (which is set to 1 at IL_0006). This is not false, so the break at IL_0017 doesn't occur. V_2's value is loaded, which is 0 (it's never changed up to this point since it's been initalized). Because brtrue won't cause a break to occur, a 1 is loaded, and you break to endfilter. Now a value of 1 is on the stack, so this causes the handler's code to execute. As before, VB .NET stores the exception information via SetProjectData(). When V_2 is loaded again at IL_002e, the following brfalse causes the code to jump to IL_0033, where V_2 is set to –1. V_3 is loaded again, and a switch statement occurs. Since V_3 is still 1, the filter block is left at IL_0047, which causes another jump at IL_000d to IL_004b, where the method finally finished execution. Just seeing this code should motivate you to use the new syntax.

Finally, here's the CIL for ResumeNextErrorHandling(), which is shown in Listing 6-10. Because the CIL gets pretty long, I've added the original VB .NET code so you can see where the CIL is added to handle the On Error Resume Next construct within the method.

Listing 6-10. "On Error Resume Next" Results in CIL

```
//  Sub ResumeNextErrorHandling(ByVal X As Integer, ByVal Y As Integer)
.method public static void  ResumeNextErrorHandling(int32 X,
    int32 Y) cil managed
{
  // Code size       113 (0x71)
  .maxstack  2
  .locals init (int32 V_0,
          int32 V_1,
          class [mscorlib]System.Exception V_2,
          int32 V_3,
          int32 V_4)
  //  On Error Resume Next
  IL_0000:  call        void [Microsoft.VisualBasic]
    Microsoft.VisualBasic.CompilerServices.ProjectData::ClearProjectError()
  IL_0005:  ldc.i4.1
  IL_0006:  stloc.s     V_4
  //  Dim Z As Integer
  //  Z = X \ Y
  IL_0008:  ldc.i4.1
  IL_0009:  stloc.1
  IL_000a:  ldarg.0
  IL_000b:  ldarg.1
  IL_000c:  div
  IL_000d:  stloc.0
  IL_000e:  leave.s     IL_0068
  IL_0010:  ldloc.3
  IL_0011:  ldc.i4.1
  IL_0012:  add
  IL_0013:  ldc.i4.0
```

```
IL_0014:  stloc.3
IL_0015:  switch     (
                        IL_0000,
                        IL_0008,
                        IL_000e)
IL_0026:  leave.s    IL_0066
IL_0028:  isinst     [mscorlib]System.Exception
IL_002d:  brfalse.s  IL_0039
IL_002f:  ldloc.s    V_4
IL_0031:  brfalse.s  IL_0039
IL_0033:  ldloc.3
IL_0034:  brtrue.s   IL_0039
IL_0036:  ldc.i4.1
IL_0037:  br.s       IL_003a
IL_0039:  ldc.i4.0
IL_003a:  endfilter
IL_003c:  castclass  [mscorlib]System.Exception
IL_0041:  dup
IL_0042:  call       void [Microsoft.VisualBasic]
  Microsoft.VisualBasic.CompilerServices.ProjectData::SetProjectError(
  class [mscorlib]System.Exception)
IL_0047:  stloc.2
IL_0048:  ldloc.3
IL_0049:  brfalse.s  IL_004d
IL_004b:  leave.s    IL_0066
IL_004d:  ldloc.1
IL_004e:  stloc.3
IL_004f:  ldloc.s    V_4
IL_0051:  switch     (
                        IL_0060,
                        IL_0062)
IL_005e:  leave.s    IL_0064
IL_0060:  leave.s    IL_0064
IL_0062:  leave.s    IL_0010
IL_0064:  rethrow
IL_0066:  ldloc.2
.try IL_0000 to IL_0028 filter IL_0028 handler IL_003c to IL_0066
IL_0067:  throw
//  End Sub
IL_0068:  ldloc.3
IL_0069:  brfalse.s  IL_0070
IL_006b:  call       void [Microsoft.VisualBasic]
  Microsoft.VisualBasic.CompilerServices.ProjectData::ClearProjectError()
IL_0070:  ret
} // end of method ErrorResumeNext::ResumeNextErrorHandling
```

Wow, did that bloat the code! If someone insists on using this approach to error handling, just ask him or her if all of this code is really worth it just to prevent an exception from being raised if someone makes the following call:

```
ResumeNextErrorHandling(3, 0)
```

I think not. If your language of choice is VB .NET, I strongly recommend using the new exception handling mechanisms rather than using the old constructs. To me, having a code size of 21 (for NewErrorHandling()) is much more appealing that 113 (for ResumeNextErrorHandling()).

 SOURCE CODE *The ErrorResumeNext project contains the methods described in this section.*

Active Objects

You may know that .NET supports threading—that is, you can create threads that will process work separate from the main thread. In C# and VB .NET, you have to manage threads in native .NET code. Oberon, however, tries to abstract some of the details away with the concept of an *active* object. Let's take a look at how this works via the example shown in Listing 6-11.

Listing 6-11. Creating an Active Object in Oberon

```
MODULE GuidGen;
    TYPE Generator* = OBJECT {ACTIVE}
        CONST waitTime = 1000;

        VAR quit : BOOLEAN;
            curGuid : System.Guid;

        PROCEDURE GetGuid*() : System.Guid;
        BEGIN
            RETURN curGuid;
        END GetGuid;

        PROCEDURE Stop*();
        BEGIN
            quit := TRUE;
        END Stop;
```

```
BEGIN
    quit := FALSE;
    WHILE ~quit DO
        curGuid := System.Guid.NewGuid();
        System.Threading.Thread.Sleep(waitTime);
    END
    END Generator;
END GuidGen.
```

This assembly will contain a type called Generator. However, note that the type is adorned with the ACTIVE directive. This attribute tells the compiler to run the code that is contained in the type's BEGIN...END block on a separate thread. This code creates a new Guid every second. To exit the loop, the client must call Stop().

From the client's perspective, it's oblivious that it spawns a new thread when it creates an instance of Generator. However, the way Oberon currently generates the code to handle this thread processing is a bit odd. Figure 6-3 shows what a typical .NET developer will see if he or she looks at Generator in VS .NET's Object Browser.

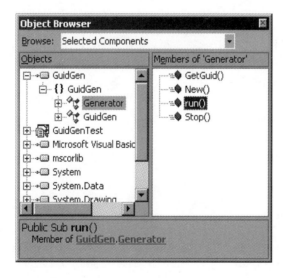

Figure 6-3. Generator's methods

See that run() method? This is the method that Generator's constructor passes to a ThreadStart delegate to state which method should be run on a separate thread:

```
.method public specialname rtspecialname
        instance void  .ctor() cil managed
{
  // Code size        39 (0x27)
  .maxstack  11
  IL_0000:  ldarg  0
  IL_0004:  call instance void [mscorlib]System.Object::.ctor()
  IL_0009:  ldarg 0
  IL_000d:  ldarg 0
  IL_0011:  ldvirtftn  instance void GuidGen.Generator::run()
  IL_0017:  newobj  instance void
    [mscorlib]System.Threading.ThreadStart::.ctor(object,
    native int)
  IL_001c:  newobj  instance void
    [mscorlib]System.Threading.Thread::.ctor(
    class [mscorlib]System.Threading.ThreadStart)
  IL_0021:  callvirt instance void
    [mscorlib]System.Threading.Thread::Start()
  IL_0026:  ret
} // end of method Generator::.ctor
```

However, there's no reason to make run() public, and in this case, it would cause the client a lot of pain if he or she called it on the same thread. run() enters a WHILE...END loop that will only stop when quit is set to TRUE. Unless the client happened to call Stop() before run(), the method would never return, and the client would hang.

Although I think there's a lot of promise for abstracting threading details away from the developer as Oberon does with active objects, I think the compiler designers of Oberon have some work to do before it becomes transparent and seamless. Giving the method that contains the threading code a public scope is dangerous at best. If you use a language construct from any language that you're not completely familiar with, make sure you create a number of test cases before you include it in a larger project. This doesn't guarantee that you will have figured out every possible problem, but you may catch potential issues when the damage caused by these problems is minimal.[10]

---

10. Right before this book was published, a research paper was released on adding constructs similar to active objects to C#. It's titled "Modern Concurrency Abstractions for C#," and you can download it at http://research.microsoft.com/Users/luca/Papers/Polyphony%20ECOOP.A4.pdf.

SOURCE CODE *The GuidGen folder contains the Oberon file to create* Generator, *and GuidGenTest contains a VB .NET test harness that allows you to play with* Generator.

Language Interoperability: The Real Story

Now that you've gone through investigating the language translations that occur from higher-level languages to CIL via the compilers, let's see what happens when types from different languages are intermixed.

Inheritance with Oberon .NET Types

Let's back up and reexamine the hypothetical coding situation I gave in Chapter 1. I had a number of languages in use to create assemblies that other languages expanded upon. Although the example was pretty basic, you may have been puzzled over one of my design decisions. Recall that I had implemented an interface called IPerson (written in C#) in Oberon. This new type was called Person. Then, I inherited from IPerson to create a new interface called ICustomer, which was implemented by a class called Customer. All of this was done in C#. Figure 6-4 shows the current design scenario.

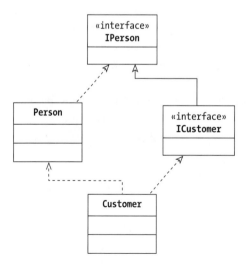

Figure 6-4. Current interface-class relationships

To be honest, I would never have done it this way. Figure 6-5 shows what I would have done if I had the choice.

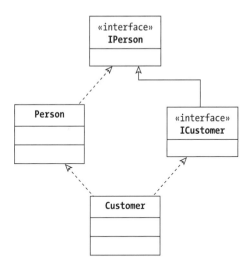

Figure 6-5. Preferred interface-class relationships

The difference is subtle, but it's there. In the first case, Customer doesn't inherit from Person; it's only using its functionality via containment. In the second case, Customer inherits from Person.

So what's stopping me from doing this? The issue lies with the Oberon language, or, to be more precise, what Oberon's compiler is doing with the Person type. Recall that Person is defined as follows:

```
MODULE PersonImpl;
    TYPE Person* = OBJECT IMPLEMENTS PersonDefinition.IPerson;
        (*  code goes here…*)
    END Person;
END PersonImpl.
```

When you load the assembly into ILDasm and look at Person, you may be surprised by what you see:

```
.class public auto ansi sealed Person
       extends [mscorlib]System.Object
       implements [PersonDefinition]PersonDefinition.IPerson
{
} // end of class Person
```

The type is sealed! Therefore, there is no way that I can legally extend this type, so that's why I had to use a combination of containment and method forwarding in Customer with respect to Person.[11]

Although language interoperability is definitely possible in .NET and is much easier than any other solution that I have seen, in some cases, things may not work as expected. I didn't expect Oberon to automatically make any type sealed, so when I tried to make Customer inherit from Person, I got an error.

Overloaded and Overridden Methods

There are some subtleties in how languages will determine which method they call with respect to types that overload methods from base types. Such subtleties can lead to some interesting discussions in the conference room if you don't look at what's really going on.

Here's a concrete example written in C#:

```
public class Chair {}
public class ComfyChair : Chair {}

public class Person
{
    public string Sit(ComfyChair c)
    {
        MethodBase mb = MethodBase.GetCurrentMethod();
        return "You called " +
            mb.DeclaringType.FullName + "\n" +
            "\t" + mb.ToString() + "\n" +
            "from type " + this.GetType().FullName + "\n";
    }
}

public class SpanishInquisitor : Person
{
    public string Sit(Chair c)
    {
        MethodBase mb = MethodBase.GetCurrentMethod();
        return "You called " +
            mb.DeclaringType.FullName + "\n" +
            "\t" + mb.ToString() + "\n" +
            "from type " + this.GetType().FullName + "\n";
    }
}
```

---

11. Technically, this is documented behavior according to a white paper from the makers of the Oberon compiler for .NET (http://www.oberon.ethz.ch/oberon.net/whitepaper/ActiveOberonNetWhitePaper.pdf). See Section 6.1 in the paper for details.

Both Sit() methods are nonvirtual, so Sit() in SpanishInquisitor is not over-riding Person's Sit() implementation. Also note that Sit() in SpanishInquisitor takes a Chair instance, but Sit() in Person takes a more specific type—that is, ComfyChair.

Let's create a small test harness of these types in a C# console application:

```
class OAOTest
{
    static void Main(string[] args)
    {
        Chair c = new Chair();
        ComfyChair cc = new ComfyChair();
        Person p = new Person();
        SpanishInquisitor si = new SpanishInquisitor();

        Console.WriteLine(p.Sit(cc));
        Console.WriteLine(si.Sit(cc));
        Console.WriteLine(si.Sit(c));
    }
}
```

Before this code is run, try to guess what the output is going to be. Done? Okay, here's what the console says:

```
You called OverrideAndOverload.Person
        System.String Sit(OverrideAndOverload.ComfyChair)
from type OverrideAndOverload.Person

You called OverrideAndOverload.SpanishInquisitor
        System.String Sit(OverrideAndOverload.Chair)
from type OverrideAndOverload.SpanishInquisitor

You called OverrideAndOverload.SpanishInquisitor
        System.String Sit(OverrideAndOverload.Chair)
from type OverrideAndOverload.SpanishInquisitor
```

The first and third methods aren't really open for discussion, as there are no other choices for the C# compiler to pick. Here's the pertinent CIL that represents the second method call:

```
.locals init (class [OverrideAndOverload]OverrideAndOverload.Chair V_0,
        class [OverrideAndOverload]OverrideAndOverload.ComfyChair V_1,
        class [OverrideAndOverload]OverrideAndOverload.Person V_2,
        class [OverrideAndOverload]OverrideAndOverload.SpanishInquisitor V_3)
```

```
ldloc.3
ldloc.1
callvirt    instance string [OverrideAndOverload]
  OverrideAndOverload.SpanishInquisitor::Sit(
  class [OverrideAndOverload]OverrideAndOverload.Chair)
```

In this case, C# decides to call Sit() on SpanishInquisitor. Now let's create a similar test harness in VB .NET:

```
Sub Main()
    Dim c As Chair = New Chair()
    Dim cc As ComfyChair = New ComfyChair()
    Dim p As Person = New Person()
    Dim si As SpanishInquisitor = New SpanishInquisitor()

    Console.WriteLine(p.Sit(cc))
    Console.WriteLine(si.Sit(cc))
    Console.WriteLine(si.Sit(c))
End Sub
```

Looks like the same code, right? But the results are a little different—here's the output:

```
You called OverrideAndOverload.Person
       System.String Sit(OverrideAndOverload.ComfyChair)
from type OverrideAndOverload.Person

You called OverrideAndOverload.Person
       System.String Sit(OverrideAndOverload.ComfyChair)
from type OverrideAndOverload.SpanishInquisitor

You called OverrideAndOverload.SpanishInquisitor
       System.String Sit(OverrideAndOverload.Chair)
from type OverrideAndOverload.SpanishInquisitor
```

And here's the CIL:

```
.locals init (class [OverrideAndOverload]OverrideAndOverload.Chair V_0,
        class [OverrideAndOverload]OverrideAndOverload.ComfyChair V_1,
        class [OverrideAndOverload]OverrideAndOverload.Person V_2,
        class [OverrideAndOverload]OverrideAndOverload.SpanishInquisitor V_3)
ldloc.3
ldloc.1
callvirt    instance string
  [OverrideAndOverload]OverrideAndOverload.Person::Sit(
  class [OverrideAndOverload]OverrideAndOverload.ComfyChair)
```

VB .NET decides to call Sit() on Person and not on SpanishInquisitor. Note that a similar test harness in Oberon yields the same result as the VB .NET test code:

```
MODULE OberonOverrideAndOverloadTest;
VAR
    c: OverrideAndOverload.Chair;
    cc: OverrideAndOverload.ComfyChair;
    p: OverrideAndOverload.Person;
    si: OverrideAndOverload.SpanishInquisitor;
BEGIN
    NEW(c);
    NEW(cc);
    NEW(p);
    NEW(si);
    System.Console.WriteLine{(System.String)}(p.Sit(cc));
    System.Console.WriteLine{(System.String)}(si.Sit(cc));
    System.Console.WriteLine{(System.String)}(si.Sit(c));
END OberonOverrideAndOverloadTest.
```

So what gives? Why do Oberon and VB .NET decide to use the Sit() method on Person, but C# uses Sit() on SpanishInquisitor? The reason is that it's purely a language choice—both "sides" make a valid argument. C#'s compiler looks at each object in the inheritance tree, and as soon as it finds a match that's good enough, the compiler calls it. That's why C#'s compiler calls Sit() on SpanishInquisitor; ComfyChair descends from Chair, so that call is perfectly valid. Oberon's and VB .NET's compilers look through the tree until they find the best match they can. They therefore call Sit() on Person because that method signature takes a ComfyChair type.

Note that *nothing* in the Partition docs requires a language to take one approach or another.[12] Nor could it—different languages have made different choices in this situation before .NET came along, so it couldn't mandate a rule in this case. If you're on a project where developers insist on using multiple languages and you run into situations where discrepancies arise in behavior, distill the problem down to its essence and consult the Partition docs. You may find other cases where there is no hard-and-fast rule, so keep this technique in mind.

---

12. See Section 9.2 of Partition I.

SOURCE CODE *The OverrideAndOverload folder contains the class definitions used in this section (Chair, Person, and so on). The OverrideAndOverloadTest, VBOverrideAndOverloadTest, and OberonOverrideAndOverloadTest folders contain the test harnesses.*

The Other Property

In Chapter 2 I said in the section "Defining Properties in Types" that I would show you how a higher-level language would handle extended property information. That is, if a property is defined with the .other directive, what does C# do with it, if anything? I'll show you in a rather unexpected way via a COM server written in VB 6.

Let's say you have two classes in a COM server called GetLetSet: GLS and GLSTest. Here's the definition of GLS:

```
Private m_Def As Long

Public Property Let ThisIsTheDefault(ByVal Value As Long)
m_Def = Value
End Property

Public Property Get ThisIsTheDefault() As Long
ThisIsTheDefault = m_Def
End Property
```

GLS has one property, ThisIsTheDefault. Now, you can't see this from the code, but this property is set as the default property. You can do this in the Procedure Attributes dialog box, which you bring up by selecting Tools ➤ Procedure Attributes. Figure 6-6 shows you where you can make a property the default one for a class.

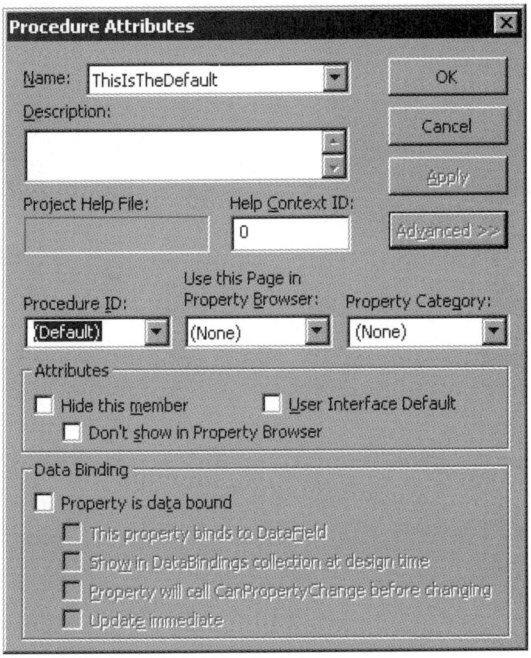

Figure 6-6. Setting the default property in VB 6

When (Default) is selected in the Procedure ID drop-down box, that property will become the default.

If a property is set up as the default property, you don't have to specify the property name to use it. Therefore, the following code in VB 6 is perfectly valid (albeit very confusing):

```
Dim g As GLS
Set g = New GLS
g = 4
```

After this code is complete, the private field m_Def will be set to 4. Again, this is not obvious to a developer seeing the code for the first time, which is why few VB 6 developers ever used default properties. And it can be even worse if a developer adds a class like GLSTest:

```
Dim m_GLS As GLS

Public Property Let MyGLS(Value As GLS)
m_GLS = Value
End Property
```

```
Public Property Set MyGLS(Value As GLS)
Set m_GLS = Value
End Property

Public Property Get MyGLS() As GLS
Set MyGLS = m_GLS
End Property

Private Sub Class_Initialize()
Set m_GLS = New GLS
End Sub
```

By having a Let property defined for MyGLS, a VB 6 client can write convoluted code like this:

```
Dim g As GLS
Set g = New GLS
g = 4
Dim gt As GLSTest
Set gt = New GLSTest
gt.MyGLS = g
```

At first glance, it looks like GLSTest's private field m_GLS is being set to g, when in reality, the last line of code is calling ThisIsTheDefault on m_GLS, setting m_Def equal to 4. This is not what I consider self-documenting code.

However, get/set/let properties lead to an interesting scenario with COM interoperability in .NET. If you reference the GetLetSet.dll COM server in a C# project, you can write C# that does the same thing as the last VB 6 code snippet, but be careful! It's not as straightforward as it may look at first glance:

```
static void Main(string[] args)
{
    GLS gls = new GLSClass();
    gls.ThisIsTheDefault = 4;

    GLSTest gt = new GLSTestClass();
    GLS glRet = gt.get_MyGLS();
    Console.WriteLine("Before:  " +
        glRet.ThisIsTheDefault.ToString());

    gt.let_MyGLS(ref gls);
    glRet = gt.get_MyGLS();
    Console.WriteLine("After:  " +
        glRet.ThisIsTheDefault.ToString());
}
```

The first aspect that's different is that you must explicitly call the property ThisIsTheDefault on gls. But the real twister is that you can't use the property MyGLS; you have to call the get_MyGLS() and let_MyGLS() methods. The reason is found when you look at the .NET-to-COM interop assembly that C# creates so you can access GetLetSet. This assembly is called Interop.GetLetSet.dll, and you can find it in the bin directories. If you open it up in ILDasm, here's what the MyGLS property looks like:

```
.property class GetLetSet.GLS MyGLS()
{
  .custom instance void
    [mscorlib]System.Runtime.InteropServices.DispIdAttribute::.ctor(int32) =
    ( 01 00 00 00 03 68 00 00 )                        // .....h..
  .get instance class
    GetLetSet.GLS GetLetSet._GLSTest::get_MyGLS()
  .set instance void
    GetLetSet._GLSTest::set_MyGLS(class GetLetSet.GLS&)
  .other instance void
    GetLetSet._GLSTest::let_MyGLS(class GetLetSet.GLS&)
} // end of property _GLSTest::MyGLS
```

The .other directive is used to represent the Let version of MyGLS. However, C# gets confused when you try to use MyGLS, as it can't figure out if you're really trying to call the set_MyGLS() method or the let_MyGLS() method. That's why an explicit call to the property's method is necessary.[13]

Admittedly, this is something you probably won't see very often (at least, I hope you won't). But if you ever need to use a COM server where a property allows you to get, let, and set a value, you'll know how to handle it.

SOURCE CODE *The GetLetSet folder contains the VB 6 definitions of GLS and GLSTest. The GLSClient subfolder contains the C# client code.*

---

13. Unfortunately, IntelliSense won't show the property methods, even though they're public. But if you simply type them in, everything will compile normally.

Overloading Methods in CIL

Let's close out this chapter with a discussion on overloading methods in CIL. Way back in Chapter 2 in the section "Overriding Methods," I gave a definition of a method signature. One of the parts that made up the signature was the return type. I didn't make it explicit in Chapter 2, but now I'm going to show you how you can overload methods in which the return type alone distinguishes the method and how C# and VB .NET each handle these methods.

Let's create a class that has two methods named GiveMeANumber(). One returns an int32, and the other returns a float64:

```
.class public GetNumbers
{
    .method public hidebysig
        specialname rtspecialname
        instance void .ctor() cil managed
    {
        .maxstack 1
        ldarg.0
        call instance void [mscorlib]System.Object::.ctor()
        ret
    }

    .method public instance int32
        GiveMeANumber() cil managed
    {
        .maxstack 1
        ldc.i4 24
        ret
    }

    .method public instance float64
        GiveMeANumber() cil managed
    {
        .maxstack 1
        ldc.r8 42
        ret
    }
}
```

The implementations are pretty easy. The int32 version will always return 24, and the float64 version will always return 42.

To call these methods from another assembly written in CIL should be second nature for you by now. As you know, calling methods in CIL requires you to give the type of the return value, so the ilasm compiler will have enough information to discern which GiveMeANumber() method you're calling, as demonstrated in Listing 6-12.

Listing 6-12. Resolving Method Calls Based on the Return Value Types

```
.class public OBRTester
{
    .method private hidebysig
        specialname rtspecialname
        instance void .ctor() cil managed
    {
        .maxstack 1
        ldarg.0
        call instance void [mscorlib]System.Object::.ctor()
        ret
    }

    .method public static void Main()
        cil managed
    {
        .entrypoint
        .maxstack 2
        .locals init (class [OverloadByReturn]GetNumbers gn)
        newobj instance void [OverloadByReturn]GetNumbers::.ctor()
        stloc gn
        ldloc gn
        call instance int32 [OverloadByReturn]GetNumbers::GiveMeANumber()
        call void [mscorlib]System.Console::WriteLine(int32)
        ldloc gn
        call instance float64 [OverloadByReturn]GetNumbers::GiveMeANumber()
        call void [mscorlib]System.Console::WriteLine(float64)
        ret
    }
}
```

When the application is run that contains OBRTester, the console should look like this:

```
C:\OBRTester>OBRClient
24
42
```

You get the int32 first, and then you obtain the float64 value. At each call opcode, the return type is specified, so all is well in the .NET world.

However, things get pretty ugly in both C# and VB .NET if they encounter GetNumbers:

```
//  C#
class OBRTester
{
    static void Main(string[] args)
    {
        GetNumbers gn = new GetNumbers();
        int gnInt = gn.GiveMeANumber();
        Console.WriteLine(gnInt);
        double gnDouble = gn.GiveMeANumber();
        Console.WriteLine(gnDouble);
    }
}


'  VB . NET
Module OBRTester

    Sub Main()
        Dim gn As GetNumbers = New GetNumbers()
        Dim gnInt As Integer = gn.GiveMeANumber()
        Console.WriteLine(gnInt)
        Dim gnDouble As Double = gn.GiveMeANumber()
        Console.WriteLine(gnDouble)
    End Sub

End Module
```

Unfortunately, neither one of these code snippets will compile. When you compile the C# code, the compiler gives you the following error:

```
The call is ambiguous between the following methods or properties:
'GetNumbers.GiveMeANumber()' and 'GetNumbers.GiveMeANumber()'
```

VB .NET's error message is similar (although it's a bit more verbose):

```
Overload resolution failed because no accessible 'GiveMeANumber'
is most specific for these arguments:
'Public Function GiveMeANumber() As Double': Not most specific.
'Public Function GiveMeANumber() As Integer': Not most specific.
```

In both cases, the compiler can't resolve the call you're trying to make. Neither C# nor VB .NET supports overloading methods by return value. As overloading methods based on the return value is not CLS compliant,[14] you should not expose any methods in CIL that do this. Instead, provide a method that can internally resolve which method should be called—this will allow languages like C# and VB .NET to indirectly call these overloaded methods.

SOURCE CODE *The OverloadByReturn folder contains the IL files that define GetNumbers and OBRTester. The CSharpTester and VBTester projects show how you can write code to call* GetNumbers*'s methods (although the projects won't compile).*

Conclusion

In this chapter, you looked at a number of different language constructs and interoperability situations and how they really worked at a CIL level. By knowing how CIL works, you could easily determine why compilers make the choices that they do to implement the developer's wishes in a higher-level language. In the next chapter, you're going to start making those choices yourself when you create your own assemblies via the Emitter classes.

---

14.   See Section 9.2 of Partition I.

CHAPTER 7

Emitting Types

In this chapter, I'll show you the Emitter classes in .NET and how you can use your newfound knowledge of CIL to use these types effectively. I'll go over each type in detail, discussing how they work to build assemblies and types on the fly. I'll also explain ways to debug these dynamic assemblies.

Applying CIL

By this time, you should be fairly fluent in the ways of CIL. If you ever see ILDasm output, you should have no problem being able to read it, and if needed, you could write your .NET project in CIL. However, let's be honest. You're probably not going to write many applications in CIL. Although I personally find CIL to be easier to write than x86 assembly, I also find it much easier to write this:

```
Dim aString As String = New String()
```

than this:

```
.locals init ([0] string aString)
newobj instance void [mscorlib]System.String::.ctor()
stloc.0
```

And when it comes to writing a GUI-based application in CIL (as demonstrated in Chapter 4), it gets downright tedious.

So why learn CIL in the first place? There are a couple of reasons why I think it's important. One, you get to see what's going on at the lowest possible level in .NET. Personally, I think my understanding of .NET increased dramatically the more I learned about how the different CIL opcodes worked. Playing with C# or VB .NET was interesting, but I didn't immediately get the subtle differences between the languages (especially in regard to overriding interface methods). Seeing those differences in CIL made the rules of overriding methods much clearer.

But I think an even bigger reason is the ability to emit code at runtime. .NET defines a number of classes that allow you to create types during code execution. These classes enable you to do all sorts of tricks that would be downright difficult to pull off otherwise. To use these classes, you need to have a good understanding of CIL because the method implementations are all done using the CIL opcodes. By learning CIL, you have the ability to take this knowledge and apply it to the classes.

I'd like to make one comment about dynamic code generation before continuing. If your code relies on the ability to make types at runtime, then your code will need the proper permission—specifically, the `ReflectionPermission` with the `Flags` attribute set to `ReflectionEmit`. This is not a permission that you will automatically get in every scenario (for example, downloaded code from the Internet), as this technique is extremely powerful and can be used fairly easily for malicious purposes. You should always ensure that your code has this permission via the `ReflectionPermissionAttribute`—I'll show you how to do this in the next section.

Emitter Basics

I'll start by explaining where the code-generation classes are in the .NET Framework, and how to get the fundamental parts of a dynamic type in place.

> **NOTE** *Throughout this section, I'm going to create a very simple example in VB .NET that will create an implementation of an* `ICustomer` *interface on the fly. As you peruse each code snippet, keep this in mind so you can see how the example is completed in each section.*

Defining the Essentials

To begin, let's make sure your references are in place:

```
Imports System.Reflection
Imports System.Reflection.Emit
Imports System.Security.Permissions
```

All of the code-generation classes (which I'll classify as the Emitter classes from now on) are located in mscorlib within the `System.Reflection.Emit` namespace. Technically, you don't need to import `System.Reflection`, but I've found that I usually need to perform some kind of introspection of predefined types when I'm creating dynamic types, so that's why you're also importing `System.Reflection`.

The `System.Security.Permission` namespace is imported so you can make the following attribute declaration:

```
<Assembly: ReflectionPermissionAttribute(SecurityAction.RequestMinimum, _
    ReflectionEmit:=True)>
```

As I mentioned in the last section, this attribute should always be declared when you're emitting code. If the assembly isn't granted this permission, you won't be able to do anything. You can add the following attribute to a class definition or a method, which will check to see if clients of your code have the `ReflectionPermissionAttribute`:

```
<Type: ReflectionPermissionAttribute(SecurityAction.Demand, _
    ReflectionEmit:=True)>
```

If the calling code does not have the permission, the type will not be loaded and a `SecurityExecption` will be generated.

I'll also show some of the VB .NET code that defines several types that you'll use later on:

```
Public Class DynamicImplCustomer

    Private Const CUST_MODULE As String = "DynamicCustomerModule"
    Private Const CUST_ASM As String = "DynamicCustomer"
    Private Const CUST_FIRST_NAME_FIELD As String = "m_FirstName"
    Private Const CUST_LAST_NAME_FIELD As String = "m_LastName"
    Private Const CUST_AGE_FIELD As String = "m_Age"


    Private Shared m_FirstNameField As FieldInfo
    Private Shared m_LastNameField As FieldInfo
    Private Shared m_AgeField As FieldInfo
End Class
```

There's also an `ICustomer` interface that you'll implement later on:

```
Public Interface ICustomer
    Property FirstName() As String
    Property LastName() As String
    Property Age() As Integer
    Function IsAdult() As Boolean
End Interface
```

Creating Assemblies

When you define a new type, it needs to live within a module, which exists within an assembly. To create the new assembly, you call `DefineDynamicAssembly()` on an `AppDomain` object:

```
Public Shared Function Create(ByVal FirstName As String, _
    ByVal LastName As String) As ICustomer

    Dim m_DynCustAsm As AssemblyBuilder
    Dim m_DynCustAsmModule As ModuleBuilder
    Dim m_DynCustAsmName As AssemblyName

    m_DynCustAsmName = New AssemblyName()

    With m_DynCustAsmName
        .Name = CUST_ASM
        .Version = New Version(1, 0, 0, 0)
    End With

    Dim uniqueCustName As String = Guid.NewGuid().ToString()

    m_DynCustAsm = AppDomain.CurrentDomain.DefineDynamicAssembly( _
        m_DynCustAsmName, AssemblyBuilderAccess.Save)
    m_DynCustAsmModule = m_DynCustAsm.DefineDynamicModule(CUST_MODULE)
```

This is the easiest of DefineDynamicAssembly()'s nine overloads. All of them
take as their first two parameters the values shown in Create(). The first is an
AssemblyName reference—this type allows you to define a number of properties that
end up in an assembly's manifest, like the hash algorithm (HashAlgorithm), the
version number (Version), and so on. As you can see in the type initializer, you set
the version number (via a Version type instance) and the name.

The second argument to DefineDynamicAssembly() states how the assembly should
be persisted. There are three values for AssemblyBuilderAccess: Save, RunAndSave, and
Run. Run specifies that any types within the assembly can be executed once the
assembly has been saved. Save means that the assembly will be saved to a physical
disk location. If you use the RunAndSave combination, the assembly will be saved
and you can immediately use types from the assembly. Currently, you're using a
transient assembly, so the second argument is set to AssemblyBuilderAccess.Run.
Therefore, once the AppDomain that the dynamic assembly lives in is unloaded, all of
the generated code goes with it. I'll show you how the assembly is saved to disk
later on in the section "Persisting the Results."

The other eight DefineDynamicAssembly() overloads allow you to define a
number of security aspects for the new assembly. You can define the evidence (for
example, certificate information, zone of origin, and so on) for the new assembly
via an Evidence type, the permissions that you hope the assembly will be granted
via PermissionSet types, and whether type creations within the assembly should be
synchronized or not.

Once the assembly is defined, you need to declare at least one module to be able to create types. There are four overloads for DefineDynamicModule()—I've picked the easiest of the four for this example, where I define the name of the module. Other overloads allow you to define the filename for the module if the assembly is persisted and whether symbol information should be created. I'll cover debugging emitted types later on in the section "Debugging Dynamic Assemblies."

Building Types

You have your assembly and module in place. Now you can define a new type that implements the ICustomer interface:

```
Dim newCustInterfaces(0) As Type
newCustInterfaces(0) = GetType(ICustomer)

Dim newCust As TypeBuilder
Dim uniqueCustName As String = Guid.NewGuid().ToString()
newCust = DynCustAsmModule.DefineType("Customer" + uniqueCustName, _
    TypeAttributes.Class Or TypeAttributes.Public, _
    GetType(System.Object), newCustInterfaces)
```

DefineType() has seven overrides—I'm using one of the more complex ones in the code snippet. All of them have as their first argument the name of the new type. Six overrides allow you to define different type attributes via the TypeAttribute enumeration (such as Interface and Sealed). Five overrides let you define the base type that you want to derive from. In this case, I'm explicitly deriving from System.Object; if you use a DefineType() override where you can't specify the base type, it'll automatically be System.Object. The last argument is available in one override: you provide it with a list of interface types that the dynamic type will implement.[1]

---

1. Other DefineType() overrides allow you to specify the packing size or the total size of the type, but I won't cover those scenarios in this book.

Adding Fields

The new type is defined—now you can start to add some structure to it. Let's add three fields that you can use to store relevant customer information:

```
' Called in Create()…
BuildFields(newCust)

Private Shared Sub BuildFields(ByVal NewCust As TypeBuilder)
    '  Add the fields to store
    '  the first and last names
    '  along with the age.
    m_FirstNameField = NewCust.DefineField(CUST_FIRST_NAME_FIELD, _
        GetType(System.String), FieldAttributes.Private)
    m_LastNameField = NewCust.DefineField(CUST_LAST_NAME_FIELD, _
        GetType(System.String), FieldAttributes.Private)
    m_AgeField = NewCust.DefineField(CUST_AGE_FIELD, _
        GetType(System.Int32), FieldAttributes.Private)
End Sub
```

DefineField() allows you to define a new field within the type. Fortunately, there are no overrides in this case; only one version of this method exists. You give the field a name, its type, and any attributes that the field should have via the FieldAttributes enumeration. The method returns a reference to a FieldBuilder instance, but that's something that you don't need in BuildFields(). Later on in the section "Implementing Methods" I'll show you how you can use this FieldBuilder reference to retrieve and modify its value.

Emitting Methods

So far, you've been able to create a type and give it some fields. Let's move on to giving your types some behavior by looking at method creation.

Adding Methods

To add methods, you have a couple of options at your disposal. First, let's see how you would create the default constructor for a type:

```
' Called in Create()…
BuildConstructor(newCust, FirstName, LastName)
```

```
Private Shared Sub BuildConstructor(ByVal NewCust As TypeBuilder, _
    ByVal FirstName As String, ByVal LastName As String)
    Dim custCtor As ConstructorBuilder

    custCtor = NewCust.DefineConstructor(MethodAttributes.Public Or _
            MethodAttributes.SpecialName Or MethodAttributes.RTSpecialName Or _
            MethodAttributes.HideBySig, CallingConventions.Standard, Nothing)
    ' Constructor's implementation goes here…
End Sub
```

Recall from Chapter 2 that constructors must have the specialname and
rtspecialname attributes—that's why they're included in the first argument.
The last argument allows you to define the types that will be passed to the
constructor via a Type array—in this case, you're defining the default constructor,
which takes no arguments.

For this type, you don't need a type initializer, but if you did, you'd call
DefineTypeInitializer():

```
custTypeCtor = NewCust.DefineTypeInitializer()
```

Both DefineConstructor() and DefineTypeInitializer() return a
ConstructorBuilder instance.

If you need to define a regular method, use DefineMethod():

```
' Called in Create()…
BuildIsAdult(newCust)

Private Shared Sub BuildIsAdultMethod(ByVal NewCust As TypeBuilder)
    Dim isAdultMethod As MethodBuilder

    isAdultMethod = NewCust.DefineMethod("IsAdultImpl", _
        MethodAttributes.HideBySig Or _
        MethodAttributes.NewSlot Or MethodAttributes.Virtual Or _
        MethodAttributes.Public, GetType(System.Boolean), Nothing)
End Sub
```

DefineMethod() has another signature with which you can define the calling
convention, but usually you'll use the default .NET calling convention. The third
argument defines the return type, and the last argument specifies the argument
types.

Now, if you look at the ICustomer specification, you'll notice that you need to
implement IsAdult(). Therefore, let's make this new IsAdultImpl() method override
IsAdult():

```
Private Shared Sub BuildIsAdultMethod(ByVal NewCust As TypeBuilder)
    Dim isAdultMethod As MethodBuilder
    Dim parentMethod As MethodInfo
    Dim isAdultIL As ILGenerator
    Dim isTrue As Label
    Dim finishMethod As Label
    Dim ILretVal As LocalBuilder

    parentMethod = GetType(ICustomer).GetMethod("IsAdult")
    isAdultMethod = NewCust.DefineMethod("IsAdultImpl", _
        MethodAttributes.HideBySig Or _
        MethodAttributes.NewSlot Or MethodAttributes.Virtual Or _
        MethodAttributes.Public, GetType(System.Boolean), Nothing)

    NewCust.DefineMethodOverride(isAdultMethod, parentMethod)
    '  CIL implementation goes here…
End Sub
```

All this does is make the override relationship between the two methods explicit via the .override directive.

You can also define new properties via DefineProperty(). DefineProperty() has only one definition, and it's the same as the one shown for DefineMethod() previously. The only difference is that the second argument is a PropertyAttribute enumeration. However, to override the FirstName and LastName properties in ICustomer, you need to actually override the get and set methods via the technique I just described.[2]

Implementing Methods

Once you've defined a method, you can add code to implement that method. You do this by first calling GetILGenerator() on a MethodBuilder reference:

```
isAdultIL = isAdultMethod.GetILGenerator()
```

With this reference, you can add pretty much any method implementation detail you want. Let's start by adding a local variable: a Boolean that you'll use as the return value:

```
ILretVal = isAdultIL.DeclareLocal(GetType(System.Boolean))
```

---

2.   See the BuildProperties() method in the code sample for this chapter for the code to override the base property's methods.

All you need to do is specify the local's type in DeclareLocal(). If you want to scope local variables to a scope block, you use a combination of BeginScope() and EndScope() methods:

```
anILGenerator.BeginScope()
aLocalInt = anILGenerator.DefineLocal(GetType(System.String))
'  CIL implementation goes here…
anILGenerator.EndScope()
```

Of course, you can always emit the CIL code whenever you want by calling Emit():

```
'  Initialize the local to false.
isAdultIL.Emit(OpCodes.Ldc_I4_0)
isAdultIL.Emit(OpCodes.Stloc_0)
```

Emit() has 17 different versions—I'll cover a couple of them in this section. All of them take as their first argument an OpCode value. Yes, this is not a misprint— I mean OpCode. So what's this OpCodes type doing in the Emit() calls?

This probably seems a little weird to you at first glance. There are two relevant types to this discussion in the Emitter namespace: an OpCode structure and an OpCodes class.[3] Emit()'s first argument is a reference to an OpCode instance, but OpCodes defines a number of prebuilt OpCode instances as static fields (for example, Stloc_0, Ldc_I4_0, and so on), so you can just pass these fields to Emit(). In fact, you really don't have a choice. If you tried to create an instance of OpCode, you'd find out that the only custom constructor on OpCode has assembly accessibility, so you'd never be able to call it.

Let's see what some of the other Emit() overrides can do. Most of them simply change the type of the second argument so you can pass the correct information to the Emitter. For example, if you wanted to set a field's value in a type, here's how you'd do it:

```
isAdultIL.Emit(OpCodes.Ldarg_0)
isAdultIL.Emit(OpCodes.Ldfld, m_AgeField)
isAdultIL.Emit(OpCodes.Ldc_I4_S, 18)
```

You can also set up labels for condition breakpoints. First, you define the label via DefineLabel() on the ILGenerator reference. Then, you pass that LabelInfo reference to Emit() at the proper time:

```
isTrue = isAdultIL.DefineLabel()
finishMethod = isAdultIL.DefineLabel()
isAdultIL.Emit(OpCodes.Bge, isTrue)
isAdultIL.Emit(OpCodes.Br, finishMethod)
```

---

3.   Note that OpCodes is *not* an enumeration; I assumed this at first glance, which really left me confused the more I dug into this.

Later on in the code, you need to set where the label is in the CIL stream via `MarkLabel()`:

```
isAdultIL.MarkLabel(isTrue)
```

For the sake of completeness, here's the rest of `BuildIsAdultMethod()`:

```
isAdultIL.Emit(OpCodes.Ldc_I4_1)
isAdultIL.Emit(OpCodes.Stloc_0)
isAdultIL.MarkLabel(finishMethod)
isAdultIL.Emit(OpCodes.Ldloc_0)
isAdultIL.Emit(OpCodes.Ret)
```

Now, in the `IsAdult()` method just generated, you don't need to call any other methods on an object. However, in the dynamic type's constructor, you have to call the base type's constructor as well as create a random age value for the m_Age field. Let's look at the implementation of `BuildConstructor()`—I'll pick up the VB .NET code stream from the section "Adding Methods":

```
custIL = custCtor.GetILGenerator()
rndAge = custIL.DeclareLocal(GetType(System.Random))
custIL.Emit(OpCodes.Ldarg_0)
custIL.Emit(OpCodes.Call, _
    GetType(System.Object).GetConstructor(System.Type.EmptyTypes))
```

One of `Emit()`'s overloads takes a `ConstructorInfo` reference as its second argument. Use the code I just demonstrated to call any type's constructor. If the constructor takes arguments, set the argument to `GetConstructor()` to an array of `Type` references that represent the types of the custom constructor's arguments.

I'll skip a couple of lines of VB .NET code that set up the first and last name fields and get right to the code that calculates the random age:

```
custIL.Emit(OpCodes.Newobj, _
    GetType(System.Random).GetConstructor(System.Type.EmptyTypes))
custIL.Emit(OpCodes.Stloc_0)
custIL.Emit(OpCodes.Ldarg_0)
custIL.Emit(OpCodes.Ldloc_0)
custIL.Emit(OpCodes.Ldc_I4, 100)
Dim rndArgTypes(0) As Type
rndArgTypes(0) = GetType(System.Int32)
custIL.Emit(OpCodes.Callvirt, _
    GetType(System.Random).GetMethod("Next", rndArgTypes))
custIL.Emit(OpCodes.Stfld, m_AgeField)
custIL.Emit(OpCodes.Ret)
```

When you invoke a method, you can use the Call, Callvirt, or Calli field on OpCodes. You then pass a MethodInfo object as the second argument. That's it—assuming that you've pushed the correct values onto the stack, the call will work.

You could also make the same call with EmitCall():

```
custIL.EmitCall(OpCodes.Callvirt, _
    GetType(System.Random).GetMethod("Next", rndArgTypes), _
    Nothing)
```

EmitCall() takes three arguments: the OpCode, a MethodInfo object, and a Type array if the method is a vararg method and optional values will be passed. In this case, Next() isn't a vararg method, so you can set this to Nothing (or System.Types.EmptyTypes).[4] There's also an EmitCalli() method in case you need to invoke a method via its pointer (as you saw with the delegate calls in Chapter 4).

Before moving on to another method implementation detail, I'd like to make note of a couple of ILGenerator features. First, if you need to print out the value of a field or a local variable to the console along with a descriptive piece of information, you can use the EmitWriteLine() call:

```
isAdultIL.EmitWriteLine("The first name is…")
isAdultIL.EmitWriteLine(m_FirstNameField)
isAdultIL.EmitWriteLine("The return value is…")
isAdultIL.EmitWriteLine(ILretVal)
```

EmitWriteLine() has three overloads: a string value, a FieldInfo object, and a LocalBuilder object. In all three cases, all you need to do is call EmitWriteLine(); you don't need to push the Me instance onto the stack to access the field or push the local variable's value onto the stack. EmitWriteLine() takes care of the necessary CIL for you.

The other nice feature is the transparent calculation of the .maxstack directive. You may have noticed that I never call a method like SetMaxstackSize() for an emitted method. The nice thing is that, somewhere within the Emitter classes, it's automagically figured out for you.[5]

---

4. I've seen no difference in the resulting assemblies between the two techniques. Personally, I like using Emit() to call methods, as I usually don't call vararg methods on a regular basis, so it saves on some coding keystrokes.

5. This leads to an interesting proposal of writing all of your CIL code via the Emitter classes in the .NET language of your choice so you don't have to figure out what .maxstack should be.

Exception Handling

Currently, IsAdultImpl() has no exception handling. Although the code is pretty simplistic and shouldn't cause an exception, let's add an exception handler to demonstrate how you would do it with the Emitter. I'll start by showing you where the exception block begins in the original BuildIsAdultImpl():

```
isAdultIL.Emit(OpCodes.Ldc_I4_0)
isAdultIL.Emit(OpCodes.Stloc_0)
exceptionLabel = isAdultIL.BeginExceptionBlock()
isAdultIL.Emit(OpCodes.Ldarg_0)
isAdultIL.Emit(OpCodes.Ldfld, m_AgeField)
```

When you call BeginExceptionBlock(), a try block is started at the point of the call. It gives you a Label object that you can use to get out of the try block, but you usually won't need it—I'll explain why in a moment.

Once you're done with all of your exception handling, call EndExceptionBlock():

```
isAdultIL.EndExceptionBlock()
isAdultIL.Emit(OpCodes.Ldloc_0)
isAdultIL.Emit(OpCodes.Ret)
```

Note that EndExceptionBlock() will automatically emit a leave opcode at the end of the try block that points to a label marking the first line of code outside of the exception block. That's why you don't need to emit a leave opcode in the try block, so the label given to you by BeginExceptionBlock() is usually not necessary (unless you need to get out of a try block halfway through its execution).

While you're in the exception block, you can call BeginCatchBlock() to catch any thrown exceptions:

```
isAdultIL.BeginCatchBlock(GetType(System.Exception))
```

You specify the type of exception you'd like to catch for its only argument. Note that there is no EndCatchBlock(); the catch block ends when another catch block has begun, or EndExceptionBlock() has been called. You can also define a finally or fault block within the exception block with BeginFinallyBlock() and BeginFaultBlock(), respectively. The blocks are closed when the EndExceptionBlock() is called.

If you catch an exception in a catch block, remember that the exception is at the top of stack in case you want to use it:

```
Dim anException As LocalBuilder
anException = isAdultIL.DeclareLocal(GetType(System.Exception))
'   VB .NET code goes here…
isAdultIL.BeginCatchBlock()
isAdultIL.Emit(OpCodes.Stloc, anException)
```

Throwing an exception is no different from what you saw earlier in the section "Handling Exceptions" in Chapter 3. You create the proper exception, push it onto the stack, and call throw:

```
isAdultIL.Emit(OpCodes.Newobj, _
    GetType(System.ArgumentException).GetConstructor(System.Type.EmptyTypes))
isAdultIL.Emit(OpCodes.Throw)
```

You can also rethrow an exception within a catch block by emitting a Rethrow OpCode:

```
isAdultIL.BeginCatchBlock()
isAdultIL.Emit(OpCodes.Rethrow)
```

Persisting the Results

Once you have all of the code set up for the dynamic types, you need to persist them. However, what is meant by "persist" depends on the type of assembly and module you are creating. Let's look at all of the options.

Baking Types

No matter which assembly persistence mechanism you use, in all three cases you must save the type so clients can create instances. To "bake" the type, you call CreateType():

```
Dim newCustType As Type = newCust.CreateType()
```

At this point, you can create new type instances; it doesn't matter what kind of assembly you have. The easiest way to do this is to call CreateInstance() on the dynamic assembly:

```
Return CType(m_DynCustAsm.CreateInstance("Customer" + uniqueCustName), _
    ICustomer)
```

 NOTE *Andrew Troelsen, in his book,* **C# and the .NET Platform**, *called this process "baking." I didn't understand what he meant by that until I attempted my own dynamic type creation—I would see a call to* BakeByteArray() *on an* ILGenerator *object in the stack trace when I'd mess things up and cause an exception. If you take a look at the* CreateType() *method in ILDasm, you'll see that this method is the one that finalizes the CIL stream.*

Transient-Only Assemblies

This is the kind of assembly that is created when you pass
`AssemblyBuilderAccess.Run` to `DefineDynamicAssembly()`. In this case, you don't need
to do anything with the dynamic assembly. Simply create your types, bake them,
and you're done. Specifically, you must use a `DefineDynamicAssembly()` method that
does not take file information when you define the module, as the module will also
be transient and cannot be persisted to a file. If you try to give a filename for a
module, or you accidentally try to save the assembly to disk (which is covered in
the next section) when your assembly is transient, you'll get an exception.

Transient assemblies are great if you're creating code that performs a dynamic
service-oriented task for a client. If the service needs to change considerably
depending on the configuration given to you by the client and performance is a
must, I'd go with a transient assembly. Essentially, you can wire the configurations
in at runtime, perform the service, and let the dynamic code disappear when all is
said and done.[6]

Persistent-Only Assemblies

If you have to create an assembly that must stick around for quite some time and
you do not need it right away, then you should pass in `AssemblyBuilderAccess.Save`
to `DefineDynamicAssembly()` (which is what is currently being done in the
`DynamicCustomer` assembly). Then, to save the assembly, you must call `Save()`
on the `AssemblyBuilder` reference, passing in the filename of the assembly.

The directory that the assembly will be saved in depends on which
`DefineDynamicAssembly()` method you call. If you specify the directory in its
`dir` argument, the assembly will be saved there. If you either invoke a
`DefineDynamicAssembly()` method that doesn't have a `dir` argument or set `dir` to
`Nothing`, the current directory will be used to store the assembly.

Now, in this case, you can create either transient or persistable modules.
To create a persistent module, use a version of `DefineDynamicModule()` that has a
`fileName` parameter, and set this argument to the appropriate filename. When
`Save()` is called on the `AssemblyBuilder`, the persistent modules will be written to
disk. However, the filenames that you give the module and the assembly affect the
persisting process. If the module filename given in `DefineDynamicModule()` matches
the assembly filename given in `Save()`, one PE file will be created. If the filenames
differ, two PE files will be created. All of the type information will be stored in the
module; the assembly PE file will only contain manifest information.

---

6. In the next chapter, you'll see an ideal candidate for such a service: method interception.

Let's go over a couple of code snippets to review what happens with persistable assemblies and modules. Here's the first example:

```
Dim asm As AssemblyBuilder = _
    AppDomain.CurrentDomain.DefineDyanmicAssembly(_
    "AnAssembly", AssemblyBuilderAccess.Save)
Dim m As ModuleBuilder = _
    asm.DefineDynamicModule("AModule", "AModule.dll")
' …
asm.Save("ANewModule.dll")
```

In this case, the result will be two DLLs in the current directory. The ANewModule.dll file will only contain the assembly manifest information; the AModule.dll file will contain all of the type information.

Here's the second example:

```
Dim asm As AssemblyBuilder = _
    AppDomain.CurrentDomain.DefineDyanmicAssembly(_
    "AnAssembly", AssemblyBuilderAccess.Save)
Dim m As ModuleBuilder = _
    asm.DefineDynamicModule("AModule")
' …
asm.Save("ANewModule.dll")
```

This time, only one DLL will be created. It will contain no module or type information, as the module is transient.

Finally, here's the third example:

```
Dim asm As AssemblyBuilder = _
    AppDomain.CurrentDomain.DefineDyanmicAssembly(_
    "AnAssembly", AssemblyBuilderAccess.Save)
Dim m As ModuleBuilder = _
    asm.DefineDynamicModule("AModule", "AModule.dll")
' …
asm.Save("AModule.dll")
```

Only one DLL will exist, and it will contain the assembly manifest, module, and type information.

Transient, Persistent Assemblies

The third `AssemblyBuilderAccess` option is `RunAndSave`. This is a combination of the first two options. It's ideal in instances where you may need a combination of transient and persistable modules. When `Save()` is called on the `AssemblyBuilder` object, the persistent modules will be saved to disk (following the same rules that you saw in the last section), but the transient modules won't.

 SOURCE CODE *The DynamicCustomer project contains the assembly to create the dynamic customer type along with a test UI client project.*

Beyond the Basics

Now that I've covered the fundamentals of emitting code, let's look at some other features of the Emitter classes.

Setting Entry Points

So far, I've shown you how to create DLL-type assemblies. It's also possible to create a dynamic assembly that's of the EXE PE flavor. Essentially, the code is exactly the same as you've seen before; you only need to specify the method that's the entry point of the EXE. You do this by calling `SetEntryPoint()` on the `AssemblyBuilder` reference, passing it the appropriate `MethodBuilder` object:

```
Sub Main()
    Dim an As AssemblyName = New AssemblyName()
    an.Name = "NewAssembly"

    Dim ab As AssemblyBuilder = AppDomain.CurrentDomain.DefineDynamicAssembly( _
        an, AssemblyBuilderAccess.Save)

    Dim mb As ModuleBuilder = ab.DefineDynamicModule( _
        "NewAssembly", "NewAssembly.exe")
    Dim tb As TypeBuilder = mb.DefineType("RunThis")
    Dim mthb As MethodBuilder = tb.DefineMethod("Go", MethodAttributes.Static Or _
        MethodAttributes.Public, Nothing, System.Type.EmptyTypes)
```

```
    Dim mImpl As ILGenerator = mthb.GetILGenerator()
    mImpl.EmitWriteLine("I'm here.")
    mImpl.Emit(OpCodes.Ret)

    tb.CreateType()
    ab.SetEntryPoint(mthb)

    ab.Save("NewAssembly.exe")

    AppDomain.CurrentDomain.ExecuteAssembly("NewAssembly.exe")
End Sub
```

When NewAssembly.EXE is executed, you'll see "I'm here." show up in the console window. Note that if you have a Windows GUI-type application, you should use an overloaded version of SetEntryPoint():

```
ab.SetEntryPoint(mthb, PEFileKinds.WindowApplication)
```

PEFileKinds is an enumeration that defines three different PE types: ConsoleApplication, Dll, and WindowApplication.

Adding Attributes

If you want to add attributes to any member of your assembly, you can call SetCustomAttribute() on any of the Builder types. There are two overloads for this method—the first version adds the attribute information via a CustomAttributeBuilder type. For example, let's update the previous code snippet to add the CLSCompliant attribute to the assembly and the LoaderOptimization attribute to the entry point method. Here's how the CLSCompliant attribute is added:

```
Private Shared Sub AddCLSComplianceAttribute( _
    ByRef TargetAssembly As AssemblyBuilder)
    Dim ctorArgs(0) As Type
    ctorArgs(0) = GetType(System.Boolean)

    Dim clsAttrib As Type
    clsAttrib = GetType(System.CLSCompliantAttribute)

    Dim clsAttribCtor As ConstructorInfo
    clsAttribCtor = clsAttrib.GetConstructor(ctorArgs)

    Dim clsAttribBuilder As CustomAttributeBuilder
```

```
        Dim clsArgs(0) As Object
        clsArgs(0) = False

        clsAttribBuilder = New CustomAttributeBuilder(clsAttribCtor, clsArgs)
        TargetAssembly.SetCustomAttribute(clsAttribBuilder)
    End Sub
```

It's pretty easy. You create the `CustomAttributeBuilder` reference from `CLSCompliant`'s constructor, setting `isCompliant` to `True` (that is, `clsArgs(0)` = `True`). Next, you call `SetCustomAttribute()` on the target assembly. The code is the same for `AddLoaderOptimizationAttribute()`, except that you pass in a `MethodBuilder` object:

```
Private Shared Sub AddLoaderOptimizationAttribute( _
    ByRef TargetEntryPoint As MethodBuilder)
```

You can also add attribute information by using a byte array, similar to how you would define attributes in ilasm, as demonstrated in Chapter 2. Here's how it's done in `AddLoaderOptimizationAttribute()`:

```
Private Shared Sub AddLoaderOptimizationAttribute( _
    ByRef TargetEntryPoint As MethodBuilder)
    Dim ctorArgs(0) As Type
    ctorArgs(0) = GetType(System.Byte)

    Dim loaderAttrib As Type
    loaderAttrib = GetType(System.LoaderOptimizationAttribute)

    Dim loaderAttribCtor As ConstructorInfo
    loaderAttribCtor = loaderAttrib.GetConstructor(ctorArgs)

    Dim attribInfo() As Byte = {1, 0, 1, 0, 0}

    TargetEntryPoint.SetCustomAttribute(loaderAttribCtor, attribInfo)
End Sub
```

This ends up setting the value argument of `LoaderOptimization`'s constructor to `SingleDomain`.

Modifying Method Parameter Information

If you need to pass an argument with by-reference semantics, or you want to make an argument optional, you'll need to make some augmentations to the method's arguments. You can do this by calling `DefineParameter()` on either a `MethodBuilder` or `ConstructorBuilder` object. Let's create a method that takes one optional argument:

```
Private Shared Function MultiplyByTwoMethod( _
    ByRef TargetType As TypeBuilder) As MethodBuilder
    Dim argTypes() As Type = {Type.GetType("System.Int32")}

    Dim elseMethod As MethodBuilder = TargetType.DefineMethod("MultiplyByTwo", _
        MethodAttributes.Static Or MethodAttributes.Public, _
        GetType(System.Int32), argTypes)

    Dim paramInfo As ParameterBuilder = elseMethod.DefineParameter(1, _
        ParameterAttributes.Optional Or ParameterAttributes.HasDefault, _
        "ANumber")

    paramInfo.SetConstant(CInt(25))
    Dim elseIL As ILGenerator = elseMethod.GetILGenerator()
    elseIL.Emit(OpCodes.Ldarg_0)
    elseIL.Emit(OpCodes.Ldc_I4_2)
    elseIL.Emit(OpCodes.Mul)
    elseIL.Emit(OpCodes.Ret)

    Return elseMethod
End Function
```

The first argument to `DefineParameter()` is the index value. It always starts with 1, regardless of whether the method is static or not (as you cannot modify the "this" parameter with `DefineParameter()`). The second argument allows you to set a number of parameter attributes—in this case, I'm stating that the argument is optional and has a default value. The third argument allows you to name the argument so it'll show up in the ILDasm dump with a descriptive name. If you define an optional parameter, you can use `SetConstant()` to define the default value.

When the assembly is created, you should see this metadata show up in ILDasm:

```
.method public static int32
    MultiplyByTwo([opt] int32 ANumber) cil managed
{
  .param [1] = int32(0x00000019)
  //…
}
```

SOURCE CODE *The BTB project contains the code discussed in this section.*

Debugging Dynamic Assemblies

Although creating dynamic assemblies and modules is a great capability to have, the elation of creating your first dynamic assembly may taper off a bit after you get your first InvalidProgramException (or any exception for that matter). In this section, I'll show you how you can debug your dynamic code.

Emitting Debug Information

The first thing you must do to be able to debug your code is use a version of DefineDynamicModule() that has the emitSymbolInfo argument set to True:[7]

```
Private Const RETURN_MODULE_NAME As String = "ReturnModule"
' …
ReturnAsmModule = ReturnAsm.DefineDynamicModule( _
    RETURN_MODULE_NAME, _
    RETURN_MODULE_NAME + ".dll", True)
```

After you're done emitting your CIL and you've called Save() on the AssemblyBuilder reference, you'll see a PDB file in the same directory with the module file. It'll also have the same name as the module's name (in this case that would be ReturnModule.pdb).[8]

Adding to the Symbol Writer

As you saw in Chapter 5, it's preferable to debug your code using a source code file rather than x86 assembly. To do this requires a bit more work than working with the /debug option for ilasm, but it's not too difficult using the Emitter classes.

After you make your dynamic module with symbol information, you can call DefineDocument() on the module:

---

7. Please refer to the Source Code description at the end of the section "Debugging Dynamic Assemblies" to see where the code snippets in this section come from.

8. There is a version of DefineDynamicModule() to emit debug information for transient modules, which I'll cover at the end of this chapter.

```
Private Shared m_symDoc As ISymbolDocumentWriter
Private Const IL_FILE As String = "c:\returnimpl.il"
'  …
m_symDoc = ReturnAsmModule.DefineDocument(IL_FILE, _
    SymLanguageType.ILAssembly, _
    SymLanguageVendor.Microsoft, _
    SymDocumentType.Text)
```

This returns a reference to a type that implements the ISymbolDocumentWriter interface. The four parameters allow you to define the location of the source code file, the language in which the source code is written, the language vendor, and the document type. The last three parameters all take GUIDs to identify the attribute in question. Currently, SymLanguageType defines eleven language GUIDs (for example, Basic, C, SMC, and so on), whereas SymLanguageVendor only defines Microsoft and SymDocumentType only defines Text. Note that the source code file doesn't need to exist when you call DefineDocument(). It only needs to exist when the assembly is debugged, as the file location will be stored in the symbol file.

Once you have the document writer, you can use it to map source code lines with CIL instructions. After you get an ILGenerator object, you can call MarkSequencePoint() to create these mappings. For example, let's say you had the following method defined in an IL file:

```
.method public hidebysig newslot virtual
        instance float64 ReturnTheDoubleImpl(float64 A_1) cil managed
{
    .override [Debugging]Debugging.IReturn::ReturnTheDouble
    .maxstack  2
    .locals init ([0] int32 uselessInt)
    ldc.i4.3
    ldc.i4.0
    div
    pop
    ldarg.1
    ret
}
```

Let's assume that the first text line is line 35 in the IL file. When you emit the first two instructions of ReturnTheDoubleImpl, here's how you'd call MarkSequencePoint():

```
'  Assume rtdIL is an ILGenerator type.
rtdIL.MarkSequencePoint(m_symDoc, 41, 5, 41, 13)
rtdIL.Emit(OpCodes.Ldc_I4_3)
rtdIL.MarkSequencePoint(m_symDoc, 42, 5, 42, 13)
rtdIL.Emit(OpCodes.Ldc_I4_0)
```

The magic numbers in MarkSequencePoint() define where the text is that matches to this opcode. The first two numbers define the start line and column position; the last two define the endpoints. You must mark the sequence points immediately before you apply Emit() to the opcode. This is *very* important; if you don't, the debugger won't be able to map the current instruction to the correct place in code, and you'll end up wondering why a CIL opcode five lines deep in the method is highlighted when you know that's incorrect.

There are other ways to add information to the symbol writer. If you declare a local variable, you can call SetLocalSymInfo() on the LocalBuilder object to give it a friendly name:

```
Dim uselessInt As LocalBuilder
uselessInt = rtdIL.DeclareLocal(GetType(System.Int32))
uselessInt.SetLocalSymInfo("uselessInt")
```

In this case, the debugger (along with ILDasm) will show the friendly name.

Reloading the Assembly

After you're done defining the module's types, you can generate the symbol file by calling Save() on the dynamic assembly. However, you're not quite done yet. Currently, I've used CreateInstance() on the assembly to create type instances:

```
Return CType(ReturnAsm.CreateInstance("ReturnImpl"), IReturn)
```

Let's say your ReturnImpl method has the ReturnTheDoubleImpl() method mentioned before implemented (which will cause a DivideByZeroException). If your client calls ReturnTheDoubleImpl(), they'll end up in the debugger as Figure 7-1 shows.

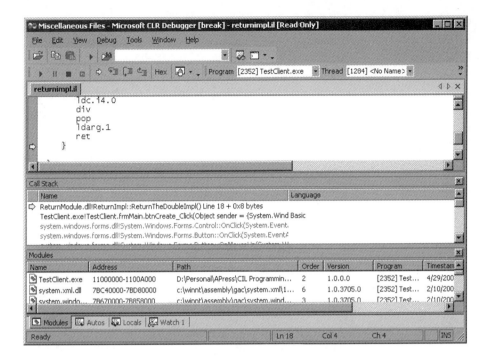

Figure 7-1. Wrong CIL target

Note that the debugger is at the end of the method; it should be on `div`. If you also look in the Call Stack window, you'll see that the byte offset value is 0x8, which is incorrect. It should be 3 bytes, as that's where `div` is located in `ReturnTheDoubleImpl()`'s CIL stream.

To get the breakpoint to end up in the right spot, you need to reload the assembly after you've created it:

```
Dim newAsm As [Assembly] = [Assembly].LoadFrom(RETURN_ASM_NAME + ".dll")
Return CType(newAsm.CreateInstance("ReturnImpl"), IReturn)
```

Figure 7-2 shows the results.

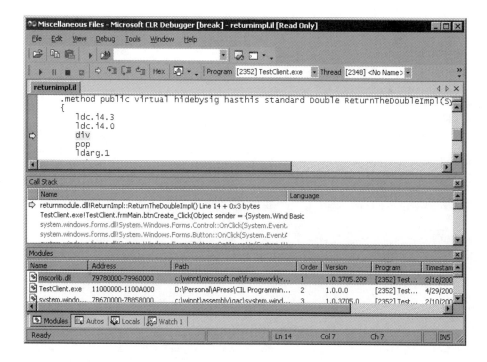

Figure 7-2. Correct CIL target

Now the breakpoint ends up on `div`.

Where's the Target IL File?

Now, if you've marked sequence points correctly, your IL file is in the correct directory, and your assembly is still causing an error, you should be able to jump to the correct opcode in the IL file. However, there's one assumption I've made throughout this discussion: the IL file already exists! What happens if the code is dynamically generated on the fly without parsing an IL file?

Unfortunately, in this case there's not much you can do. The Emitter classes don't provide a way to create an IL file on-the-fly given a newly baked type. Therefore, you're going to need to roll your own code to generate a "mini" IL file to give you a source code file.

NOTE *If you dig around in the SDK for the Emitter classes, you may notice the* SetSource() *method on the* ISymbolDocumentWriter *interface. I tried to use this to see if I could embed source code in the symbol file so I wouldn't need to keep a physical source code file around, but to no avail; I ended up getting a* NotSupportException *when I would call this method.*

Creating the DebugFile Class

What I mean by a "mini" IL file is that you want to generate the minimal amount of CIL that is needed (or miniCIL if you will). You don't have to include any assembly manifest information; all you really need is the CIL in the methods and the types that they contain. Therefore, I created a class called DebugFile that handles the generation of the miniCIL for you. It will also add sequence points for you so you don't need to handle that as well. Let's go through the inner working of this class—as you'll see from its implementation, there were a fair amount of minor snags and "gotchas" that I had to work around to get this to function.

First, here's what its constructor looks like:

```
Public Sub New(ByVal ILFile As String, ByVal CanOverwrite As Boolean, _
    ByVal SymDoc As ISymbolDocumentWriter)
    If SymDoc Is Nothing Then
        Throw New Exception("The symbol document writer reference cannot be null.")
    End If

    If File.Exists(ILFile) = True And CanOverwrite = False Then
        Throw New Exception("The given file exists and cannot be overwritten.")
    End If

    If CanOverwrite = True And File.Exists(ILFile) = True Then
        File.Delete(ILFile)
    End If

    m_ILWriter = New StreamWriter(ILFile, CanOverwrite)
    Me.m_symDoc = SymDoc
    Me.m_methodParams = New Hashtable()
End Sub
```

m_ILWriter is a TextWriter object that you use to write the miniCIL to the given file. m_methodParams stores the argument types of dynamic methods—you'll see why you need this in a moment.

Once the DebugFile instance is obtained, you can add type and method information. Types are added via StartType():

```
Public Sub StartType(ByVal NewType As TypeBuilder)
    Dim TypeInfo As StringBuilder = New StringBuilder()

    TypeInfo.Append(CLASS_IL).Append(SP)
    TypeInfo.Append(GetAttributeString(NewType))
```

```
        TypeInfo.Append(NewType.FullName).Append(SP)
        TypeInfo.Append(CLASS_EXTENDS_IL).Append(SP). _
            Append(NewType.BaseType().FullName).Append(SP)

    Dim typeInterface As Type
    If Not NewType.GetInterfaces() Is Nothing Then
        For Each typeInterface In NewType.GetInterfaces()
            TypeInfo.Append(CLASS_IMPLEMENTS_IL).Append(SP). _
                Append(typeInterface.FullName).Append(SP)
        Next
    End If

    Me.WriteText(TypeInfo.ToString())
    Me.WriteText(BEGIN_SCOPE)
    m_IndentLevel = m_IndentLevel + 1
End Sub
```

The type's information is parsed and added to a string that is sent to m_ILFile via WriteText(), which is a private method that handles text writing with proper indentation:

```
Private Sub WriteText(ByVal TextData As String)
    m_ILWriter.WriteLine(GetIndent() + TextData)
    m_LineCount = m_LineCount + 1
End Sub
```

You'll see this method called throughout DebugFile to format the output correctly. GetIndent() simply returns a string containing a number of spaces to indent the given text.

Now, in StartType() you'll notice that three specific pieces of information are written to the miniCIL file: the type attribute information, the base type name, and the names of any interfaces that the type extends. The last two pieces of information are handled with Reflection code; the attribute information is handled by GetAttributeString(), which is shown in Listing 7-1.

Listing 7-1. Discovering Type Attribute Information

```
Private Function GetAttributeString(ByVal Attrib As Type) As String
    Dim sb As StringBuilder = New StringBuilder()

    With Attrib
        '  Is is public, private, nested...?
        If .IsPublic Then
            sb.Append("public").Append(" ")
```

```
        ElseIf .IsNestedAssembly Then
            sb.Append("nestedassembly").Append(" ")
        ElseIf .IsNestedFamANDAssem Then
            sb.Append("nestedfamandassembly").Append(" ")
        ElseIf .IsNestedFamily Then
            sb.Append("nestedfamily").Append(" ")
        ElseIf .IsNestedFamORAssem Then
            sb.Append("nestedfamorassembly").Append(" ")
        ElseIf .IsNestedPrivate Then
            sb.Append("nestedprivate").Append(" ")
        Else
            sb.Append("private").Append(" ")
        End If


        ' Other attribute parsing goes here...
    End With
    Return sb.ToString()
End Function
```

More attributes are parsed than what I'm showing here, but you get the general idea. You'll see what the results of this attribute parsing are when you generate a miniCIL file.

Let's move on to methods. As new methods are created for a dynamic type, StartMethod() (which is shown in Listing 7-2) should be called.

Listing 7-2. Writing Method Information

```
Public Sub StartMethod(ByVal NewMethod As MethodBase, _
    ByVal MethodArgs() As Type, ByVal ILGen As ILGenerator)
    m_ILGen = ILGen

    Dim MethodInfo As StringBuilder = New StringBuilder()

    MethodInfo.Append(METHOD_IL).Append(SP)
    MethodInfo.Append(GetAttributeString(NewMethod))

    If TypeOf NewMethod Is MethodInfo Then
        MethodInfo.Append(CType(NewMethod, MethodInfo).ReturnType.Name).Append(SP)
    End If

    MethodInfo.Append(Me.GetMethodArgInfo(NewMethod.Name, MethodArgs))

    Me.AddMethodArgs(NewMethod, MethodArgs)
```

```
    Me.WriteText(MethodInfo.ToString())
    Me.WriteText(BEGIN_SCOPE)
    m_IndentLevel = m_IndentLevel + 1
End Sub
```

It's similar to StartType() in that you add the method's definition to the miniCIL file. An overloaded version of GetAttributeString() that takes a MethodBase object is called to glean the method's attribute information. However, there are some aspects to methods that you need to handle differently. First, if the method is a MethodInfo type, you need to add return type information to the line of code. Also, you need to add method argument information as well, which is what GetMethodArgInfo() is for; its implementation is shown in Listing 7-3.

Listing 7-3. Retrieving Method Argument Information

```
Private Function GetMethodArgInfo(ByVal TargetMethodName As String, _
    ByVal MethodArgs() As Type) As String
    Dim MethodInfo As StringBuilder = New StringBuilder()

    MethodInfo.Append(TargetMethodName)
    MethodInfo.Append(BEGIN_ARGS)

    Dim argType As Type
    Dim argC As Integer = 0

    If Not MethodArgs Is Nothing And MethodArgs.Length > 0 Then
        For Each argType In MethodArgs
            argC = argC + 1
            MethodInfo.Append(argType.FullName).Append(SP). _
                Append(ARG).Append(argC.ToString())
            If (argC < MethodArgs.Length) Then
                MethodInfo.Append(ARG_DLM).Append(SP)
            End If
        Next
    End If

    MethodInfo.Append(END_ARGS)

    Return MethodInfo.ToString()
End Function
```

Now, you may wonder why you need to force the client to provide the method's argument type information when there's the GetParameters() method on the MethodBase type. Normally, you would use GetParameters(), but before a dynamic type is baked, calling this method will cause an exception. That's also why you store the type information into a hash table via AddMethodArgs(). If a type ends up calling this method, you can find the argument type array in the hash table so you can add the argument list to the method during a call, calli, or callvirt instruction.

After either a method or type is finished, the client should call EndScope():

```
Public Sub EndScope(Optional ByVal IsMethod As Boolean = False)
    m_IndentLevel = m_IndentLevel - 1
    Me.WriteText(END_SCOPE)

    If IsMethod = True Then
        Me.MarkSequencePoint(END_SCOPE.Length)
    End If

    Me.WriteText(vbNullString)
End Sub
```

If the ending scope is for a method, the client should set IsMethod to True so a final sequence point can be added for method clean-up code.

Finally, whenever an opcode is added, the client should call AddOpCode(). Just as there are a number of Emit() overloads, so there are a number of AddOpCode() overloads—I'll show the one that handles method invocation opcodes in Listing 7-4.

Listing 7-4. Handling Method Invocation-Based Opcodes

```
Public Sub AddOpCode(ByVal NewOpCode As OpCode, _
    ByVal InvokedMethod As MethodBase)
    Dim opBuilder As StringBuilder = New StringBuilder()

    opBuilder.Append(NewOpCode.ToString()).Append(SP)

    Dim argTypes() As Type

    Try
        If Not InvokedMethod.GetParameters() Is Nothing _
            And InvokedMethod.GetParameters().Length > 0 Then
            ReDim argTypes(InvokedMethod.GetParameters().Length - 1)

            Dim argC As Integer = 0
            Dim paramInfo As ParameterInfo
            For Each paramInfo In InvokedMethod.GetParameters()
                argTypes(argC) = paramInfo.ParameterType
            Next
        End If
```

```
Catch e As Exception
    ' See if the method arg info is in the hashtable.
    Dim sig As String = Me.GetMethodSignature(InvokedMethod)
    If Me.m_methodParams.ContainsKey(sig) = True Then
        argTypes = CType(Me.m_methodParams.Item(sig), Type())
    End If
End Try

opBuilder.Append(Me.GetMethodArgInfo(InvokedMethod.Name, argTypes))

Me.WriteText(opBuilder.ToString())
Me.MarkSequencePoint(opBuilder.ToString().Length)
End Sub
```

As you can see in the catch block, you're trying to retrieve the argument type list if the called method is a dynamic method. There's no guarantee that it'll be in there, but at least this is an attempt to show as much information in the miniCIL file as possible. GetMethodSignature() is a utility method used to retrieve the signature of a method:[9]

```
Private Function GetMethodSignature(ByVal TargetMethod As MethodBase) As String
    Dim sig As String

    If TypeOf TargetMethod Is MethodBuilder Then
        sig = CType(TargetMethod, MethodBuilder).Signature
    Else
        sig = CType(TargetMethod, ConstructorBuilder).Signature
    End If

    Return sig
End Function
```

The AddOpCode() method should be called before the client calls Emit(), as AddOpCode() will set the sequence point. As I stated before, the location of the MarkSequencePoint() calls are critical, so make sure these calls are done in the correct spot.

Now, if you use DebugFile in an assembly that generates a type that contains ReturnTheMethodImpl(), you should see a miniCIL file that looks like this:

---

9.   I find it odd that the Signature property is not defined on MethodBase or MethodInfo; if it were, the need for this method and its contained type casting would be unnecessary.

```
.class public ansi class ReturnImpl extends System.Object
    implements Debugging.IReturn
{
    .method public constructor hidebysig
        specialname standard .ctor()
    {
        ldarg.0
        call .ctor()
        ret
    }

    .method public virtual hidebysig hasthis
        standard Double ReturnTheDoubleImpl(System.Double V_1)
    {
        ldc.i4.3
        ldc.i4.0
        div
        pop
        ldarg.1
        ret
    }

}
```

The `.type` and `.method` definitions are actually on one line in the file; space constraints prevent me from showing that in this book. It's not pretty, but it works—in fact, the CIL shown in Figures 7-1 and 7-2 is generated from DebugFile.

SOURCE CODE *The ILDebug project contains the* DebugFile *class, which is used in the Debugging project. That project contains the code that implements* ReturnTheDoubleImpl()*. There's also a* TestClient *project that allows you to test the IL file generation and subsequent debugging.*

Debugging Transient Modules

As I mentioned in the section "Emitting Debug Information," there's another overload for DefineDynamicModule() that allows you to emit symbolic information for a transient module:

```
ReturnAsmModule = ReturnAsm.DefineDynamicModule( _
    RETURN_MODULE_NAME, True)
```

However, with respect to the source code file, transient modules act differently from persistent ones. If your emitted code causes an exception or you have a `break` opcode in the method, the debugger will not be able to find the source code file even if you called `DefineDocument()`. The debugger will report that the symbols were loaded for that module, but it will only be able to show the native assembly.

I wish I could give a concrete reason as to why this doesn't work. My best estimation[10] is that the file path is not added to the symbol store until the symbol store is closed by calling `Close()` on the `m_iSymWriter` field in the `Module` type. However, since `m_iSymWriter` is an interface type, there's no way to determine if that is the case. Furthermore, even if `m_iSymWriter` was a concrete type (that is, a class) that allows you to find out what `Close()` does, you can't determine when it would be called as there are methods on the `Module` type that can't be disassembled in ILDasm (for example, `InternalPreSavePEFile()` and `InternalSavePEFile()`).

> **NOTE** `DefineDynamicModuleInternal()` on `ModuleBuilder` *creates an* `ISymbolWriter`-*based type via* `GetInteralType()` *on an* `Assembly` *instance. However, this is also hidden in ILDasm, so I can't figure out what type the* `System.Diagnostics.SymbolStore.SymWriter` *string causes* `GetInternalType()` *to produce (and there's no* `SymWriter` *type in* `System.Diagnostics.SymbolStore` *either).*

Even if it could be determined when the source file path is saved to the symbol store, the fact of the matter is you can't get the debugger to find your source code file with symbol information emitted by a transient module. Therefore, if you need to debug your emitted code and you want to be able to step through source code, you'll need to make a persistable module.

Conclusion

In this chapter, you saw how you could use the Emitter classes to create new assemblies during the execution of your code. I covered the all aspects of assembly creation, including type definitions, method implementations, and debugging. In the next chapter, I'll tie all of the concepts covered in this book together in an example using dynamic code to intercept method invocation.

---

10. This information was found by digging around in mscorlib.dll using reverse-engineering tools; it's not something you'd find by using the .NET SDK.

CHAPTER 8

Dynamic Proxies
in .NET

In this chapter, I'll take everything that was discussed in the previous chapters and use that knowledge to create a real-world example. I'll create a dynamic type via the Emitter classes that allows you to intercept method invocations. I'll cover the design and its implementation along with other options that come with .NET.

Separating Concerns

How many times have you run into situations on a project where your methods are doing similar work? Consider the following C# method (which is a member of the SomeClass type):

```
public void StoreAnInt(int arg1)
{
    m_internalValue = arg1;
}
```

Since the Director of Software Engineering from Way Up High has just decided that every method needs some kind of tracing mechanism to make debugging problems easier, you need to add some logging code:

```
public void StoreAnInt (int arg1)
{
    TextWriter logFile = File.Append(@"c:\somedir\somelogfile.txt");
    logFile.WriteText((new StackFrame()).GetMethod().Name +
        " was invoked.");
    m_internalValue = arg1;
    logFile.WriteText ((new StackFrame()).GetMethod().Name +
        " is finished.");
    logFile.Close();
}
```

But it doesn't stop there. A week later, another mandate has been made: all critical method implementation code must be made synchronous to avoid potential threading problems:

```
public void StoreAnInt (int arg1)
{
    Monitor.Enter(this);
    TextWriter logFile = File.Append(@"c:\somedir\somelogfile.txt");
    logFile.WriteText((new StackFrame()).GetMethod().Name +
        " was invoked.");
    m_internalValue = arg1;
    logFile.WriteText ((new StackFrame()).GetMethod().Name +
        " is finished.");
    logFile.Close();
    Monitor.Exit(this);
}
```

By this time, the implementation of StoreAnInt() has grown from one line of code to six. Furthermore, my implementation of the mandates may be different from that of other developers. For example, I've chosen to log method activity to a local text file; another developer may choose to use a database, and yet another may use an XML file. I've also decided to use the Monitor type to lock the entire method; another developer may use a different locking mechanism, or vary when the locking occurs in the method. Finally, there's no definition as to when each requirement should occur. I've decided to lock the tracing code, but neither requirement states whether that's correct or not. Without any standards in place, the potential for discrepancies in implementation increases along with the possibility of bugs.

What would be nice is having some kind of mechanism in place that would add these trace statements and synchronization mechanisms generically, regardless of the class. That is, StoreAnInt() would store the value, and the generic code would log that StoreAnInt() was called with a particular value. One possible solution is to have two methods handle the requirements separately:

```
public void LockMethod(MethodBase LockedMethod,
    params object[] args)
{
    Monitor.Enter(this);
    LockedMethod.Invoke(this, args);
    Monitor.Exit(this);
}
```

```
public void TraceMethod(MethodBase TracedMethod,
    params object[] args)
{
    File logFile = new File(@"c:\somedir\somelogfile.txt",
        FileMode.Append);
    logFile.AppendText(TracedMethod.Name +
        " was invoked.");
    TracedMethod.Invoke(this, args);
    logFile.AppendText(TracedMethod.Name +
        " is finished.");
    logFile.Close();
}
```

However, the client is now responsible for knowing which method should be called first:

```
static void Main(string[] args)
{
    SomeClass sc = new SomeClass();
    MethodBase scMtd =
        sc.GetType().GetMethod("StoreAnInt");
    MethodBase scTrace =
        sc.GetType().GetMethod("TraceMethod");

    object[] intArgs = {42};
    object[] mthArgs = {scMtd, intArgs};

    sc.LockMethod(scTrace,  mthArgs);
}
```

You've now abstracted the implementations to methods that can be reused by other type methods. However, this is not the ideal solution by any means. All you've really done is move the majority of the complexity and responsibility to the client, which is not desirable.

What you really want is to move these concerns to a type such that the client and the server do not know, or care, that they are being used. In other words, when a client makes an instance of SomeClass, you need an "in-between" type that manages the synchronization and logging as shown in Figure 8-1.

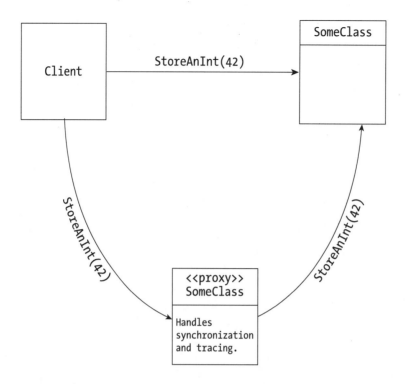

Figure 8-1. Intercepting StoreAnInt()

To the client, it appears to be making a normal StoreAnInt() call. However, the middle-man type intercepts that method invocation, handles the concerns, and then makes the actual StoreAnInt() call. Neither one knows, or cares, that the method has been synchronized or traced. In fact, you can choose not to invoke the method at all, which will make it appear to the client that the method suddenly had a no-op implementation.

This is great! As this simple example demonstrates, dynamic proxies allow the developer to extend a class's capabilities as well as separate aspects and services (for example, security, transactions, design-by-contract, and code adaptation) out of a class and make them generic to any class that needs them.

Functional Specifications

Given what you now know about CIL and the Emitter classes, you should be able to create an interceptor type as demonstrated earlier. Let's start by listing a number of specifications that you want this example app to accomplish, as this will help in designing the system:

- Given an object whose class has at least one accessible virtual method and is not sealed, create an object that extends and wraps that given object and forwards method invocations to the inner object's virtual methods.

- If a class has already had a proxy generated, simply generate the proxy object off of a cached proxy type.

- Before the method is invoked, let an invocation handler know which method will be invoked, and the method argument's values. Allow the client to prevent the method from being invoked.

- Once the method has been invoked, let the client know that it was invoked. Also, let the client know if the method generated an exception.

After I listed these specs, I came to the following conclusions:

- This application needs an interface that a client could implement in a class. This interface would be the link from the proxy object to the client to inform him or her of the pre- and post-method invocation events.

- To generate the proxy object, the application would have one static method on a class to keep things simple.

Class Design and Method Call Conditions

Now that I've outlined the design, let's make a class model, as that will give you a good foundation to work off of. You'll create a class called Proxy that has only one method: Create(). This method takes two parameters: the object to base the proxy code on and an array of InvocationHandler interface references. If Create() is successful, you'll get a reference to a new proxy object (NewProxy). However, since the NewProxy type is dynamic in that it'll be different for each given type, the return type is object; the client is responsible for casting the generated proxy to the correct type. The design is shown in Figure 8-2.

NOTE *If you want to view the source code as you read the chapter, the Proxy class is in the Proxies project, which is contained in the source code.*

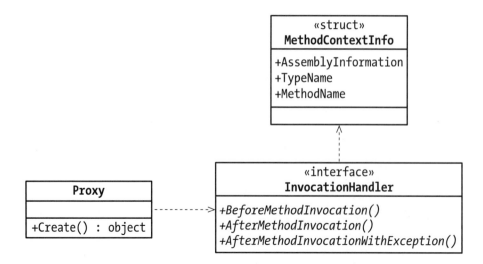

Figure 8-2. Proxy class diagram

Well, for the client there's not much to do—just call one method and the client's done. But what does an InvocationHandler implementor (or IH implementor for brevity's sake) do? Creating a class that inherits from InvocationHandler is trivial, but the issue you need to know here is how the methods work. Let's take each one step by step in the order you would get them if a method in a wrapped object was going to be invoked.

Receiving a Notification before Method Invocation

Before a method on the target object is invoked, the proxy object calls BeforeMethodInvocation(). This method takes four arguments. The first one, CurrentMethod, gives you information about the target method. It's of type MethodContextInfo, which has three read-only properties: AssemblyInformation (which is typed as an AssemblyName), TypeName, and MethodName (the latter two are strings). MethodArgs is the second argument—it contains the values for all of the arguments if any exist. Note that I do not provide the actual MethodInfo object that represents the method to be invoked, because I didn't want the client to have the ability to invoke the method.

The last two arguments, CallMethod and BubbleException, give the IH implementor some choices in the call flow. Specifically, the implementor has two choices to make. It can let the proxy object invoke the method by setting CallMethod to true. However, if the implementor doesn't want the real method to be invoked, it can prevent the call from occurring by setting CallMethod to false. The other argument,

BubbleException, tells the proxy object that if it catches an exception when BeforeMethodInvocation is called, it should rethrow the exception if the argument is true; otherwise, suppress the exception. This allows the implementor to not only prevent the call from being made, but also create an exception to the client. By default, Proxy will set CallMethod to true and BubbleException to false.

Let's look at two code snippets to demonstrate how these Boolean arguments work:

```
public void BeforeMethodInvocation(MethodContextInfo CurrentMethod,
    ref object[] MethodArgs, ref bool CallMethod, ref bool BubbleException)
{
    CallMethod = false;
    BubbleException = false;
}
```

The IH implementor doesn't want any generated exceptions to be rethrown to the proxy client, but he or she doesn't want the method invoked. Now take a look at this snippet:

```
public void BeforeMethodInvocation(MethodContextInfo CurrentMethod,
    ref object[] MethodArgs, ref bool CallMethod, ref bool BubbleException)
{
    CallMethod = true;
    BubbleException = true;
}
```

In this case, if an exception is created, the proxy should throw it to the client and not call the method. However, if no exception occurs, call the method.

Receiving a Notification after Method Invocation

If the IH implementor allows the method to be invoked in BeforeMethodInvocation(), the target method will be called. If the invocation did not throw an exception, then the proxy object will call AfterMethodInvocation(). The first two arguments are similar to the first two in BeforeMethodInvocation(). The arguments are given to allow the handler to change any by-reference arguments after the target method is finished. The third argument, ReturnValue, contains the return value of the method. If the method doesn't have a return value or the method didn't return a value, this will be equal to null. Again, the handler has the option to create an exception and rethrow it by setting BubbleException appropriately.

When Method Invocations Go Bad

Not every method invocation will happen without an exception occurring.
If a method throws an exception, AfterMethodInvocationWithException() will be
called. This method gives the IH implementor the method information and a reference to an Exception-based object called GeneratedException that was thrown by the
proxy's wrapped object's method. There are two by-reference Boolean types,
BubbleGeneratedException and BubbleException. The first one, if set to true, will
rethrow GeneratedException. If it's false and BubbleException is true, any exception
generated by AfterMethodInvocationWithException() will be rethrown. By default,
BubbleException will be true, as there needs to be a directed decision to not throw
an exception that the target method generated. However, BubbleGeneratedException
is false by default.

Proxy Call Flow

To make the method call transition clearer, I've created a call flow diagram illustrating a simple method invocation on a dynamic proxy (see Figure 8-3).

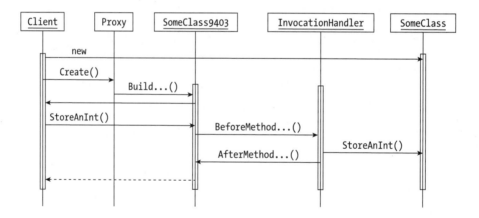

Figure 8-3. Dynamic proxy call flow

In this case, the client creates an instance of SomeClass and passes it on to
Proxy's Create(). Create() calls a bunch of internal Build...() methods to create the
proxy for SomeClass() (which is what the rest of the chapter will show). This proxy
instance is returned to the client, which then calls StoreAnInt(). The call is inter-
cepted, and BeforeMethodInvocation() is called. The underlying implementation is
then called, and the appropriate AfterMethod...() call is made. Finally, if a return
value is needed, it is returned to the client.

Implementing Proxy Creation

It's one thing to talk about what you'd like to have Create() do. It's quite another to actually implement the design decisions. Therefore, I'm going to break down each part of Create() and discuss in detail what you need to do to create a proxy.

Preconditional Checks

Before any proxy generation code is run, make a couple of checks on the given arguments to Create():

```
public static Object Create(Object BaseObject, InvocationHandler[] Handlers)
// Local variables are declared here...
if(null == BaseObject) {
    throw new ArgumentNullException(BASE_OBJECT_ARG_NAME,
        ERROR_BASE_OBJECT_NULL);
}

if(null == Handlers) {
    throw new ArgumentNullException(HANDLERS_ARG_NAME,
        ERROR_HANDLERS_NULL);
}

if(0 == Handlers.Length) {
    throw new ArgumentException(ERROR_HANDLERS_NONE,
        HANDLERS_ARG_NAME);
}

if(BaseObject.GetType().IsAbstract) {
    throw new ArgumentException(ERROR_BASE_OBJECT_ABSTRACT,
        BASE_OBJECT_ARG_NAME);
}

if(BaseObject.GetType().IsSealed) {
    throw new ArgumentException(ERROR_BASE_OBJECT_SEALED,
        BASE_OBJECT_ARG_NAME);
}

Hashtable targets = GetTargetMethods(BaseObject);
if(0 == targets.Count) {
    throw new ArgumentException(ERROR_BASE_OBJECT_NO_METHODS,
        BASE_OBJECT_ARG_NAME);
}
```

Most of the method preconditions are self-explanatory (for example, it doesn't make sense to create a proxy for a given object if the given reference is null). However, the last one isn't as obvious. A call is made to GetTargetMethods(), and if the resulting hashtable has no items, an exception is thrown. What GetTargetMethods() does is create a list of methods on the base object that you can hook. However, it's not as simple as iterating through all of the methods on the base object and selecting all the virtual ones. You have to be careful to not select virtual methods that are not public, as there's no way for you to access them. As you saw in the last chapter, VB .NET and C# can create public virtual methods that implement interface methods, but the compilers make the methods final by default. Therefore, you have to ignore the implementation method, but you must hook the interface methods. Furthermore, you know that a method can implement a number of interface methods, so you should try to have your proxy class reflect that design as well.

Let's see what GetTargetMethods() looks like:

```
private static Hashtable GetTargetMethods(Object BaseObject)
{
    Type baseType = BaseObject.GetType();
    Hashtable retVal = new Hashtable();

    foreach(Type itf in baseType.GetInterfaces())
    {
        InterfaceMapping imap = baseType.GetInterfaceMap(itf);
        for(int i = 0; i < imap.InterfaceMethods.Length; i++)
        {
            MethodInfo trueTarget;
            if(true == imap.TargetMethods[i].IsPublic)
            {
                trueTarget = imap.TargetMethods[i];
            }
            else
            {
                trueTarget = imap.InterfaceMethods[i];
            }

            MethodMappings itfMM = (MethodMappings)retVal[trueTarget];
            if(null == itfMM)
            {
                itfMM = new MethodMappings(trueTarget, true);
                retVal.Add(trueTarget, itfMM);
            }

            itfMM.MappedMethods.Add(imap.InterfaceMethods[i]);
        }
    }
```

This is half of the implementation code for `GetTargetMethods()`. In this section, you iterate through all of the interfaces that the base object implements. For each interface, you get a mapping of interface methods to target methods via the `InterfaceMapping` structure. Next, you iterate through each interface method. If the interface's target method is public, then you know you can invoke that method rather than the interface's method. If not, then you have no choice but to hook the interface method itself. Of course, a number of interface methods can be implemented by one method, so you create a `MethodMappings` class that allows you to keep track of which methods the target method overrides. That's what the hashtable contains—a list of `MethodMappings` objects that are keyed off of the target method.

Let's take a look at the other half of `GetTargetMethods()`:

```
foreach(MethodInfo mi in baseType.GetMethods())
{
    if(mi.IsPublic && mi.IsVirtual && !mi.IsFinal)
    {
        MethodMappings baseMM = (MethodMappings)retVal[mi];
        if(null == baseMM)
        {
            baseMM = new MethodMappings(mi, false);
            retVal.Add(mi, baseMM);
            baseMM.MappedMethods.Add(mi);
        }
    }
}
return retVal;
}
```

Now turn your attention to the base methods. If the method is virtual and public but not final, you can hook it. In this case, the target method is the same as the mapped method.

Note that in both sections, the second value to the `MethodMappings` constructor is different. For interface methods, it's true, but for base methods, it's false. This is reflected in the read-only `OverridesInterfaceMethods`. This property will become important when you actually hook the methods later on.

Caching Types, Modules, and Assemblies

Assuming that the given object satisfies all of the preconditions in Create(), you can now start creating the proxy:

```
baseType = BaseObject.GetType();

typeKey = baseType.Assembly.FullName + "::" +
    baseType.FullName;
typeKey = typeKey.GetHashCode().ToString();

proxyCtorArgs = new Object[2];
proxyCtorArgs[0] = BaseObject;
proxyCtorArgs[1] = Handlers;

if(true == createdTypes.ContainsKey(typeKey))
{
    newProxy = Activator.CreateInstance(
        (Type)createdTypes[typeKey], proxyCtorArgs);
}
else
{
```

I'll cover the else block in a moment; I want to make a brief point about the CreateInstance() call first. Note that you use the hash code of the assembly name plus the type name to see if you've already made a proxy for the given type. It takes some time to create a proxy, and if a client is trying to create 20 proxies for the same type, there's no reason to regenerate the proxy code every time. Therefore, you store the generated proxy in a hashtable and, if you find it, you create an instance of the cached type (passing in the appropriate constructor values). You use the hash code values to mangle assembly, type, and method names. You want to reduce the chance of creating items that may collide with preexisting items, so you append these hash codes at the appropriate times. Ultimately, the client should never call the generated proxy, so it won't see a bunch of oddly named methods that it has to call.

Of course, if you haven't encountered this type yet, you need to create the proxy for it, so you need to make a dynamic assembly and module:

```
assemblyKey = baseType.Assembly.FullName.GetHashCode().ToString();

if(true == createdModules.ContainsKey(assemblyKey))
{
```

```
        proxyModule = (ModuleBuilder)createdModules[assemblyKey];
}
else
{
    newAssemblyName = new AssemblyName();
    baseAssemblyName = baseType.Assembly.GetName();
    newAssemblyName.Name = baseAssemblyName.Name + assemblyKey;
    newAssemblyName.Version = baseAssemblyName.Version;

    #if DEBUG
    proxyAssembly = AppDomain.CurrentDomain.DefineDynamicAssembly(
        newAssemblyName, AssemblyBuilderAccess.RunAndSave);

    proxyModule = proxyAssembly.DefineDynamicModule(
        newAssemblyName.Name,
        newAssemblyName.Name + ".dll");
    #else
    proxyAssembly = AppDomain.CurrentDomain.DefineDynamicAssembly(
        newAssemblyName, AssemblyBuilderAccess.Run);

    proxyModule = proxyAssembly.DefineDynamicModule(
        newAssemblyName.Name);
    #endif
    createdModules.Add(assemblyKey, proxyModule);
}
```

Along with types, you also cache dynamic modules. If you encounter two different types from the same module, you might as well put them into the same dynamic module, so that's why the dynamic module is cached.

You'll note that I've left in the conditional compilations in the code snippet. For a debug build of the Proxies assembly, you use assemblies and modules that can be run but also saved. In a release build, you don't want to write anything to disk, so leave them as transients. When constructing this application, I noticed that as I developed the Proxy class it was easier to just persist the generated code and examine it with ILDasm and PEVerify to rectify any bugs, so this example doesn't contain debug builds of the dynamic assemblies for a Proxies debug build. You can change this if you want—just use the DebugFile class from Chapter 7 and set emitSymbolInformation to true—but I personally didn't see the need for it here.

Of course, if you're using the debug build of the Proxies assembly, you'll want to save the dynamic assemblies eventually. However, you can't do it in Create(), as it's possible that the method may be given another type from the same module.

If you persist it, you'd get an error. Therefore, you also need to cache the dynamic assemblies in debug mode:

```
proxyType = proxyModule.DefineType(
    baseType.Namespace.ToString() + "." + baseType.Name + typeKey,
    TypeAttributes.Class | TypeAttributes.Sealed |
    TypeAttributes.Public, baseType);

invokeHandlers = proxyType.DefineField(INVOKE_HANDLER_FIELD,
    Handlers.GetType(), FieldAttributes.Private);
wrappedObject = proxyType.DefineField(WRAPPED_OBJECT_FIELD,
    BaseObject.GetType(), FieldAttributes.Private);

BuildParameterlessConstructor(proxyType, baseType);
BuildConstructor(baseType, proxyType, wrappedObject, invokeHandlers);
AddInterfaces(baseType, proxyType);
invokeMethod = BuildInvokeMethod(proxyType, invokeHandlers,
    wrappedObject);

BuildTargetMethods(proxyType, invokeMethod, wrappedObject, targets);
newProxyType = proxyType.CreateType();

#if DEBUG
if(null == createdAssemblies[assemblyKey])
{
    createdAssemblies.Add(assemblyKey, proxyAssembly);
}
#endif

newProxy = Activator.CreateInstance(newProxyType, proxyCtorArgs);
createdTypes.Add(typeKey, newProxyType);
```

Ignore the first two-thirds of this code snippet as I'm only showing it to finish out Create(); I'll cover that code in the section "Defining the Constructors." As you can see, once the proxy is created, you store that type in the appropriate hashtable. However, if this is a debug build, you also store the assembly. To actually persist the assemblies, you add another method to Proxy called Persist():

```
#if DEBUG
public static void Persist()
{
    foreach(AssemblyBuilder ab in createdAssemblies.Values)
    {
        ab.Save(ab.GetName().Name + ".dll");
    }
}
#endif
```

Note that I would never intentionally release a debug build of Proxy to anyone because of this method, and you shouldn't either. A client may get confused as to why this method is there. This is only for debugging purposes—it allows you to save proxy-generated code when you are ready to do so in a test client.

Defining the Constructors

You've now seen what Create() does at a somewhat high-level to optimize proxy type generation and assembly persistence. Now let's start uncovering how the proxy is actually created. You already saw in the last section that when you create a proxy type, it inherits from the given type and it is defined as being public as well as sealed.[1] You don't want to take the proxy you just created and try to extend it in any way, but the client will need to be able to access it. Next, you create two fields—invokeHandlers, which will store the InvocationHandler references, and wrappedObject, which will reference the given object.

Once the proxy type is defined, you create two constructors. One is the default no-argument constructor, and the other takes two arguments. Let's take a look at how the default constructor is made:

```
private static void BuildParameterlessConstructor(
    TypeBuilder BaseProxy, Type BaseType)
{
    ConstructorBuilder proxyCtor =
        BaseProxy.DefineConstructor(MethodAttributes.Private |
        MethodAttributes.SpecialName | MethodAttributes.RTSpecialName |
        MethodAttributes.HideBySig, CallingConventions.Standard,
        System.Type.EmptyTypes);
```

---

1. That code was in the section I asked you to ignore. Usually if someone tells me to ignore a piece of information, I immediately look at it, and I'm guessing that you probably did as well!

```
    ILGenerator proxyCtorIL = proxyCtor.GetILGenerator();
    proxyCtorIL.Emit(OpCodes.Ldarg_0);
    ConstructorInfo objectCtor = BaseType.GetConstructor(
        System.Type.EmptyTypes);
    proxyCtorIL.Emit(OpCodes.Call, objectCtor);
    proxyCtorIL.Emit(OpCodes.Ret);
}
```

This is pretty simple as far as the CIL generation for a proxy goes. All you do is invoke the parent's constructor. Note, though, that the default constructor is private—I'll explain why after I cover the second constructor's construction:

```
private static void BuildConstructor(
    Type BaseObjectType, TypeBuilder BaseProxy,
    FieldBuilder WrappedType, FieldBuilder InvokeHandlers)
{
    Type[] proxyCtorArgs = new Type[2];
    proxyCtorArgs[0] = BaseObjectType;
    proxyCtorArgs[1] = typeof(Proxies.InvocationHandler[]);
    ConstructorBuilder proxyCtor =
        BaseProxy.DefineConstructor(MethodAttributes.Public |
            MethodAttributes.SpecialName | MethodAttributes.RTSpecialName |
            MethodAttributes.HideBySig, CallingConventions.Standard,
            proxyCtorArgs);

    ILGenerator proxyCtorIL = proxyCtor.GetILGenerator();
    proxyCtorIL.Emit(OpCodes.Ldarg_0);
    ConstructorInfo objectCtor =
        BaseObjectType.GetConstructor(System.Type.EmptyTypes);
    proxyCtorIL.Emit(OpCodes.Call, objectCtor);
    proxyCtorIL.Emit(OpCodes.Ldarg_0);
    proxyCtorIL.Emit(OpCodes.Ldarg_1);
    proxyCtorIL.Emit(OpCodes.Stfld, WrappedType);
    proxyCtorIL.Emit(OpCodes.Ldarg_0);
    proxyCtorIL.Emit(OpCodes.Ldarg_2);
    proxyCtorIL.Emit(OpCodes.Stfld, InvokeHandlers);
    proxyCtorIL.Emit(OpCodes.Ret);
}
```

This is the only public constructor on the proxy. If a client really wants to cache the generated proxy types, the only way they'd be able to create new instances is by passing in the appropriate type along with an InvocationHandler-based array, which is what you should do with a cached proxy anyway when Create() is called. At least you're protecting yourself a bit from a user creating the proxy via the default constructor, which would leave the fields uninitialized. That would not be a good thing.

Implementing the Interfaces

After the constructors are defined, you need to have the proxy type implement the base object's interfaces:

```
private static void AddInterfaces(Type BaseObjectType, TypeBuilder BaseProxy)
{
    foreach(Type baseInterface in BaseObjectType.GetInterfaces())
    {
        if(true == baseInterface.IsPublic)
        {
            BaseProxy.AddInterfaceImplementation(baseInterface);
        }
    }
}
```

This is very straightforward. If a given interface is public, you call AddInterfaceImplementation on the TypeBuilder reference. By doing this, you ensure that you've implemented the same interfaces as the base type.

Invoking Target Methods

Finally, we get to the heart of the matter: invoking the target method on the base object. Each proxy has a private method called InvokeMethod() that handles the pre- and post-processing for any method hook in the proxy. This method is rather large—in fact, you'll notice in the source code that I use regions to divide the code into logical groups. I'll mimic that grouping by covering each section of code separately.

Defining InvokeMethod()

Before anything else happens, InvokeMethod() needs to be defined:

```
private static MethodInfo BuildInvokeMethod(TypeBuilder BaseProxy,
    FieldBuilder InvokeHandlers, FieldBuilder WrappedObject)
{
    Type[] invokeArgTypes = new Type[3];
    invokeArgTypes[0] = typeof(System.Reflection.MethodInfo);
    invokeArgTypes[1] = Type.GetType("System.Object[]&");
    invokeArgTypes[2] = typeof(Proxies.MethodContextInfo);

    MethodBuilder invokeMethod = BaseProxy.DefineMethod(INVOKE_METHOD,
        MethodAttributes.Private | MethodAttributes.HideBySig,
        CallingConventions.HasThis,
        typeof(System.Object), invokeArgTypes);

    invokeMethod.DefineParameter(2,
        (ParameterAttributes.In | ParameterAttributes.Out),
        "methodArgs");
```

InvokeMethod() takes three arguments. The first one is the target method to invoke. The second argument is the target method's arguments. Note that the array will be passed by reference so the IH implementors will be able to alter the argument values if they need to. The third argument is a MethodContextInfo object that will be passed to the InvocationHandler methods so the implementors of that interface will know which method is the current target.

There are also a number of local variables for InvokeMethod():

```
LocalBuilder raiseException = invokeMethodIL.DeclareLocal(typeof(System.Boolean));
LocalBuilder doInvoke = invokeMethodIL.DeclareLocal(typeof(System.Boolean));
LocalBuilder bubbleEx = invokeMethodIL.DeclareLocal(typeof(System.Boolean));
LocalBuilder bubbleGenEx = invokeMethodIL.DeclareLocal(typeof(System.Boolean));
LocalBuilder success = invokeMethodIL.DeclareLocal(typeof(System.Boolean));
LocalBuilder retVal = invokeMethodIL.DeclareLocal(typeof(System.Object));
LocalBuilder invokeEx = invokeMethodIL.DeclareLocal(typeof(System.Exception));
LocalBuilder i = invokeMethodIL.DeclareLocal(typeof(System.Int32));
```

I'll leave their initialization out of the discussion. You'll see them appear in the following code snippets.

Calling BeforeMethodInvocation()

The first real activity that goes on in InvokeMethod() is that BeforeMethodInvocation() must be called on each InvocationHandler reference. To iterate through the array, a couple of labels need to be defined:

```
Label doNextHandlerBefore = invokeMethodIL.DefineLabel();
Label finishBefore = invokeMethodIL.DefineLabel();
Label incrementIBefore = invokeMethodIL.DefineLabel();
Label preventInvokeBefore = invokeMethodIL.DefineLabel();
Label ignoreBeforeEx = invokeMethodIL.DefineLabel();
```

Now the processing can begin:

```
invokeMethodIL.BeginExceptionBlock();
invokeMethodIL.MarkLabel(doNextHandlerBefore);
//  Reset the by-ref booleans.
invokeMethodIL.Emit(OpCodes.Ldc_I4_1);
invokeMethodIL.Emit(OpCodes.Stloc, doInvoke);
invokeMethodIL.Emit(OpCodes.Ldc_I4_0);
invokeMethodIL.Emit(OpCodes.Stloc, raiseException);
//  Load the next handler.
invokeMethodIL.Emit(OpCodes.Ldarg_0);
invokeMethodIL.Emit(OpCodes.Ldfld, InvokeHandlers);
invokeMethodIL.Emit(OpCodes.Ldloc, i);
invokeMethodIL.Emit(OpCodes.Ldelem_Ref);
//  Load the handler's arguments.
invokeMethodIL.Emit(OpCodes.Ldarg_3);
invokeMethodIL.Emit(OpCodes.Ldarg_2);
invokeMethodIL.Emit(OpCodes.Ldloca, doInvoke);
invokeMethodIL.Emit(OpCodes.Ldloca, raiseException);
//  BeforeInvocationHandler.
invokeMethodIL.Emit(OpCodes.Callvirt,
    typeof(Proxies.InvocationHandler).GetMethod(BEFORE_INVOKE));
```

I'm going to leave the comments in for most of the InvokeMethod() code snippets. It can become rather difficult to follow what you're doing when you're implementing a method in CIL via the Emitter classes, so I think the comments serve as helpful reference points.

Anyway, as you can see, an exception block is set up, and then each InvocationHandler reference is pushed onto the stack via the Ldarg_0, Ldfld, Ldloc, and Ldeleme_Ref OpCode values so BeforeMethodInvocation() can be invoked. The

reason why all of the processing takes place within an exception block is to catch
any exceptions that BeforeMethodInvocation() may throw:

```
//  If doInvoke == false, stop loop.
//  Note that the "br finishBefore" will keep
//  doInvoke == false.
invokeMethodIL.Emit(OpCodes.Ldloc, doInvoke);
invokeMethodIL.Emit(OpCodes.Brtrue, incrementIBefore);
invokeMethodIL.Emit(OpCodes.Br, finishBefore);
//  Increment i.
invokeMethodIL.MarkLabel(incrementIBefore);
invokeMethodIL.Emit(OpCodes.Ldloc, i);
invokeMethodIL.Emit(OpCodes.Ldc_I4_1);
invokeMethodIL.Emit(OpCodes.Add);
invokeMethodIL.Emit(OpCodes.Stloc, i);
//  See if i < invokeHandlers.Length.
invokeMethodIL.Emit(OpCodes.Ldloc, i);
invokeMethodIL.Emit(OpCodes.Ldarg_0);
invokeMethodIL.Emit(OpCodes.Ldfld, InvokeHandlers);
invokeMethodIL.Emit(OpCodes.Ldlen);
invokeMethodIL.Emit(OpCodes.Conv_I4);
invokeMethodIL.Emit(OpCodes.Blt, doNextHandlerBefore);
//  Exit loop.
invokeMethodIL.MarkLabel(finishBefore);
invokeMethodIL.BeginCatchBlock(typeof(System.Exception));
//  If raiseException == true, rethrow exception.
invokeMethodIL.Emit(OpCodes.Ldloc, raiseException);
invokeMethodIL.Emit(OpCodes.Brfalse, ignoreBeforeEx);
//  Note that the exception is on the stack here.
invokeMethodIL.Emit(OpCodes.Throw);
invokeMethodIL.MarkLabel(ignoreBeforeEx);
invokeMethodIL.EndExceptionBlock();
```

Even if an exception occurs, raiseException (which translates into the
BubbleException argument value) may still be false, so you don't want bad code in
BeforeMethodInvocation() to prevent the actual method invocation.

Calling the Target Method

Once the preprocessing is finished and an exception isn't raised, you need to check to see if CallMethod (or doInvoke) is true. If it is, you can make the invocation:

```
// OK, all the Before...() methods were called,
// and we got here.  If doInvoke == true,
// call the method.
Label performInvoke = invokeMethodIL.DefineLabel();
Label doNotPerformInvoke = invokeMethodIL.DefineLabel();
invokeMethodIL.Emit(OpCodes.Ldloc, doInvoke);
invokeMethodIL.Emit(OpCodes.Brtrue, performInvoke);
// Set success to false, since the method will not be invoked.
invokeMethodIL.Emit(OpCodes.Ldc_I4_0);
invokeMethodIL.Emit(OpCodes.Stloc, success);
invokeMethodIL.Emit(OpCodes.Br, doNotPerformInvoke);
invokeMethodIL.MarkLabel(performInvoke);
invokeMethodIL.BeginExceptionBlock();
// Load the target method and its associated object.
invokeMethodIL.Emit(OpCodes.Ldarg_1);
invokeMethodIL.Emit(OpCodes.Ldarg_0);
invokeMethodIL.Emit(OpCodes.Ldfld, WrappedObject);
invokeMethodIL.Emit(OpCodes.Ldarg_2);
invokeMethodIL.Emit(OpCodes.Ldind_Ref);
// Invoke...
argTypes = new Type[2];
argTypes[0] = typeof(System.Object);
argTypes[1] = typeof(System.Object[]);
    invokeMethodIL.Emit(OpCodes.Callvirt,
    typeof(System.Reflection.MethodInfo).GetMethod(INVOKE, argTypes));
invokeMethodIL.Emit(OpCodes.Stloc, retVal);
// Set success to true.
invokeMethodIL.Emit(OpCodes.Ldc_I4_1);
invokeMethodIL.Emit(OpCodes.Stloc, success);
```

Note that if doInvoke is false, you set success to false as well. This will prevent any post-processing from occurring. Calling the target method is actually pretty easy. You get the target object reference loaded (via Ldarg_0 and Ldfld) along with the by-reference argument array (Ldind_Ref), and then you call Invoke() on the given target method.

Handling Exceptional Target Method Invocations

If the target method throws an exception, you need to call all the
AfterMethodInvocationWithException() methods:

```
invokeMethodIL.BeginCatchBlock(typeof(System.Exception));
invokeMethodIL.Emit(OpCodes.Stloc, invokeEx);
//  The invoked method caused an exception.
//  We need to iterate through each After...Ex() method
//  and throw the appropriate exception.
invokeMethodIL.BeginExceptionBlock();
Label doNextHandlerAfterEx = invokeMethodIL.DefineLabel();
Label incrementIAfterEx = invokeMethodIL.DefineLabel();
//  Reset i = 0;
invokeMethodIL.Emit(OpCodes.Ldc_I4_0);
invokeMethodIL.Emit(OpCodes.Stloc, i);
invokeMethodIL.MarkLabel(doNextHandlerAfterEx);
//  Reset the by-ref booleans.
invokeMethodIL.Emit(OpCodes.Ldc_I4_1);
invokeMethodIL.Emit(OpCodes.Stloc, bubbleEx);
invokeMethodIL.Emit(OpCodes.Ldc_I4_0);
invokeMethodIL.Emit(OpCodes.Stloc, bubbleGenEx);
//  Load the next handler.
invokeMethodIL.Emit(OpCodes.Ldarg_0);
invokeMethodIL.Emit(OpCodes.Ldfld, InvokeHandlers);
invokeMethodIL.Emit(OpCodes.Ldloc, i);
invokeMethodIL.Emit(OpCodes.Ldelem_Ref);
//  Load the handler's arguments.
invokeMethodIL.Emit(OpCodes.Ldarg_3);
invokeMethodIL.Emit(OpCodes.Ldloc, invokeEx);
invokeMethodIL.Emit(OpCodes.Ldloca, bubbleGenEx);
invokeMethodIL.Emit(OpCodes.Ldloca, bubbleEx);
//  AfterInvocationHandlerWithException.
invokeMethodIL.Emit(OpCodes.Callvirt,
    typeof(Proxies.InvocationHandler).GetMethod(AFTER_INVOKE_EX));
```

This is where it gets tricky. You're trying to tell the InvocationHandler implementors that the target method failed, but AfterMethodInvocationWithException() may throw an exception as well. That's why another try block was created. Now, if the interface method doesn't throw an exception, you look at what the IH implementor wants to do:

```
Label rethrowEx = invokeMethodIL.DefineLabel();
invokeMethodIL.Emit(OpCodes.Ldloc, bubbleGenEx);
invokeMethodIL.Emit(OpCodes.Brtrue, rethrowEx);
invokeMethodIL.Emit(OpCodes.Ldloc, bubbleEx);
invokeMethodIL.Emit(OpCodes.Brfalse, incrementIAfterEx);
invokeMethodIL.MarkLabel(rethrowEx);
invokeMethodIL.Emit(OpCodes.Rethrow);
// Increment i.
invokeMethodIL.MarkLabel(incrementIAfterEx);
invokeMethodIL.Emit(OpCodes.Ldloc, i);
invokeMethodIL.Emit(OpCodes.Ldc_I4_1);
invokeMethodIL.Emit(OpCodes.Add);
invokeMethodIL.Emit(OpCodes.Stloc, i);
// See if i < invokeHandlers.Length.
invokeMethodIL.Emit(OpCodes.Ldloc, i);
invokeMethodIL.Emit(OpCodes.Ldarg_0);
invokeMethodIL.Emit(OpCodes.Ldfld, InvokeHandlers);
invokeMethodIL.Emit(OpCodes.Ldlen);
invokeMethodIL.Emit(OpCodes.Conv_I4);
invokeMethodIL.Emit(OpCodes.Blt, doNextHandlerAfterEx);
```

If the IH implementor that's currently referenced wants the method exception thrown, then you call Throw. Otherwise, keep on iterating through the interface references.

Now, if the interface method threw an exception or the interface method results said that the method exception should be thrown, you'll jump into your second catch block:

```
invokeMethodIL.BeginCatchBlock(typeof(System.Exception));
// If bubbleEx == true or bubbleGenEx == true, rethrow exception.
Label throwIt = invokeMethodIL.DefineLabel();
Label doNotThrowIt = invokeMethodIL.DefineLabel();
invokeMethodIL.Emit(OpCodes.Ldloc, bubbleGenEx);
invokeMethodIL.Emit(OpCodes.Brtrue, throwIt);
invokeMethodIL.Emit(OpCodes.Ldloc, bubbleEx);
invokeMethodIL.Emit(OpCodes.Brfalse, doNotThrowIt);
// Note that the exception is on the stack here...
invokeMethodIL.MarkLabel(throwIt);
invokeMethodIL.Emit(OpCodes.Rethrow);
invokeMethodIL.MarkLabel(doNotThrowIt);
invokeMethodIL.EndExceptionBlock();
invokeMethodIL.EndExceptionBlock();
invokeMethodIL.MarkLabel(doNotPerformInvoke);
```

The logic is the same as before—the exception is rethrown only if the implementation of `AfterMethodInvocationWithException()` says so.

Handling Exception-Free Target Method Invocations

If the target method was successful, you need to iterate through the `InvocationHandler` references and call `AfterMethodInvocation()`. The logic is virtually the same as what I've already covered for the other two interface methods so I won't show it again here.

Setting Up the Method Hooks

Once `BuildInvokeMethod()` is done, you need to set up the method hooks so they call `InvokeMethod()`, which is performed in `BuildTargetMethods()`. However, as every method is different, you need to adjust the generated CIL for each method. As with `InvokeMethod()`, I'll break down how the hook methods are generated into subsections.

Defining Method Overrides

Remember when you got a list of target methods to determine if you should even create a proxy for a given object? Well, now you're going to use that list to set up the hooks; this implementation is shown in Listing 8-1.

Listing 8-1. Setting Up the Method Hooks

```
private static void BuildTargetMethods(TypeBuilder BaseProxy,
    MethodInfo InvokeMethod, FieldBuilder WrappedObject,
    Hashtable TargetMethods)
{
    methodAttribs = MethodAttributes.HideBySig |
        MethodAttributes.Virtual | MethodAttributes.Private;

    foreach(DictionaryEntry de in TargetMethods)
    {
        mi = (MethodInfo)de.Key;

        argTypes = new Type[mi.GetParameters().Length];
```

```
for(int i = 0; i < mi.GetParameters().Length; i++)
{
    argTypes[i] = mi.GetParameters()[i].ParameterType;
}

proxyMethod = BaseProxy.DefineMethod(mi.Name + mi.GetHashCode(),
    methodAttribs, mi.ReturnType, argTypes);

MethodMappings mm = (MethodMappings)de.Value;

if(false == mm.OverridesInterfaceMethods)
{
    BaseProxy.DefineMethodOverride(proxyMethod, mi);
}
else
{
    for(int itfs = 0; itfs < mm.MappedMethods.Count; itfs++)
    {
        MethodInfo itfMth =
            (MethodInfo)mm.MappedMethods[itfs];
        BaseProxy.DefineMethodOverride(proxyMethod, itfMth);
    }
}
```

All of the target methods are duplicated as private methods in the proxy type. Once the method is defined on the proxy itself via DefineMethod(), you need to determine if the target method overrides interface methods or not. If it doesn't, then you know that you're overriding a nonfinal, public virtual method on the base type. If it does, then you iterate through each method in MappedMethods and override each interface method.

Base Method Invocation Setup

As I mentioned before, each method will be different in argument composition. Therefore, how you put values into the object array will vary from method to method; this logic is shown in Listing 8-2.

Listing 8-2. Handling Different Method Argument Compositions

```
argValues = proxyMthIL.DeclareLocal(typeof(System.Object[]));
methodCxtInfo = proxyMthIL.DeclareLocal(typeof(Proxies.MethodContextInfo));
targetMethod = proxyMthIL.DeclareLocal(typeof(System.Reflection.MethodInfo));
wrappedType = proxyMthIL.DeclareLocal(typeof(System.Type));

// Check for a return value.
if(typeof(void) != mi.ReturnType)
{
    tempRetVal = proxyMthIL.DeclareLocal(typeof(System.Object));
    retVal = proxyMthIL.DeclareLocal(mi.ReturnType);
}

proxyMthIL.Emit(OpCodes.Ldc_I4, mi.GetParameters().Length);
proxyMthIL.Emit(OpCodes.Newarr, typeof(System.Object));

// Set up the arg array
if(0 == mi.GetParameters().Length)
{
    // Store in argValues - there's no values
    // to put into the array.
    proxyMthIL.Emit(OpCodes.Stloc, argValues);
}
else
{
    proxyMthIL.Emit(OpCodes.Stloc, argValues);
    for(int argLoad = 0; argLoad < mi.GetParameters().Length; argLoad++)
    {
        proxyMthIL.Emit(OpCodes.Ldloc, argValues);
        proxyMthIL.Emit(OpCodes.Ldc_I4, argLoad);
        proxyMthIL.Emit(OpCodes.Ldarg, argLoad + 1);
        pi = mi.GetParameters()[argLoad];

        paramTypeName = pi.ParameterType.ToString();
        paramTypeName = paramTypeName.Replace("&", "");
        paramType = Type.GetType(paramTypeName);

        if(pi.ParameterType.IsByRef)
        {
            proxyMthIL.Emit(OpCodes.Ldobj, paramType);
        }
```

```
        if(paramType.IsValueType)
        {
            proxyMthIL.Emit(OpCodes.Box, paramType);
        }

        proxyMthIL.Emit(OpCodes.Stelem_Ref);
    }
}
```

The first problem is the return value of the method. Either a method will return nothing (or void), or it will return a value. In the case of a return value existing, you need to declare two extra local variables to handle value and reference types correctly—you'll see how these work when I get to the code that calls the target method, which is in the section "Calling InvokeMethod()."

Now, if the target method takes no parameters, you leave argValues as a new object array with no elements. If there are arguments, you store them in the object array. Note that you have to handle value type accordingly by boxing the value into an object type. Also note that all array elements are stored by-reference (Stelem_Ref) to enable argument value manipulation in IH implementations.

Configuring the Method Context Object

Before you call InvokeMethod(), you need to create a MethodContextInfo object. You have to be a bit careful with the values that you use—for example, you can't get the name of the type where the code for the hook method exists, because that's the proxy object and not the target object. The client would get pretty confused if it saw Person65734829 show up as the type name, so you have to make sure that you grab the "right" values:

```
// Get the target method.
proxyMthIL.Emit(OpCodes.Ldtoken, mi);
proxyMthIL.Emit(OpCodes.Call,
    typeof(System.Reflection.MethodBase).GetMethod(GET_METHOD_FROM_HANDLE));
proxyMthIL.Emit(OpCodes.Castclass,
    typeof(System.Reflection.MethodInfo));
proxyMthIL.Emit(OpCodes.Stloc, targetMethod);

// Set up the method context object.
proxyMthIL.Emit(OpCodes.Ldloca, methodCxtInfo);
proxyMthIL.Emit(OpCodes.Ldarg_0);
proxyMthIL.Emit(OpCodes.Ldfld, WrappedObject);
proxyMthIL.Emit(OpCodes.Callvirt,
    typeof(System.Object).GetMethod(GET_TYPE));
```

```
proxyMthIL.Emit(OpCodes.Stloc, wrappedType);
proxyMthIL.Emit(OpCodes.Ldloc, wrappedType);
proxyMthIL.Emit(OpCodes.Callvirt,
    typeof(System.Type).GetMethod(GET_ASSEMBLY_PROP));
proxyMthIL.Emit(OpCodes.Callvirt,
    typeof(System.Reflection.Assembly).GetMethod(
    GET_NAME, System.Type.EmptyTypes));
proxyMthIL.Emit(OpCodes.Ldloc, wrappedType);
proxyMthIL.Emit(OpCodes.Callvirt,
    typeof(System.Type).GetMethod(GET_FULL_NAME_PROP));
proxyMthIL.Emit(OpCodes.Ldloc, targetMethod);
proxyMthIL.Emit(OpCodes.Callvirt,
    typeof(System.Reflection.MemberInfo).GetMethod(GET_NAME_PROP));
argTypes = new Type[3];
argTypes[0] = typeof(System.Reflection.AssemblyName);
argTypes[1] = typeof(System.String);
argTypes[2] = typeof(System.String);
proxyMthIL.Emit(OpCodes.Call,
    typeof(Proxies.MethodContextInfo).GetConstructor(argTypes));
```

You may be a bit confused by the first four lines of code. This is where Emitter coding can really twist your head around if you don't keep your code locations straight. In BuildTargetMethods(), you have the correct MethodInfo object, but when the proxy code is executing, this value is long gone. You need some way to generically create the right MethodInfo object at runtime. Fortunately, the Ldtoken OpCode in concert with GetMethodFromHandle() on System.Type allow you to transform the MethodInfo object that you have into a token that can be reconstituted into a MethodInfo object at runtime. Since MethodContextInfo will need this value, you store it in a local variable.

Once you have your target method, you can create your MethodContextInfo object. The first value is the AssemblyName, which you get by loading the wrapped object's assembly value onto the stack, and then calling GetName() on the Assembly reference. The type name is retrieved in a similar fashion by calling the FullName property on the wrapped object's type. Finally, the method name is obtained by calling Name on the recently acquired target method (stored in targetMethod).

Calling InvokeMethod()

Finally, you're ready to call InvokeMethod(); this is shown in Listing 8-3.

Listing 8-3. Calling the Target Method

```
proxyMthIL.Emit(OpCodes.Ldarg_0);
proxyMthIL.Emit(OpCodes.Ldloc, targetMethod);
proxyMthIL.Emit(OpCodes.Ldloca, argValues);
proxyMthIL.Emit(OpCodes.Ldloc, methodCxtInfo);
proxyMthIL.Emit(OpCodes.Call, InvokeMethod);

// Set the method value (if any exists).
if(typeof(void) != mi.ReturnType)
{
    // Need to be careful here.  If the return type
    // is null, then we leave retVal as-is.
    Label retIsNull = proxyMthIL.DefineLabel();
    proxyMthIL.Emit(OpCodes.Stloc, tempRetVal);
    proxyMthIL.Emit(OpCodes.Ldloc, tempRetVal);
    proxyMthIL.Emit(OpCodes.Brfalse, retIsNull);
    proxyMthIL.Emit(OpCodes.Ldloc, tempRetVal);

    if(true == mi.ReturnType.IsValueType)
    {
        // Unbox whatever is on the stack.
        proxyMthIL.Emit(OpCodes.Unbox, mi.ReturnType);
        // Note:  See Section 3.42 of Partition III to see why
        // I chose the general ldobj over ldind.
        proxyMthIL.Emit(OpCodes.Ldobj, mi.ReturnType);
    }
    else
    {
        proxyMthIL.Emit(OpCodes.Castclass, mi.ReturnType);
    }

    proxyMthIL.Emit(OpCodes.Stloc, retVal);
    proxyMthIL.MarkLabel(retIsNull);
}
else
{
    proxyMthIL.Emit(OpCodes.Pop);
}
```

Calling `InvokeMethod()` isn't the hard part; it's dealing with the return value. If there's a return value but it's null, you don't do a thing, as the local `retVal` will already be null. But if there's a value, you transform that value to its appropriate

form through either an Unbox (for value types) or a Castclass (for reference types). If
there isn't a return value, you must clear the stack by using the Pop OpCode value, as
InvokeMethod() will always return some kind of value (even if it is a null) and you
must manage the stack properly.

Resetting the Argument Stack

As it's possible that the stack values may have changed, you need to reset all the
given argument values to reflect those changes, which is what the code in
Listing 8-4 does.

Listing 8-4. Adjusting the Argument Values

```
// Move the ByRef or out arg values from the array
// to the arg values.
foreach(ParameterInfo argValueByRef in mi.GetParameters())
{
    if((true == argValueByRef.ParameterType.IsByRef) ||
       (true == argValueByRef.IsOut))
    {
        paramRetTypeName = argValueByRef.ParameterType.ToString();
        paramRetTypeName = paramRetTypeName.Replace("&", "");
        paramRetType = Type.GetType(paramRetTypeName);
        proxyMthIL.Emit(OpCodes.Ldarg, argValueByRef.Position + 1);
        proxyMthIL.Emit(OpCodes.Ldloc, argValues);
        proxyMthIL.Emit(OpCodes.Ldc_I4, argValueByRef.Position);
        proxyMthIL.Emit(OpCodes.Ldelem_Ref);
        if(true == paramRetType.IsValueType)
        {
            proxyMthIL.Emit(OpCodes.Unbox, paramRetType);
            proxyMthIL.Emit(OpCodes.Ldobj, paramRetType);
            proxyMthIL.Emit(OpCodes.Stobj, paramRetType);
        }
        else
        {
            if(paramRetType != typeof(System.Object))
            {
                proxyMthIL.Emit(OpCodes.Castclass, paramRetType);
            }
            proxyMthIL.Emit(OpCodes.Stind_Ref);
        }
    }
}
```

```
    //  Finally...return.
    if(typeof(void) != mi.ReturnType)
    {
        proxyMthIL.Emit(OpCodes.Ldloc, retVal);
    }

    proxyMthIL.Emit(OpCodes.Ret);
    }
}
```

It's basically the same code that was used to build the argument array before InvokeMethod() was called, except now it's pulling the values out and putting their values into the correct argument.

Testing the Solution

I've covered the hard part: how a proxy is created. Now let's have some fun and create some proxies. I've come up with a sample application called ProxyTest that you can use to test the proxy generation—Figure 8-4 shows the application in action.

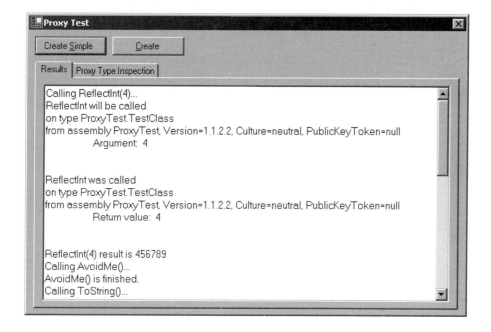

Figure 8-4. ProxyTest application

I'll walk though the application so you can see how you can load your own types to hook method invocations.

Loading the Form

Recall from the discussion on `Proxy` in the section "Caching Types, Modules, and Assemblies" that you add a method called `Persist()` if you're creating a debug build. You want to make the ability to call this method as painless as possible for a `ProxyTest` user, so you need to use a bit of reflection to make this work:

```
private void frmMain_Load(object sender, System.EventArgs e)
{
    try
    {
        this.m_ProxyPersist = typeof(Proxies.Proxy).GetMethod("Persist");

        if(null == this.m_ProxyPersist)
        {
            this.btnPersist.Visible = false;
        }
    }
    catch(Exception ex) {}
}
```

When the form is loaded, you check to see if the method exists. If it doesn't, make the `Persist` button invisible. If it does, store the `MethodInfo` reference to a private field in `frmMain`, which is used in the button's `Click()` event:

```
private void btnPersist_Click(object sender, System.EventArgs e)
{
    this.m_ProxyPersist.Invoke(null, System.Type.EmptyTypes);
}
```

Creating Proxies

I've included a number of simple types in the `ProxyTest` assembly to generate proxies for. For example, here's the definition of one of the classes, `TestClass`:

```
public class TestClass
{
    public virtual int ReflectInt(int AValue)
    {
        return AValue;
    }

    public void AvoidMe() {}

    public virtual void ExceptionGeneration()
    {
        throw new Exception("Exception occurred.");
    }
}
```

The Click() event for btnCreateSimple generates a proxy for this type:

```
private void btnCreateSimple_Click(object sender, System.EventArgs e)
{
    try
    {
        txtResults.Text = "";

        TestClass tc = new TestClass();
        InvocationHandler[] ih = {new UITraceHandler(this.txtResults)};
        TestClass tcProxy = (TestClass)Proxy.Create(tc, ih);
        InspectType(tcProxy);

        txtResults.Text += "Calling ReflectInt(4)...\r\n";
        int retVal = tcProxy.ReflectInt(4);
        txtResults.Text += "ReflectInt(4) result is " +
            retVal + "\r\n";
        txtResults.Text += "Calling AvoidMe()...\r\n";
        tcProxy.AvoidMe();
        txtResults.Text += "AvoidMe() is finished.\r\n";
        txtResults.Text += "Calling ToString()...\r\n";
        tcProxy.ToString();
        txtResults.Text += "ToString() is finished.\r\n";
        txtResults.Text += "Calling ExceptionGeneration()...\r\n";
        tcProxy.ExceptionGeneration();
        txtResults.Text += "ExceptionGeneration() is finished.\r\n";
```

```
    }
    catch(Exception ex)
    {
        ErrorForm ef = new ErrorForm(ex);
         ef.ShowDialog(this);
    }
}
```

An instance of TestClass is created, and then a proxy is made via Create(). The UITraceHandler class is used to add information to the text box when the InvocationHandler methods are called. In fact, if you go back to Figure 8-4 you'll see that the text that is added to txtResults in this event is interspersed with text from UITraceHandler.[2]

You'll also see in that figure that ReflectInt() doesn't return the right value. In AfterMethodInvocation(), you look for that method and then you alter the return value (note that I've cut out the tracing code here, but it does exist in the actual method):

```
public void AfterMethodInvocation(MethodContextInfo CurrentMethod,
    ref Object[] MethodArgs,
    ref Object ReturnValue,
    ref bool BubbleException)
{
    //  Tracing code goes here...
    if(CurrentMethod.MethodName.Equals("ReflectInt"))
    {
        ReturnValue = (int)456789;
    }
    this.m_TBox.Text += "\r\n\r\n";
}
```

So no matter what TestClass sends to ReflectInt, it'll always get 456789. You also do some method argument shenanigans with Add() on the MathOps class in BeforeMethodInvocation():

```
public void BeforeMethodInvocation(MethodContextInfo CurrentMethod,
    ref Object[] MethodArgs, ref bool CallMethod,
    ref bool BubbleException)
```

---

2.   ErrorForm is from an assembly called ErrorDialog that I created to show exception information.

I've included the binary in this book—you can find a detailed description of this class at my Web site: http://www.jasonbock.net.

```
{
    // Tracing code goes here...
    if(CurrentMethod.MethodName.Equals("Add"))
    {
        MethodArgs[0] = 33;
        MethodArgs[1] = 44;
    }
}
```

The results will look quite odd to a user:

```
Calling Add()...
Add will be called
on type ProxyTest.MathOps
from assembly ProxyTest, Version=1.1.2.2, Culture=neutral, PublicKeyToken=null
    Argument:  3
    Argument:  4

Add was called
on type ProxyTest.MathOps
from assembly ProxyTest, Version=1.1.2.2, Culture=neutral, PublicKeyToken=null
    Return value:  77

Add(3, 4) result is 77
```

Sneaky. Very sneaky.

Type Inspection

A method called InspectType() is added so you can see what the proxy looks like—it's shown in Listing 8-5.

Listing 8-5. Inspecting the Proxy Type

```
private void InspectType(Object Base)
{
    Type target = Base.GetType();
    this.txtTypeInspect.Text = "";
```

```
            txtTypeInspect.Text += "Inspecting " +
                target.FullName + " in assembly " +
                target.Assembly.FullName + "\r\n";

            txtTypeInspect.Text += "\r\n";
            txtTypeInspect.Text += "Public Methods\r\n";

            foreach(MethodInfo mi in target.GetMethods(BindingFlags.Instance |
                BindingFlags.Public))
            {
                txtTypeInspect.Text += "Method:  " + mi.Name + "\r\n";
                txtTypeInspect.Text += "\tVirtual:  " +
                    mi.IsVirtual + "\r\n";
            }

            txtTypeInspect.Text += "\r\n";
            txtTypeInspect.Text += "Private Methods\r\n";

            foreach(MethodInfo mi in target.GetMethods(BindingFlags.Instance |
                BindingFlags.NonPublic))
            {
                txtTypeInspect.Text += "Method:  " + mi.Name + "\r\n";
                txtTypeInspect.Text += "\tVirtual:  " +
                    mi.IsVirtual + "\r\n";
            }

            txtTypeInspect.Text += "\r\n";

            foreach(Type itf in target.GetInterfaces())
            {
                txtTypeInspect.Text += "Interface:  " + itf.Name + "\r\n";

                InterfaceMapping imap = target.GetInterfaceMap(itf);

                for(int i = 0; i < imap.InterfaceMethods.Length; i++)
                {
                    txtTypeInspect.Text += "\tInterface Method:  " +
                        imap.InterfaceMethods[i].DeclaringType + "\r\n";
                    txtTypeInspect.Text += "\tTarget Method:  " +
                        imap.TargetMethods[i].Name + "\r\n";
                    txtTypeInspect.Text += "\tIs Target Method Public:  " +
                        imap.TargetMethods[i].IsPublic + "\r\n";
                }
            }
        }
    }
```

It's standard reflection code, but it's interesting to see the differences with the two example classes in ProxyTest. For instance, here's what InspectType() generated for a TestClass proxy:

```
Inspecting ProxyTest.TestClass1342891065
    in assembly ProxyTest339640661, Version=1.1.2.2

Public Methods
Method:  AvoidMe
    Virtual:  False
Method:  GetType
    Virtual:  False


Private Methods
Method:  ToString107649916
    Virtual:  True
Method:  Equals107649876
    Virtual:  True
Method:  ReflectInt107649756
    Virtual:  True
Method:  GetHashCode107649836
    Virtual:  True
Method:  ExceptionGeneration107649716
    Virtual:  True
Method:  Finalize
    Virtual:  True
Method:  InvokeMethod
    Virtual:  False
Method:  MemberwiseClone
    Virtual:  False
```

Note that the two nonvirtual methods are not hooked, which is to be expected. Also, note that every public virtual method on the base type has a corresponding private method with a mangled name. This is the desired effect, as you don't want a client to be able to call your virtual methods that override the base class's virtual methods.

Listing 8-6 shows the results of an inspection on the MathOps class.

Listing 8-6. Proxy Inspection Results for the MathOps Class

```
Inspecting ProxyTest.MathOps913267613
    in assembly ProxyTest339640661, Version=1.1.2.2

Public Methods
Method:  Subtract
    Virtual:  True
Method:  Add
    Virtual:  True
Method:  Divide
    Virtual:  False
Method:  GetType
    Virtual:  False


Private Methods
Method:  ToString122817552
    Virtual:  True
Method:  Subtract122817312
    Virtual:  True
Method:  Equals122817512
    Virtual:  True
Method:  Multiply122817392
    Virtual:  True
Method:  GetHashCode122817472
    Virtual:  True
Method:  Add122817352
    Virtual:  True
Method:  Finalize
    Virtual:  True
Method:  InvokeMethod
    Virtual:  False
Method:  MemberwiseClone
    Virtual:  False

Interface:  IMathOps
    Interface Method:  ProxyTest.IMathOps
    Target Method:  Add122817352
    Is Target Method Public:  False
    Interface Method:  ProxyTest.IMathOps
    Target Method:  Subtract122817312
    Is Target Method Public:  False
```

The Add() and Subtract() methods are final, so that's why they weren't hooked. You'll also notice that the IMathOps interface pops up, which is to be expected, as MathOps implements this interface.

SOURCE CODE *The Proxies folder contains the proxy-generation code. ProxyTest is the test client.*

Contexts and .NET

I hope that this example shows the power that the runtime generation of code gives you as a .NET developer. However, there's another way to hook a method if you're willing to make your object context-bound. Although I don't have the space in this book to discuss contexts and remoting in depth,[3] I'll at least show you how you can mimic what I just did with .NET classes.

If a class derives from ContextBoundObject, .NET sets up a proxy object called __TransparentProxy, which is returned to the client after object construction. As with the dynamic proxy, the client is oblivious that it actually has a reference to the proxy rather than to the desired object. Behind the scenes the method invocations are carried along a number of registered sink objects. Fortunately, .NET allows you to participate in this call chain—let's see how this is done.

First, you need to define an attribute that inherits from ContextAttribute so ContextBoundObject-based objects can specify which sinks they want to add via a context property:

```
[AttributeUsage(AttributeTargets.Class)]
public class TypeInterceptionAttribute : ContextAttribute
{
    private const string ATTRIB_NAME = "TypeInterceptionAttribute";

    public TypeInterceptionAttribute() : base(ATTRIB_NAME) {}

    public override void GetPropertiesForNewContext
        (IConstructionCallMessage ctorMsg)
    {
        ctorMsg.ContextProperties.Add(new TypeInterceptionProperty());
    }
}
```

---

3. For more information on these topics, I recommend picking up a copy of Ingo Rammer's book, *Advanced .NET Remoting* (Apress, 2002).

GetPropertiesForNewContext() is invoked whenever a new context-bound object is created. When this is done, you can add your context property, which puts your code into the sink chain:

```
public class TypeInterceptionProperty : IContextProperty, IContributeObjectSink
{
    private const string PROP_NAME = "TypeInterceptionProperty";

    public TypeInterceptionProperty() : base() {}

    public IMessageSink GetObjectSink(MarshalByRefObject obj,
        IMessageSink nextSink)
    {
        return new TypeInterceptionMessage(nextSink);
    }

    public bool IsNewContextOK(Context newCtx)
    {
        return true;
    }

    public void Freeze(Context newContext) {}

    public string Name
    {
        get
        {
            return PROP_NAME;
        }
    }
}
```

The most important method that you have to be concerned about implementing is GetObjectSink(), which allows you to specify the class that will receive method invocations. Here, that class is TypeInterceptionMessage, which implements IMessageSink:

```
public class TypeInterceptionMessage : IMessageSink {}
```

Again, I'll keep the conversation focused on the essentials. The first thing you must do is pass the message along the sink chain, which is done when the runtime calls your NextSink property:

```
internal TypeInterceptionMessage(IMessageSink NextSink)
{
    this.m_NextSink = NextSink;
}

public IMessageSink NextSink
{
    get
    {
        return this.m_NextSink;
    }
}
```

Now, when a method is called, your sink will receive the call via two methods, SyncProcessMessage() and AsyncProcessMessage(). For this example, you'll only support synchronous calls:

```
public IMessage SyncProcessMessage(IMessage msg)
{
    IMessage retVal = null;

    if(msg is IMethodMessage)
    {
        BeforeInvocation(msg);
        retVal = this.m_NextSink.SyncProcessMessage(msg);
        AfterInvocation(msg, retVal);
    }

    return retVal;
}
```

Notice something familiar? The BeforeInvocation() and AfterInvocation() methods are methods you defined internally to TypeInterceptionMessage. They act just like your InvocationHandler interface methods—they allow you to perform pre- and post-processing on method invocations. Let's see what BeforeInvocation() does:

```
private void BeforeInvocation(IMessage msg)
{
    IMethodMessage targetCall = msg as IMethodMessage;
    Type targetType = Type.GetType(targetCall.TypeName);

    this.m_MCI = new MethodContextInfo(
        (AssemblyName)targetType.Assembly.GetName().Clone(),
        targetType.FullName, targetCall.MethodName);

    if(null != this.m_Notify)
    {
        this.m_Notify.Notify(this.m_MCI, targetCall.Args);
    }

    targetCall.LogicalCallContext.SetData(
        TypeInterceptionMessage.ContextName,
        this);
}
```

You include MethodContextInfo again so you can notify clients of the state of the method invocation. By the way, this notification process is done via a custom IMessageNotification interface:

```
public interface IMessageNotification
{
    void Notify(MethodContextInfo MethodInformation,
        Exception MethodException);
    void Notify(MethodContextInfo MethodInformation,
        string Message);
    void Notify(MethodContextInfo MethodInformation,
        object[] MethodArgs);
    void Notify(MethodContextInfo MethodInformation,
        object[] MethodArgs, object MethodRetVal);
}
```

Clients can register and unregister method state information notifications by calling RegisterNotify() and UnregisterNotify() on the sink object:

```
public void RegisterNotify(IMessageNotification NotifyClient)
{
    this.m_Notify = NotifyClient;
}
```

```
public void UnregisterNotify()
{
    this.m_Notify = null;
}
```

But how can you call these two methods when you're in a method from your context-bound object? I'll show you how you can do this in a moment, but the only way a client will be able to reach up into the context stream and call these methods is by identifying the correct sink object. That's why the SetData() call on the LogicalCallContext object in BeforeInvocation() was made. This adds the sink to the context such that a method can retrieve it via a GetData() call.

Although I've glossed over the details, this is all you need to do to hook method calls. And to have a class use your TypeInterception scheme is extremely easy:

```
using TypeInterception;

[TypeInterception()]
public class TestClass : ContextBoundObject
{
    // Method def's go here…
}
```

Here's how you reach up into context to get notification of the interception at work:

```
public void SetUp(IMessageNotification MessageNotify)
{
    TypeInterceptionMessage tim =
        (TypeInterceptionMessage)CallContext.GetData(
        TypeInterceptionMessage.ContextName);
    tim.RegisterNotify(MessageNotify);
}
```

The same code is used to call DuringInvocation() so a method can notify the sink of certain information.

I've created a test harness application so you can see method interception via contexts in action. Figure 8-5 shows the application at work.

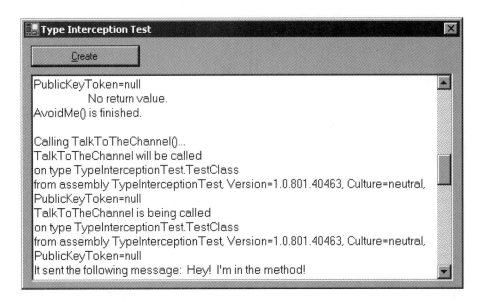

Figure 8-5. Type interception test application

SOURCE CODE *The TypeInterception folder contains context attributes and sink definitions. TypeInterceptionTest is the test client of these classes.*

Dynamic Proxies and Contexts

Before this chapter ends, I want to spend some time discussing the differences between the architecture of the example application and the technique via context-bound objects and message sinks. If you look closely at Figure 8-5, you'll see that AvoidMe() was hooked, even though that is a nonvirtual method. This is something that you can't do with the dynamic proxies architecture. Furthermore, methods can send information to the interception sink code, which is something that you can't do either. However, one thing to note is that the context approach is a design-time decision. You have to derive your classes from ContextBoundObject, and since .NET only supports single inheritance, this may not be a feasible option depending on preexisting frameworks and architecture. However, with your dynamic proxy, you can turn this on or off as you see fit; it doesn't matter what the class derives from.

I'm not trying to encourage or discourage you from using one approach over another. However, keep in mind that .NET allows for alternatives, and with the Emitter classes, you have the power to implement all sorts of ideas and configurations.

Conclusion

In this chapter, you saw how you could use the Emitter classes to hook method invocations. You went through the design and implementation of the Proxy class, and you saw how the CIL works to make the interception happen. You also saw how .NET provides a framework that allows you to receive method calls via its own proxy classes. In the next and final chapter of this book, I'll give you some suggestions to make your CIL coding experience easier.

CHAPTER 9

CIL Tips

With this chapter, the book comes to an end. I hope I've been able to give you some insight into the inner workings of .NET via CIL. It's been an incredible learning experience for me to dive into the world of .NET at a rather low level, and it's my sincere wish that I've been able to transfer some of my hard-won knowledge to you so you don't have to suffer as much. Before I end the book, I want to share some heuristics I developed as I coded more and more in CIL and with the Emitter classes. I think that if you try to follow them, you'll make your CIL-based development experiences a lot less frustrating.

Be CLS-Compliant Aware

As you know, when you code in CIL, you can do anything you want that is defined in the Partition documents. However, some constructs cannot be accessed in some languages—for example, you cannot call a vararg method in VB .NET. If you're creating assemblies for public usage, I'd strongly urge you to become familiar with Section 10 of Partition I, as it defines all the rules that an assembly must pass to be considered CLS compliant.

I'm not suggesting that you don't use the full power available to you in CIL. Just make sure that if you're using a feature that isn't allowed via the CLS rules that you provide some mechanism to use the feature that is CLS compliant.

Use Verification Tools

I don't know how many times I caused an InvalidProgramException to be thrown as I developed the code samples for this book. ilasm allows you to create assemblies where the types or the code within their methods aren't valid; when you're coding in C# or Component Pascal, you're relying on the compiler to generate a valid assembly. Although compilers are not exempt from making mistakes, it's harder to make sure your CIL-based assemblies are okay. I strongly suggest running PEVerify on any assembly that you create via ilasm. You'll catch a lot of mistakes in your code before you run it. I'd also recommend using FxCop, a tool created by Microsoft to catch other errors in your assemblies. You can download it at http://www.gotdotnet.com/team/libraries/default.aspx.

Comments and Code Regions

You may have your own personal views on comments, but I strongly suggest you comment your CIL code thoroughly. It's very easy to get lost in your CIL code, especially when you're in a loop and you're jumping all over the place. I usually try to keep comments to a minimum, but in CIL I tend to add more comments, and I'd suggest you do the same. It also makes it easier when I come back to my CIL code months later to figure out what possessed me to come up with the implementation that I did.

Also, if you're using the Emitter classes, I'd recommend using code regions (#region/#endregion) within your methods. Method implementations tend to get quite long (remember BuildInvokeMethod() in Proxy from Chapter 8?), and using code regions allow you to view smaller pieces of the implementation when you need to.

Stay Location Savvy When Emitting Assemblies

When I created the Proxy class, I really had to focus to remember where the code was going to execute. Although I may have had an object reference in the Proxy code, it wouldn't be there in the emitted code, so I needed to figure out a way to translate the information I had in the static code to the dynamic code. It can get awfully frustrating, but remember that the boundary is always there. When you know you must emit assemblies, make sure you are able to generate the code that you need given the information that you have.

Final Thoughts

I don't have any wild thoughts that I'm going to make millions of .NET developers suddenly switch over to CIL as their primary language of choice. But knowing how the language works gives you a number of advanced tools in your development skill set that you may not have had before. If you ever run into odd behavior with your assembly, you now know how to dive into its CIL and figure out where the problem lies. And if you need to generate code at runtime to optimize the performance of an algorithm, you'll know what you need to do. With that, I wish you well, and have fun coding your next project in CIL!

The Future of CIL

Although CIL was finalized with the release of .NET early in 2002, that doesn't mean work has stopped on improving the opcode set. Research efforts are currently underway to add instructions that would expand the abilities of CIL. Furthermore, developers are already asking for new features that would allow them greater access to the executing instructions. In this appendix, I'll take you on a brief tour of where CIL may be headed in the near future.

 CAUTION *I make no guarantees that the ideas presented in this appendix will ever become available for commercial use. As far as I know, at the time I wrote this appendix there are no absolute commitments from Microsoft on any new changes to CIL. Although I think the ideas will eventually see the light of day, please don't base any system design decisions on them.*

Generics in CIL

If you use collections or any kind of object containers in .NET, you are responsible for making sure you know what gets put into the collection as well as extracting it in a type-safe manner. For example, take a look at the following code snippet:

```
public class Lists
{
    public ArrayList CreateList()
    {
        ArrayList objectList = new ArrayList();

        objectList.Add(Guid.NewGuid());
        objectList.Add(Guid.NewGuid());

        return objectList
    }
}
```

Let's try to retrieve the list:

```
Lists l = new Lists();
ArrayList al = l.CreateList();
```

The problem is that unless you have the source code to `Lists` or you're willing to use ILDasm to figure out what `CreateList()` does, you have no idea what is contained within `al`. Even if you know that the list only contains objects that are of a specific type, you still have to do a cast:

```
for(int i = 0; i < al.Count; i++)
{
    Guid aGuid = (Guid)al[i];
}
```

Furthermore, with value types you have to box the values to store the value in the list, and then you must unbox the value to retrieve it from the list. If you have a lot of items in the list, this can get pretty processor-intensive. Of course, you could simply create a specialized `ArrayList` that would only handle `Guid` references (`GuidArrayList`), but then a specialized class must be explicitly defined every time a new type-specific container is needed.[1]

With generics, though, type-guessing and hand-coded specialization becomes a thing of the past. `CreateList()` would be redefined as follows:[2]

```
public ArrayList<Guid> CreateList()
{
    ArrayList<Guid> guidList = new ArrayList();

    guidList.Add(Guid.NewGuid());
    guidList.Add(Guid.NewGuid());

    return objectList
}
```

---

1. There is a free tool available that simplifies this container generation—it's called CollectionGen and you can find it at `http://www.sellsbrothers.com/tools`.

2. Just because this C# code *looks* like it supports generics does not mean it does; in fact, right now C# doesn't. I'm only adopting the syntax that its cousin C++ uses for templates for illustrative purposes.

Therefore, the client would know exactly what kind of type is contained in the ArrayList reference because it's specifying the type. Furthermore, the client would no longer need to perform any casts:

```
Lists l = new Lists();
ArrayList<Guid> al = l.CreateList();
for(int i = 0; i < al.Count; i++)
{
    Guid aGuid = al[i];
}
```

Currently, .NET does support generics, but not at the CIL level. That is, it's up to the compilers to create the parameterized types at runtime. Therefore, the support is at the high-language level and not at the CIL level. However, research has been done to determine how this support could be added to CIL.[3] Here's what your CIL code may end up looking like:

```
.class ArrayList<T>
{
    .field private !0 _items
    .method virtual instance int Add(!0 value)
    {
        ldarg.0
        ldfld !0[] ArrayList<!0>::_items
        ldlen
        add
        stelem.any !0
    }
}
```

I've glossed over a lot of technical issues here, such as initializing _items and making sure there are enough elements in _items to store the given argument value, but the important point to understand here is the new syntax. First, ArrayList is defined to take a type parameter T. This corresponds to the Guid type that you pass into ArrayList in the C# code. You also declare an array of T references. The !0 syntax is an accessor function—it states that you wish to use the first type that has been declared in ArrayList. In this case, there's only one, T, so that type defines the element's type. Therefore, _items will contain Guid references.

---

3. Please visit http://research.microsoft.com/projects/clrgen/ for more details. Specifically, download the paper "The Design and Implementation of Generics for the .NET Common Language Runtime," as it contains the essentials of the research information.

Now, when Add() is called with a Guid type, it will only allow values that are Guid-based. Therefore, a System.Integer value would be rejected. To load the field via ldfld, you must use full type information, so the !0 accessor is needed. Assuming that _items has enough slots available such that the add operation on the array's length will not cause an IndexOutOfRangeException, you store the element via a new opcode, stelem.any.

Of course, generics are not limited to class definitions. You can also make polymorphic methods as well:

```
public void ProcessArray<T>(T[] target)
{
    for(int i = 0; i < target.Lenght; i++)
    {
        //…
    }
}
```

The corresponding CIL to call this method would look something like this:

```
call void SomeClass::ProcessArray<Guid>(!!0[])
```

Note that the syntax to access method-level types uses two bangs ("!") instead of one for class-level types.

Having support for generics at the CIL level will be beneficial for developers, so long as their language of choice has the syntax necessary to use generics. What happens if C# supports generics, but VB .NET doesn't? How would VB .NET be able to consume generic classes and methods written in C#? This also raises the issue of CLS-compliance with generics—will they or won't they be compliant? I don't have the answers on any of these issues right now; I encourage you to stay aware of any future work in this area. If anything is added to CIL in the next version, I think it'll be generics.

Extended IL

Generics aren't the only addition that is being looked at for CIL. A whole slew of changes are being considered to support functional languages' constructs. Functional languages basically approach problems in a (you guessed it) functional manner. Rather than solving problems via methods on classes, you apply functions to data. For example, here's how you would sort elements in an ArrayList:

```
ArrayList al = new ArrayList();
al.Add("Left");
al.Add("Right");
al.Add("Up");
al.Add("Down");
al.Sort();
```

In Mathematica, it's a little easier:

```
Sort[{"Left", "Right", "Up", "Down"}]
```

The first example uses a method on an object to sort the data that it contains. The second example applies a function to a set of data and returns the results.[4]

The problem with functional languages is that there is not inherent support for making functions first-class .NET citizens; classes currently hold that distinction.[5] A research effort called ILX, or Extended IL, is underway to add ilasm directives and CIL opcodes so functional language compilers will have an easier time generating their code.[6]

For example, here's what Multiply() would look like in ILX:

```
.closure Multiply()
{
    .apply (int32 X, int32 Y) --> int32
    {
        ldarg X
        ldarg Y
        mul
        ret
    }
}
```

---

4. An excellent resource for information on functional languages can be found at http://www.cs.nott.ac.uk/~gmh//faq.html#functional-languages. Also check out http://directory.google.com/Top/Computers/Programming/Languages/Functional/.

5. If you've played with Mondrain for .NET (http://www.mondrain-script.org) and looked at the results when you compile Mondrain code, you'll see what the compiler has to do to map functional constructs onto the .NET substrate. It's not pretty.

6. For more information on ILX (along with a link for downloading the ILX compiler), please visit http://research.microsoft.com/projects/ilx/ilx.htm. Note that this compiler also supports the generics syntax I demonstrated in the previous section.

To apply the `Multiply()` function requires some new CIL opcodes:

```
.locals ((func (int32, int32) --> int32) MultClosure,
    int32 result)
newclo class Multiply
stloc MultClosure
ldloc MultClosure
ldc.i4.2
ldc.i4.3
callfunc (int32, int32) --> int32
stloc result
```

`newclo` loads the closure onto the stack, and then it is stored in `MultClosure`. To apply the function, you reload the closure, throw two `int32` values onto the stack, and use `callfunc` to apply the `Multiply()` function. The result is left on the stack, which is then stored in `stloc`.

There's more to functional programming than what I've shown here (such as environment values and thunks), but you can definitely see the differences. If these extensions ever make it into mainstream CIL, you'll know how to handle these functional constructs.[7]

Inline CIL

One of the statements I've often heard made from .NET developers is, "Why can't I embed CIL into my <insert favorite language here>?" Having this support would allow a VB .NET developer to do the following:

```
Function IKnowWhatIAmDoing() As Integer
Dim aValue As Integer = 456
    #CIL
    ldloc aValue
    ldc.i4.1
    add
    stloc aValue
    #ENDCIL
Return aValue
End Function
```

---

7.   Just before this book went to press, a new functional language was released that's based on the ILX work. It's called F#, and by the time you read this, a compiler should be available for download. You can find more information at http://research.microsoft.com/projects/ilx/fsharp.htm.

I have no idea what symbols would be used to embed CIL—"#" seems as good a choice as any. But you get the idea—the VB .NET developer would be able to control the CIL output of the method.

Although this enhancement is not CIL-specific, I've heard the question asked a number of times in relevant user groups. Whether this is ever added to any .NET language is up to the language designers. It's certainly something that could be done now; the compilers that parse the code would have to be able to handle the inline CIL and embed it in the PE file. Of course, verification that the CIL is correct would be a desirable feature.[8]

---

8. For an interesting discussion on this topic, please visit `http://discuss.develop.com/archives/wa.exe?A2=ind0009A&L=DOTNET&D=0&P=26793`.

.NET Languages

Following is a list of all the programming languages that are targeting or will be targeting the .NET platform. This list will change, so you may find other languages that target the .NET platform after this book has been published. Also, not all of the languages have compilers that you can download, and some of the compilers are not free. I encourage you to study and experiment with other languages to see how their idioms and styles translate into CIL constructs. Microsoft maintains a .NET language list as well—it can be found at http://msdn.microsoft.com/vstudio/ partners/language/default.asp.

Active Oberon for .NET
http://www.oberon.ethz.ch/
http://www.oberon.ethz.ch/oberon.net/

C#, C++, VB .NET
http://msdn.microsoft.com/downloads/default.asp?url=/downloads/
sample.asp?url=/msdn-files/027/000/976/msdncompositedoc.xml&frame=true

Component Pascal
http://www2.fit.qut.edu.au/CompSci/PLAS//ComponentPascal/

Delphi for .NET
http://www.borland.com/
http://www.borland.com/net/

Delta Forth .NET
http://www.dataman.ro/
http://www.dataman.ro/dforth/

Dyalog APL for .NET
http://www.dyadic.com/

Eiffel for .NET
http://www.eiffel.com
http://www.dotnet.eiffel.com

F#
http://research.microsoft.com/projects/ilx/fsharp.htm

Fortran for .NET
http://www.lahey.com/
http://www.lahey.com/net_down.htm

Fujitsu NetCOBOL for .NET

http://www.adtools.com/

http://www.adtools.com/dotnet/index.html

Mercury

http://www.cs.mu.oz.au/research/mercury/

Mondrain

http://www.mondrian-script.org/

PerlNET, PythonNET

http://www.activestate.com/

http://www.activestate.com/Initiatives/NET/

Scheme.NET

http://rover.cs.nwu.edu/~scheme/

Smalltalk.NET (or SmallScript.NET)

http://www.smallscript.org/

Standard ML

http://research.microsoft.com/Projects/SML.NET/index.htm

Visual J#

http://msdn.microsoft.com/visualj/

Index

Symbols

* (asterisk) character, using with cordbg commands, 153

/ (slash) character, using with nested types, 125

< command, using in cordbg, 162

> command, using in cordbg, 162

A

A Programmer's Introduction to C# (Eric Gunnerson), 204

abstract attribute, 58
    using with a virtual method, 60
    using with .class directive, 34

accessibility attributes, table of, 39

active objects, creating in Oberon, 221–223

add opcode
    function of, 16–17
    size of, 70
    using, 80

AddLoaderOptimizationAttribute(), adding attribute information in, 256

.addon directive, using, 66

/adv switch, defined, 19

Advanced .NET Remoting (Ingo Rammer), for information about contexts and .NET, 309

and opcode, using, 83–85

ansi (8-bit) attribute, using for marshalling, 40

AppDomainLoads mode, in cordbg, 161

Application.Run() method, in the test harness program, 136–137

arglist opcode
    size of, 70
    using, 114–116

argument stack, resetting, 300–301

argument values, code for adjusting, 300–301

ArgumentException, when thrown, 106

arguments, passing to a method, 48

arithmetic operations, performing on stack values, 80–82

ArithmeticException, when thrown, 82

arrays, creation and manipulation of, 97–99

assemblies
    code for creating types for verification testing, 178–179
    concurrent execution of, 31
    creating, 241–243
    creating persistent-only, 252–253
    creating transient-only, 252
    importance of staying location savvy when emitting, 318
    signing, 27
    strong-naming, 187–188
    verifying, 178–181

assembly, defined, 13

.assembly directive, 15
    attributes for allowing only one assembly version to run, 31
    defining an assembly with, 23–30
    for using resources in another assembly, 26
    using to reference other assemblies, 23–24

assembly hash algorithms, 25

assembly manifest, function of, 14–15

AssemblyKeyFileAttribute attribute, giving an assembly a strong name with, 24–25

attributes
    adding custom to your methods, 54
    adding information by using a byte array, 256
    adding to Emitter class assemblies, 255–256

auto layout attribute, for defining a type with the default layout, 35

autochar attribute, using for marshalling, 40

K

kill command, using, 156

L

language constructs, 205–224
language interoperability, 1–21
    in action, 1–8
    in practice, 12–21
    the real story, 224–237
    in theory, 8–12
ldarg opcode, loading an argument
    value onto the stack with, 77
ldarg.s encoding, using, 77–78
ldc (load constant) opcode, changing the
    value of a variable with, 73
ldc.i4.o opcode, size of, 70
ldelem opcode, loading array elements
    with, 98
ldelema opcode, loading an element
    address onto a stack with, 98
ldfld opcode, using, 79
ldind opcode, dereferencing a pointer
    with, 74
ldlen opcode, getting array length with,
    98
ldloc stack behavior, 71–73
ldloca opcode, pushing a variable's
    address onto a stack with, 73–74
ldloc.x, using, 72
ldnull opcode, loading a null instance
    onto the stack with, 88
ldobj opcode, using, 100
ldsfld opcode, function of, 79
ldstr opcode, for dealing with strings,
    101
*Le Ton Beau De Marot: In Praise of the
    Music of Language* (Douglas R.
    Hofstadter), 10
leave opcode, using, 109
list cl command, for getting a list of
    currently loaded classes, 160
list mod command, for getting a list of
    currently loaded modules, 160
literal attribute, defining how fields are
    initialized with, 43–44
little-endian format, 24

local variables
    declaring within your methods, 54–56
    showing values of with print
        command, 153
.locale directive, for defining culture
    your assembly is targeted for, 27
Locals debug window, for showing the
    values of local variables, 166
locals directive, adding a couple of
    variables to, 112
logging code, adding to methods, 271
LoggingMessages mode, in cordbg, 161

M

managed attribute, for method
    implementation, 46
manifest. *See* assembly manifest
MarkLabel(), setting where label is in
    CIL stream with, 248
MarkSequencePoint()
    calling to create mappings, 259–260
    importance of properly locating in
        code, 268
marshalling layer, creating, 52
.maxstack calculations
    adding branch statements to, 116
    example, 116
.maxstack directive
    specifying the maximum stack size
        with, 57
    transparent calculation of in Emitter
        classes, 249
Memory debug window, for retrieving
    memory information via address
    values, 166
memory manipulation, opcodes for,
    99–100
Metainfo
    AssemblyRef values in, 20
    illustration of screen, 19
method argument information, code
    example for retrieving, 266–267
method arguments, using, 77–79
method body directives, 53–62
.method directive, 15
    adding methods to types with, 45–62
method inlining, when it occurs, 46

Apress Titles

ISBN	PRICE	AUTHOR	TITLE
1-893115-73-9	$34.95	Abbott	Voice Enabling Web Applications: VoiceXML and Beyond
1-893115-01-1	$39.95	Appleman	Dan Appleman's Win32 API Puzzle Book and Tutorial for Visual Basic Programmers
1-893115-23-2	$29.95	Appleman	How Computer Programming Works
1-893115-97-6	$39.95	Appleman	Moving to VB .NET: Strategies, Concepts, and Code
1-59059-023-6	$39.95	Baker	Adobe Acrobat 5: The Professional User's Guide
1-59059-039-2	$49.95	Barnaby	Distributed .NET Programming
1-893115-09-7	$29.95	Baum	Dave Baum's Definitive Guide to LEGO MINDSTORMS
1-893115-84-4	$29.95	Baum, Gasperi, Hempel, and Villa	Extreme MINDSTORMS: An Advanced Guide to LEGO MINDSTORMS
1-893115-82-8	$59.95	Ben-Gan/Moreau	Advanced Transact-SQL for SQL Server 2000
1-893115-91-7	$39.95	Birmingham/Perry	Software Development on a Leash
1-893115-48-8	$29.95	Bischof	The .NET Languages: A Quick Translation Guide
1-893115-67-4	$49.95	Borge	Managing Enterprise Systems with the Windows Script Host
1-893115-28-3	$44.95	Challa/Laksberg	Essential Guide to Managed Extensions for C++
1-893115-39-9	$44.95	Chand	A Programmer's Guide to ADO.NET in C#
1-893115-44-5	$29.95	Cook	Robot Building for Beginners
1-893115-99-2	$39.95	Cornell/Morrison	Programming VB .NET: A Guide for Experienced Programmers
1-893115-72-0	$39.95	Curtin	Developing Trust: Online Privacy and Security
1-59059-014-7	$44.95	Drol	Object-Oriented Macromedia Flash MX
1-59059-008-2	$29.95	Duncan	The Career Programmer: Guerilla Tactics for an Imperfect World
1-893115-71-2	$39.95	Ferguson	Mobile .NET
1-893115-90-9	$49.95	Finsel	The Handbook for Reluctant Database Administrators
1-59059-024-4	$49.95	Fraser	Real World ASP.NET: Building a Content Management System
1-893115-42-9	$44.95	Foo/Lee	XML Programming Using the Microsoft XML Parser
1-893115-55-0	$34.95	Frenz	Visual Basic and Visual Basic .NET for Scientists and Engineers
1-893115-85-2	$34.95	Gilmore	A Programmer's Introduction to PHP 4.0
1-893115-36-4	$34.95	Goodwill	Apache Jakarta-Tomcat
1-893115-17-8	$59.95	Gross	A Programmer's Introduction to Windows DNA
1-893115-62-3	$39.95	Gunnerson	A Programmer's Introduction to C#, Second Edition
1-59059-009-0	$49.95	Harris/Macdonald	Moving to ASP.NET: Web Development with VB .NET
1-893115-30-5	$49.95	Harkins/Reid	SQL: Access to SQL Server
1-893115-10-0	$34.95	Holub	Taming Java Threads
1-893115-04-6	$34.95	Hyman/Vaddadi	Mike and Phani's Essential C++ Techniques
1-893115-96-8	$59.95	Jorelid	J2EE FrontEnd Technologies: A Programmer's Guide to Servlets, JavaServer Pages, and Enterprise JavaBeans
1-893115-49-6	$39.95	Kilburn	Palm Programming in Basic
1-893115-50-X	$34.95	Knudsen	Wireless Java: Developing with Java 2, Micro Edition
1-893115-79-8	$49.95	Kofler	Definitive Guide to Excel VBA
1-893115-57-7	$39.95	Kofler	MySQL
1-893115-87-9	$39.95	Kurata	Doing Web Development: Client-Side Techniques
1-893115-75-5	$44.95	Kurniawan	Internet Programming with VB

ISBN	PRICE	AUTHOR	TITLE
1-893115-38-0	$24.95	Lafler	Power AOL: A Survival Guide
1-893115-46-1	$36.95	Lathrop	Linux in Small Business: A Practical User's Guide
1-893115-19-4	$49.95	Macdonald	Serious ADO: Universal Data Access with Visual Basic
1-893115-06-2	$39.95	Marquis/Smith	A Visual Basic 6.0 Programmer's Toolkit
1-893115-22-4	$27.95	McCarter	David McCarter's VB Tips and Techniques
1-59059-021-X	$34.95	Moore	Karl Moore's Visual Basic .NET: The Tutorials
1-893115-76-3	$49.95	Morrison	C++ For VB Programmers
1-59059-003-1	$39.95	Nakhimovsky/Meyers	XML Programming: Web Applications and Web Services with JSP and ASP
1-893115-80-1	$39.95	Newmarch	A Programmer's Guide to Jini Technology
1-893115-58-5	$49.95	Oellermann	Architecting Web Services
1-59059-020-1	$44.95	Patzer	JSP Examples and Best Practices
1-893115-81-X	$39.95	Pike	SQL Server: Common Problems, Tested Solutions
1-59059-017-1	$34.95	Rainwater	Herding Cats: A Primer for Programmers Who Lead Programmers
1-59059-025-2	$49.95	Rammer	Advanced .NET Remoting
1-893115-20-8	$34.95	Rischpater	Wireless Web Development
1-893115-93-3	$34.95	Rischpater	Wireless Web Development with PHP and WAP
1-893115-89-5	$59.95	Shemitz	Kylix: The Professional Developer's Guide and Reference
1-893115-40-2	$39.95	Sill	The qmail Handbook
1-893115-24-0	$49.95	Sinclair	From Access to SQL Server
1-893115-94-1	$29.95	Spolsky	User Interface Design for Programmers
1-893115-53-4	$44.95	Sweeney	Visual Basic for Testers
1-59059-002-3	$44.95	Symmonds	Internationalization and Localization Using Microsoft .NET
1-59059-010-4	$54.95	Thomsen	Database Programming with C#
1-893115-29-1	$44.95	Thomsen	Database Programming with Visual Basic .NET
1-893115-65-8	$39.95	Tiffany	Pocket PC Database Development with eMbedded Visual Basic
1-893115-59-3	$59.95	Troelsen	C# and the .NET Platform
1-59059-011-2	$59.95	Troelsen	COM and .NET Interoperability
1-893115-26-7	$59.95	Troelsen	Visual Basic .NET and the .NET Platform
1-893115-54-2	$49.95	Trueblood/Lovett	Data Mining and Statistical Analysis Using SQL
1-893115-68-2	$54.95	Vaughn	ADO.NET and ADO Examples and Best Practices for VB Programmers, Second Edition
1-59059-012-0	$49.95	Vaughn/Blackburn	ADO.NET Examples and Best Practices for C# Programmers
1-893115-83-6	$44.95	Wells	Code Centric: T-SQL Programming with Stored Procedures and Triggers
1-893115-95-X	$49.95	Welschenbach	Cryptography in C and C++
1-893115-05-4	$39.95	Williamson	Writing Cross-Browser Dynamic HTML
1-893115-78-X	$49.95	Zukowski	Definitive Guide to Swing for Java 2, Second Edition
1-893115-92-5	$49.95	Zukowski	Java Collections
1-893115-98-4	$54.95	Zukowski	Learn Java with JBuilder 6

Available at bookstores nationwide or from Springer Verlag New York, Inc. at 1-800-777-4643; fax 1-212-533-3503. Contact us for more information at sales@apress.com.

Opcodes Quick Reference

 NOTE *This table is meant to serve as an aid for remembering how the various CIL opcodes are used; the descriptions are brief in nature and do not explain the entire story behind their related opcodes (Chapter 3 covers the opcodes in detail).*

NAME	DESCRIPTION
add	Adds the two values on the stack and pushes the result on the stack. Use .ovf to check for overflow conditions.
and	Performs the AND binary operation on the two values on the stack and pushes the result on the stack.
arglist	Retrieves the variable-argument list handle for a vararg method.
beq	Breaks to a code label if the two topmost values on the stack are equal.
bge	Breaks to a code label if the second topmost value on the stack is greater than or equal to the topmost stack value. Use .un to assume unsigned comparisons if the values are integers.
bgt	Breaks to a code label if the second topmost value on the stack is greater than the topmost stack value. Use .un to assume unsigned comparisons if the values are integers.
ble	Breaks to a code label if the second topmost value on the stack is less than or equal to the topmost stack value Use .un to assume unsigned comparisons if the values are integers.
blt	Breaks to a code label if the second topmost value on the stack is less than the topmost stack value. Use .un to assume unsigned comparisons if the values are integers.
bne.un	Breaks to a code label if the two topmost values are not equal.
box	Turns a value type into a reference type.
br	Breaks to a code label unconditionally.
brfalse	Breaks to a code label if the topmost value evaluates to false.
brtrue	Breaks to a code label if the topmost value evaluates to true.
call	Calls an instance method. Will not throw an exception if the instance reference is not on the stack.
calli	Calls a method via a function pointer.
callvirt	Calls an instance method. Will throw an exception if the instance reference is not on the stack.
castclass	Checks to see if a reference is of a specific type and pushes the cast result on the stack. Will throw an exception if the cast doesn't work.
ceq	Compares two values for equality and pushes the result on the stack.
cgt	Compares the topmost value and the next stack value to see if it the deeper stack value is larger. Use .un to assume unsigned comparisons if the values are integers.
ckfinite	Checks for divide-by-zero conditions on floating-point data.
clt	Compares the topmost value and the next stack value to see if it the deeper stack value is smaller. Use .un to assume unsigned comparisons if the values are integers.
conv	Converts a value to the appended type. Use .ovf to check for overflow conditions.
cpblk	Copies data from one location in memory to another.
cpobj	Takes the value from one address and copies it to the location specified with another address.
div	Divides the two values on the stack and pushes the result on the stack.
dup	Duplicates the current value on the stack.
endfault	Signals the end of a fault exception block.
endfinally	Signals the end of a finally exception block.
initblk	Initializes a block of memory.
isinst	Checks to see if a reference is of a specific type and pushes the cast result onto the stack (null if the cast didn't work).